SMP 16-19

Pure 3

Vectors and applications of calculus

CAMBRIDGE
UNIVERSITY PRESS

This book is adapted from earlier SMP books, with additional material, by Emma McCaughan.

Other material was originally contributed by

Simon Baxter
Chris Belsom
Stan Dolan
Doug French
Andy Hall
Barrie Hunt
Mike Leach
Tim Lewis
Lorna Lyons
Richard Peacock
Paul Roder
Jeff Searle
David Tall
Brian Wardle
Thelma Wilson
Phil Wood

PUBLISHED BY THE PRESS SYNDICATE OF THE UNIVERSITY OF CAMBRIDGE
The Pitt Building, Trumpington Street, Cambridge, United Kingdom

CAMBRIDGE UNIVERSITY PRESS
The Edinburgh Building, Cambridge, CB2 2RU, UK
40 West 20th Street, New York, NY 10011–4211, USA
477 Williamstown Road, Port Melbourne, VIC 3207, Australia
Ruiz de Alarcón 13, 28014 Madrid, Spain
Dock House, The Waterfront, Cape Town 8001, South Africa

http://www.cambridge.org

First published 2001

Printed in the United Kingdom at the University Press, Cambridge

Typeface Minion and Officina   *System* QuarkXpress®

A catalogue record for this book is available from the British Library

ISBN 0 521 78799 8 paperback

Cover photograph: © Digital Vision
Cover design: Angela Ashton

Contents

Using this book

Most sections within a chapter consist of work developing new ideas followed by an exercise for practice in using those ideas.

Within the development sections, some questions and activities are labelled with a **D**, for example **2D**, and are enclosed in a box. These involve issues that are worth exploring through discussion – either teacher-led discussion in the whole class or discussion by students in small groups, who may then feed back their conclusions to the whole class.

Questions labelled **E** are more demanding.

Support material appears at the end of Chapter 1. This is referred to at the point in the chapter where some students may need to consolidate their differentiation skills before moving further with the main flow of the work.

1 Cartesian and parametric equations

A Curves varying with time (answers p. 117)

The graph shows the motion of a ball thrown horizontally from the top of a building. The path it follows can be described by the equation $y = 10 - \frac{2}{5}x^2$. This equation is called a **Cartesian equation**, and describes the position of the ball in the Cartesian (x, y) plane. However, this is not always the most convenient way in which to describe the ball's motion. If you have already studied projectiles in *Mechanics 1*, you will remember finding the x- and y-coordinates separately, in terms of t, the time elapsed.

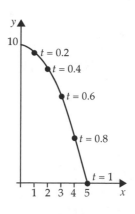

$$x = 5t$$
$$y = 10 - 10t^2$$

These equations are called **parametric equations**, and t is called the **parameter**. In this chapter, you will see that parametric equations can be used to describe many types of graph.

1D

(a) Complete this table of values for the Cartesian equation $y = 10 - \frac{2}{5}x^2$.

x	0	1	2	3	4	5
y	10					

(b) Complete this table of values for the parametric equations $x = 5t$, $y = 10 - 10t^2$.

t	0	0.2	0.4	0.6	0.8	1
x	0	1				
y	10	9.6				

(c) What do you notice about the two tables?

(d) From $x = 5t$, we know that $t = \dfrac{x}{5}$. Substitute this expression for t in $y = 10 - 10t^2$, to show that $y = 10 - \frac{2}{5}x^2$.

2D A curve is given by the parametric equations $x = 2t - 1$, $y = t^2$.

(a) Complete this table of values and plot the points on an (x, y) graph. Note that the values of t will not appear on the graph.

t	0	1	2	3	4	5
x						
y						

(b) What is the general shape of the curve?

Many graph-plotting calculators and packages will allow you to enter equations in parametric form and to plot their graphs.

3 Use a graph plotter to draw the curve given by $x = t + 1$, $y = t^2 - 1$. Experiment, using the graph plotter, to find the Cartesian equation of the curve.

Exercise A (answers p. 117)

1 (a) A curve is given by the parametric equations
$$x = 20t, \quad y = 90 - 5t^2$$
Complete this table of values and plot the points on an (x, y) graph.

t	0	1	2	3	4	5
x						
y						

(b) On the same graph, plot the points which would arise if t were to take the values -1, -2, -3, -4 and -5. You should not need to recalculate the values – look for symmetry with your answers to (a).

(c) What is the general shape of the curve?

2 By choosing suitable values of t and drawing up a table, plot the curve given by the parametric curves $x = 2t^2$, $y = 4t^3$. Check your answer using a graph plotter.

3E A curve is defined by $x = \theta - \sin \theta$, $y = 1 - \cos \theta$.

(a) Complete this table of values.

θ	0	$\dfrac{\pi}{4}$	$\dfrac{\pi}{3}$	$\dfrac{\pi}{2}$	$\dfrac{2\pi}{3}$	$\dfrac{3\pi}{4}$	π	$\dfrac{5\pi}{4}$	$\dfrac{4\pi}{3}$	$\dfrac{3\pi}{2}$	$\dfrac{5\pi}{3}$	$\dfrac{7\pi}{4}$	2π
x													
y													

(b) Plot the curve for this range of values of θ, leaving space to continue the graph at either side.

(c) Describe how the x and y values will continue.

(d) Sketch the continuation of the graph for values of θ less than zero and greater than 2π.

4E It is often possible to sketch a curve without plotting a large number of points. Consider, for example, the curve given by

$$x = \frac{1+t}{2-t}, \quad y = \frac{2+t}{4-t}$$

(a) Write down where the curve cuts the axes.

We can write $t \rightarrow 2^+$ to denote 't approaches 2 from above'. As $t \rightarrow 2^+$, $2 - t$ is a small negative quantity, so $x \rightarrow -\infty$. As $t \rightarrow 2^+$, $y \rightarrow 2$, so the curve will get closer and closer to the line $y = 2$. We call the line $y = 2$ an **asymptote**.

(b) Explain what happens as $t \rightarrow 2^-$, i.e. as t approaches 2 through values smaller than 2.

(c) Write down any further asymptotes.

(d) Write down any obvious points.

(e) Sketch the curve. (Do not plot!)

B Conic sections (answers p. 118)

1D | Imagine cutting through a cone with a sheet of metal. Picture the shape of the cone where it has been sliced. What different shapes can be created? Which of these shapes can you name?

The curves created by intersecting a cone and a plane in this way are known as **conic sections**, or conics. The family of conic sections has been studied since around 350 BC. There are three types of conic section: the ellipse (of which the circle is a particular case), the parabola and the hyperbola. In this section you will study the circle, the ellipse, the parabola and the rectangular hyperbola, a particular type of hyperbola.

The Cartesian equation of a circle of radius r centred on the origin is $x^2 + y^2 = r^2$. This can be seen clearly by considering Pythagoras' theorem.

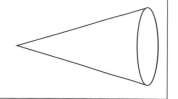

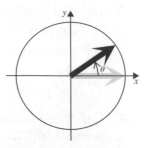

For parametric equations, you need an extra variable. Imagine that the circle is being drawn by the pointer in the diagram rotating anticlockwise about the origin. As the pointer moves, the angle θ increases, and it is this parameter which gives the usual parametric equations.

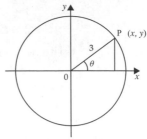

2 (a) For the circle in the diagram, radius 3, centre $(0, 0)$, use trigonometry to find $\cos\theta$ and $\sin\theta$ in terms of x and y.

(b) Rearrange these equations to find x and y in terms of θ.

(c) Find the values of x and y to complete this table.

θ	0	$\dfrac{\pi}{2}$	π	$\dfrac{3\pi}{2}$	2π	$\dfrac{5\pi}{2}$	3π
x							
y							

(d) Check that these values correspond to the graph.

(e) From your parametric equations, obtained in (b), substitute for $\cos\theta$ and $\sin\theta$ in the identity $\cos^2\theta + \sin^2\theta = 1$ and rearrange to show that $x^2 + y^2 = 9$.

3 Suppose a circle of radius 3 is stretched by a factor of 2 in the x direction, so that the point P is transformed to P' and the circle becomes an ellipse.

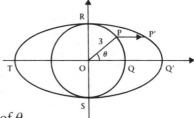

TQ' is the **major axis** of the ellipse. SR is the **minor axis**.

(a) Write down the coordinates of P in terms of θ.

(b) Write down the y-coordinate of P' in terms of θ.

(c) Write down the x-coordinate of P' in terms of θ.

(d) Write down the parametric equations of the ellipse.

(e) Write down the coordinates of R, Q and Q'.

4 A curve is given by $x = 5\cos\theta$, $y = 4\sin\theta$.

(a) Calculate the coordinates corresponding to $\theta = 0, \dfrac{\pi}{2}, \pi, \dfrac{3\pi}{2}$.

(b) Hence sketch the curve.

5 Sketch the graphs of the following curves, indicating the lengths of the major and minor axes.

(a) $x = 5 \cos \theta$, $y = 6 \sin \theta$ (b) $x = 2 \cos \theta$, $y = \sin \theta$

(c) $x = a \cos \theta$, $y = b \sin \theta$

6 (a) Complete the following argument which leads to the Cartesian equation of an ellipse.

$$x = a \cos \theta, \quad y = b \sin \theta$$

$$\Longrightarrow \quad \cos \theta = ?, \quad \sin \theta = ?$$

So, since $\cos^2 \theta + \sin^2 \theta = ?$, it follows that

$$\left(\frac{?}{?}\right)^2 + \left(\frac{?}{?}\right)^2 = 1$$

or $\quad \dfrac{x^2}{?^2} + \dfrac{y^2}{?^2} = 1$

(b) Sketch the ellipse $\dfrac{x^2}{4} + \dfrac{y^2}{9} = 1$.

7E Consider the ellipse $\dfrac{x^2}{a^2} + \dfrac{y^2}{b^2} = 1$.

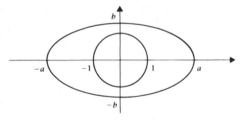

(a) This ellipse can be obtained from the circle $x^2 + y^2 = 1$ by means of a two-way stretch. What are the scale factors of this in the x and y directions?

(b) Write down the area of the circle $x^2 + y^2 = 1$. Hence write down the area of the ellipse.

For the **circle**, the Cartesian equation is

$$x^2 + y^2 = r^2$$

and the parametric equations are

$$x = r \cos \theta, \quad y = r \sin \theta$$

For the **ellipse**, the Cartesian equation is

$$\frac{x^2}{a^2} + \frac{y^2}{b^2} = 1$$

and the parametric equations are

$$x = a \cos \theta, \quad y = b \sin \theta$$

The major axis of the ellipse is of length $2a$ and its minor axis is of length $2b$.

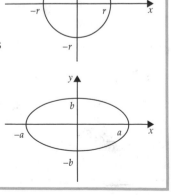

Notice that the circle is a special case of the ellipse, where $a = b = r$.

8 (a) Plot the following curve for values of t between -3 and 3.
$$x = 3t^2, \ y = 6t$$

   (b) Comment on the shape of the curve.

   (c) Express t in terms of y, and substitute for t in $x = 3t^2$. Hence show that $y^2 = 12x$.

9 (a) Plot the following curve for values of t between -3 and 3.
$$x = 5t^2, \ y = 10t.$$

   (b) Express t in terms of y, and use this to obtain an equation connecting x and y.

10 Write down the parametric equations for the curve whose Cartesian equation is $y^2 = 16x$. Use a graph plotter to check your answer.

11E (a) Show that the point P $(ap^2, 2ap)$ lies on the curve $y^2 = 4ax$.

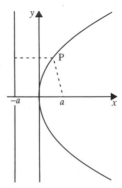

   (b) Find the distance from point P to the point $(a, 0)$, simplifying your answer.

   (c) Find the distance from point P to the line $x = -a$.

   (d) Show that your answers to (b) and (c) are equal.

This result is true for any point on the curve in question 11, as any point on this curve can be expressed as $(at^2, 2at)$ for some value of t. A parabola can be defined as the locus of those points equidistant from a fixed point (the focus) and a fixed straight line (the directrix).

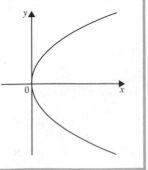

For the **parabola**, the Cartesian equation is
$$y^2 = 4ax$$
and the parametric equations are
$$x = at^2, \quad y = 2at$$

formula book

This book deals with a parabola whose axis of symmetry is horizontal, rather than vertical as in earlier books. The equations for the corresponding parabola with a vertical axis could be $x^2 = 4ay$, and $x = 2at, y = at^2$.

12D (a) Complete this table of values for the graph $y = \dfrac{1}{x}$.

x	-3	-2	-1	1	2	3	t
y							

(b) Use the last column of this table to suggest the parametric equations for this graph.

13 (a) Plot the graph given by the parametric equations $x = 2t$, $y = \dfrac{2}{t}$ for values of t between -5 and 5.

(b) Complete this working: $xy = 2t \times \left(\dfrac{?}{?} \right) = \, ?$.

14 By substituting for x and y, show that the point $\left(ct, \dfrac{c}{t} \right)$ lies on the curve $xy = c^2$.

For the **rectangular hyperbola**, the Cartesian equation is

$$xy = c^2 \qquad \text{or} \qquad y = \dfrac{c^2}{x}$$

and the parametric equations are

$$x = ct, \quad y = \dfrac{c}{t} \qquad \textit{formula box}$$

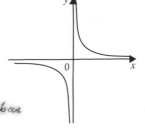

15E (a) Investigate the relationship between the hyperbola $x = 2t$, $y = \dfrac{2}{t}$ and the following curves. $\quad xy = c^2$

    (i) $\quad x = 2t$, $y = \dfrac{2}{t} + 2$ $\qquad x = ct \qquad y = \dfrac{c}{t}$

    (ii) $\quad x = 2t + 1$, $y = \dfrac{2}{t}$

(b) Investigate the relationship between the ellipse $x = 3 \cos t$, $y = 5 \sin t$ and the following curves.
    (i) $\quad x = 3 \cos t$, $y = 5 \sin t - 2$
    (ii) $\quad x = 3 \cos t + 1$, $y = 5 \sin t$

(c) Describe the effect on the parametric equations of translating the curve $x = 2 \cos t$, $y = 3 \sin t$ by the vector $\begin{pmatrix} 2 \\ 3 \end{pmatrix}$.

(d) Write down the parametric equations of a circle of radius 4 with centre $(1, -3)$.

Exercise B (answers p. 119)

1 Copy and complete this table.

Type of curve	Cartesian equation	Parametric equations
Circle	$x^2 + y^2 = 25$	
		$x = 3 \cos \theta,\ y = 5 \sin \theta$
		$x = 2t^2,\ y = 4t$
	$xy = 16$	
	$y = \dfrac{9}{x}$	

2 Rewrite $9x^2 + 4y^2 = 36$ in the form $\dfrac{x^2}{a^2} + \dfrac{y^2}{b^2} = 1$. Hence write down the parametric equations of this ellipse.

3 Find the Cartesian equation (in its simplest form) of the ellipse described by $x = \frac{1}{2} \cos \theta,\ y = \frac{1}{3} \sin \theta$.

4 Find the parametric equations of the curve $y^2 = 2x$.

5 Find the Cartesian equation of the hyperbola described by $x = \dfrac{t}{2},\ y = \dfrac{1}{2t}$.

C Conversion (answers p. 119)

You have seen how to convert parametric equations of the form $x = at^2$, $y = 2at$ into a Cartesian equation, by finding t in terms of y and substituting into $x = at^2$. In general, conversion from parametric to Cartesian form involves the removal of a parameter using simultaneous equation techniques.

1 For the parametric equations

$$x = 20t \qquad (1)$$
$$y = 90 - 5t^2 \qquad (2)$$

  (a) use equation (1) to find t in terms of x

  (b) substitute for t in equation (2) to show that $y = 90 - \dfrac{x^2}{80}$.

2 Use a similar method to find the Cartesian equations of the curves given by these parametric equations.

  (a) $x = 4t,\ y = 10t - 5t^2$

  (b) $x = 3t,\ y = 5 - \dfrac{6}{t}$

  (c) $x = 4t^2 - 3t,\ y = 2t$

3 For the parametric equations

$$x = 3 + 2t \qquad (1)$$
$$y = 6 - 4t \qquad (2)$$

(a) multiply equation (1) by 2

(b) add this equation to equation (2).

(c) What does this Cartesian equation describe?

4 Use a similar method to find the Cartesian equations corresponding to these parametric equations.

(a) $x = 2t - 1, y = 4 - 2t$

(b) $x = 3t + 2, y = 9t - 7$

You have seen that the variable θ can be eliminated from the equations $x = 3 \cos \theta, y = 3 \sin \theta$ by substituting into the trigonometric identity $\sin^2 \theta + \cos^2 \theta = 1$.

The three identities

$$\sin^2 \theta + \cos^2 \theta = 1$$
$$\tan^2 \theta + 1 \quad = \sec^2 \theta$$
$$1 + \cot^2 \theta = \operatorname{cosec}^2 \theta$$

can all be used in this way.

5E (a) By substituting into one of the identities above, convert the parametric equations $x = \cot \theta, 2y = \operatorname{cosec} \theta$ into a Cartesian equation.

(b) If $x = 2 \sec \theta, y = 3 \tan \theta$, substitute into one of the identities above to find an equation connecting x and y.

(c) Find the Cartesian equation for $x = 2 \cos \theta + 3, y = \sin \theta - 1$.

Exercise C (answers p. 120)

1 Find the Cartesian equations corresponding to these parametric equations.

(a) $x = 2 + 3t, y = 4 - 5t$

(b) $x = 2t, y = t^2 - 3t$

(c) $x = t + 1, y = t^2 - 1$

(d) $x = \frac{1}{2}t, y = \frac{1}{4}t^2 - t$

(e) $x = 6 - \dfrac{2}{t^2}, y = 3t$

(f) $x = \dfrac{1}{t}, y = 2t^2$

2E Use appropriate trigonometric identities to find the Cartesian equations corresponding to these parametric equations.

(a) $2x = \sec \theta, \dfrac{y}{3} = \tan \theta$ (b) $x = 4 \sin t, y = 3 \cos t$

(c) $x = \operatorname{cosec} \theta, y = \dfrac{1}{2} \cot \theta$ (d) $\dfrac{x}{3} = \sec \theta, y = \tan \theta + 1$

3E For the curve given by
$$y = (x - 2)^2 + 4$$
suggest two different possible sets of parametric equations.

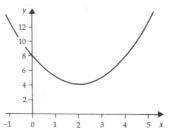

D Differentiating parametric equations (answers p. 120)

You have used the chain rule to find rates of change in cases where there were two equations involving three variables.

For example, if $y = \sin \theta$ and $\theta = 3x^2 + 2$, then

$$\frac{dy}{dx} = \frac{dy}{d\theta} \times \frac{d\theta}{dx}$$
$$= \cos \theta \times 6x$$
$$= 6x \cos \theta$$
$$= 6x \cos (3x^2 + 2)$$

Parametric equations can also give two equations with three variables. For example, a circle with centre the origin and radius 3 units has parametric equations

$$x = 3 \cos \theta, \quad y = 3 \sin \theta$$

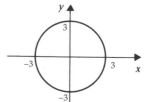

You can find $\dfrac{dy}{dx}$ using the chain rule.

$$\frac{dy}{dx} = \frac{dy}{d\theta} \times \frac{d\theta}{dx}$$

From the parametric equations, you can write down $\dfrac{dy}{d\theta}$ and $\dfrac{dx}{d\theta}$, but not $\dfrac{d\theta}{dx}$. However, you should remember that $\dfrac{d\theta}{dx} = 1 \div \dfrac{dx}{d\theta}$.

This means that the chain rule can be rewritten as

$$\frac{dy}{dx} = \frac{dy}{d\theta} \div \frac{dx}{d\theta}.$$

1D (a) For the circle given by the parametric equations $x = 3 \cos \theta$, $y = 3 \sin \theta$, use the formula $\dfrac{dy}{dx} = \dfrac{dy}{d\theta} \div \dfrac{dx}{d\theta}$ to show that $\dfrac{dy}{dx} = \dfrac{-\cos \theta}{\sin \theta}$.

(b) Check that this answer gives the correct values for the gradient of the circle when $\theta = 0, \dfrac{\pi}{2}, \pi$.

2 Consider the curve described by the parametric equations $x = 10t$, $y = 5t^2$.

(a) Find $\dfrac{dx}{dt}$.

(b) Find $\dfrac{dy}{dt}$.

(c) Use $\dfrac{dy}{dx} = \dfrac{dy}{dt} \div \dfrac{dx}{dt}$ to find $\dfrac{dy}{dx}$ in terms of t.

(d) Find the coordinates of the point on the curve where $t = 3$.

(e) Find the gradient of the curve at the point where $t = 3$.

(f) Find the equation of the tangent to the curve at the point where $t = 3$.

(g) Find the equation of the normal to the curve at the point where $t = 3$.

The process of differentiating expressions given in parametric form is known as **parametric differentiation**. It may have occurred to you that you could have found some of the gradients by first converting the parametric equations to Cartesian equations. This may occasionally be an easy method. For example, if

$$x = 2t + 3, \quad y = 6t + 9$$

you may spot at once that $y = 3x$, so $\dfrac{dy}{dx} = 3$.

Generally, however, parametric differentiation will be quicker. Further differentiation practice is provided in the support material S1.1 on p. 19.

3 (a) Find the Cartesian equation for the curve in question 2.

(b) From the Cartesian equation, find $\dfrac{dy}{dx}$, and hence find the equations of the tangent and the normal at the point where $t = 3$.

When dealing with the gradient at a point, the point may be described by its parameter or by its coordinates. If the coordinates are given, and you have used parametric differentiation, you will need to calculate the parameter at that point.

4   A curve is defined by $x = t^2$, $y = 2t + 5$.

(a) Use parametric differentiation to find the gradient at the point where $t = 2$.

(b) Find the gradient at the point $(4, 1)$. (Note that the x-coordinate gives two possible values of t, but the y-coordinate gives only one value.)

Example 1

A curve is defined by $x = t + 2$, $y = \dfrac{3}{t}$. Use parametric differentiation to find the gradient at the point $(5, 1)$.

Solution

$$\frac{dx}{dt} = 1, \quad \frac{dy}{dt} = -\frac{3}{t^2}$$

$$\Rightarrow \quad \frac{dy}{dx} = -\frac{3}{t^2} \div 1$$

$$\Rightarrow \quad \frac{dy}{dx} = -\frac{3}{t^2}$$

At $(5, 1)$, $t + 2 = 5$ and $1 = \dfrac{3}{t}$. So $t = 3$.

Hence the gradient at $(5, 1)$ is $-\frac{3}{9} = -\frac{1}{3}$.

> The gradient of a curve given in parametric form can be found using parametric differentiation.
> $$\frac{dy}{dx} = \frac{dy}{dt} \div \frac{dx}{dt}$$

Exercise D (answers p. 120)

1   A curve has parametric equations $x = t$, $y = \dfrac{1}{t}$. Write down $\dfrac{dx}{dt}$ and $\dfrac{dy}{dt}$ and hence find $\dfrac{dy}{dx}$. Calculate the gradient of the curve at $t = 2$.

2 A curve has parametric equations $x = 3\cos\theta$, $y = 4\sin\theta$.
Work out the Cartesian coordinates and gradient at the point where
$\theta = \frac{1}{2}\pi$.

3 For the curve defined by $x = 4u$, $y = u^2$, find $\dfrac{dy}{dx}$ and the equations of
the tangent and the normal to the curve at the point where $u = 2$.

4 Find the equation of the tangent to the curve $x = u^2$, $y = 2u^3$ at the
point where $u = 1$.

5 For the curve $x = 2v$, $y = v^3 - 3v$

    (a) work out $\dfrac{dy}{dx}$

    (b) write down the two values of v for which $\dfrac{dy}{dx} = 0$

    (c) write down the x- and y-coordinates of the turning points on the
curve.

6 Given that $x = 3s$, $y = s^2$, find $\dfrac{dy}{dx}$, first by parametric differentiation
and then by conversion to a Cartesian equation.
Check that both methods give the same value for the gradient of the
curve at $s = 1$.

7 For each part of this question, find $\dfrac{dy}{dx}$ by the method of your choice.
    (a) $x = (t+2)^2$, $y = t^3 - 3$
    (b) $x = 2t^2$, $y = 6t^2 - 4$
    (c) $x = 2\cos\theta - \sin\theta$, $y = 3\sin\theta$
    (d) $x = \sin 2\theta$, $y = \sin 3\theta$

8 A curve has parametric equations $x = t^2 + 4$, $y = 2t^3 + 4t$.
    (a) Find $\dfrac{dy}{dx}$ in terms of t and show that $\left(\dfrac{dy}{dx}\right)^2 \geqslant 24$.
    (b) Sketch the curve.

9E Find the equation of the tangent to the curve $x = \theta - \cos\theta$, $y = \sin\theta$ at
the point where $\theta = \frac{1}{4}\pi$. Write down the coordinates of the points A
and B at which this tangent cuts the x- and y-axes respectively and
hence find the area of the triangle OAB.

10E (a) Find the tangent to the hyperbola $xy = c^2$ at the point $P\left(cp, \dfrac{c}{p}\right)$.

    (b) This tangent meets the x-axis at A and the y-axis at B. Find the
coordinates of A and B.

    (c) Find the coordinates of the mid-point of AB and comment on the
result.

E Implicit differentiation (answers p. 121)

You know how to differentiate functions of functions, sums, differences, products and quotients of functions.

However, all the functions which you have been asked to differentiate have been stated **explicitly**, i.e. as $y = f(x)$.

Sometimes, though, functions are stated **implicitly**. For example, the equation of the circle of centre $(0, 0)$ and radius 3 units is usually given in the implicit form

$$x^2 + y^2 = 9$$

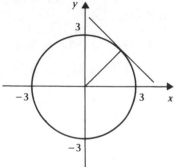

You can find $\dfrac{dy}{dx}$ from this implicit equation by finding the derivative of both sides of the equation, with respect to x.

$$\frac{d}{dx}(x^2) + \frac{d}{dx}(y^2) = \frac{d}{dx}(9)$$

The only difficulty here is with $\dfrac{d}{dx}(y^2)$, and this can be overcome by using the chain rule.

$$\frac{d}{dx}(y^2) = \frac{d}{dy}(y^2) \times \frac{dy}{dx}$$

$$\frac{d}{dx}(y^2) = 2y\frac{dy}{dx}$$

If $\qquad x^2 + y^2 = 9$

then $\qquad 2x + 2y\dfrac{dy}{dx} = 0$ (differentiate throughout with respect to x)

$\Rightarrow \qquad\qquad \dfrac{dy}{dx} = \dfrac{-x}{y}$

This is consistent with the result obtained in question 1D on page 11.

The process used here is called **implicit differentiation**. This technique is very useful for any function stated implicitly, even if it can be written explicitly.

Further differentiation practice is provided in the support material S1.1 on p. 19.

1D | Consider the ellipse $4x^2 + y^2 = 20$.

(a) Use implicit differentiation to find $\dfrac{dy}{dx}$ in terms of x and y.

(b) Find the gradient at the points $(2, 2)$ and $(2, -2)$.

(c) The equation of the ellipse can be written as $y = \pm(20 - 4x^2)^{\frac{1}{2}}$. Explain which portion of the curve is described by $y = (20 - 4x^2)^{\frac{1}{2}}$.

(d) Differentiate $y = (20 - 4x^2)^{\frac{1}{2}}$ to find $\dfrac{dy}{dx}$ in terms of x.

(e) Use this to find the gradient at the point $(2, 2)$, and explain why it does not give the gradient at the point $(2, -2)$.

Sometimes implicit differentiation gives rise to more than one term containing $\dfrac{dy}{dx}$. The following example demonstrates how to deal with this situation.

Example 2

The point $(1, 2)$ lies on the graph of $x^3 + 3y^2 - 4x + y = 11$.

(a) What is the gradient of the tangent at the point $(1, 2)$?

(b) Work out the equations of this tangent and of the normal to the curve at the same point.

Solution

(a) $\dfrac{d}{dx}(x^3) + \dfrac{d}{dx}(3y^2) - \dfrac{d}{dx}(4x) + \dfrac{d}{dx}(y) = \dfrac{d}{dx}(11)$

$\Longrightarrow \qquad 3x^2 + 6y\dfrac{dy}{dx} - 4 + \dfrac{dy}{dx} = 0$

$\Longrightarrow \qquad \dfrac{dy}{dx}(6y + 1) + 3x^2 - 4 = 0$

$\Longrightarrow \qquad \dfrac{dy}{dx}(6y + 1) = 4 - 3x^2$

$\Longrightarrow \qquad \dfrac{dy}{dx} = \dfrac{4 - 3x^2}{6y + 1}$

When $x = 1$ and $y = 2$, $\dfrac{dy}{dx} = \dfrac{1}{13}$.

The tangent at $(1, 2)$ has gradient $\dfrac{1}{13}$.

(b) The equation of the tangent is

$$\frac{y-2}{x-1} = \frac{1}{13}$$

$$\Rightarrow \quad 13(y-2) = x-1$$

$$\Rightarrow \quad 13y - 26 = x - 1$$

$$\Rightarrow \quad y = \frac{1}{13}x + \frac{25}{13}$$

The equation of the normal is

$$\frac{y-2}{x-1} = -13$$

$$\Rightarrow \quad y - 2 = 13 - 13x$$

$$\Rightarrow \quad y = 15 - 13x$$

2 Use implicit differentiation to find the gradient of the curve $6x^2 + 2y^3 = 8x + 4y$ at the point $(2, -2)$.

The equations considered so far have involved terms in x and terms in y. The product rule enables differentiation of terms such as xy.

3 (a) Consider $\dfrac{dz}{dx}$, where $z = 3xy$. Let $u = 3x$ and $v = y$.

Then $\dfrac{du}{dx} = 3$, and $\dfrac{dv}{dx} = \dfrac{dy}{dx}$.

Use the product rule $\dfrac{dz}{dx} = v\dfrac{du}{dx} + u\dfrac{dv}{dx}$ to express $\dfrac{dz}{dx}$ in terms of x, y and $\dfrac{dy}{dx}$.

(b) If $3xy = x + 2$, use implicit differentiation to show that $\dfrac{dy}{dx} = \dfrac{1-3y}{3x}$.

4 Use the product rule to differentiate the following expressions with respect to x.

(a) $x^2 y \ (u = x^2, v = y)$ (b) xy^2 (c) $e^x y$

Note that differentiating a term containing both x and y will create two terms, one containing $\dfrac{dy}{dx}$.

5 Consider the equation $y^2 + xy + x^2 = 8$.

(a) Write down the result of differentiating the following terms with respect to x.

(i) y^2 (ii) xy (iii) x^2 (iv) 8

(b) Use your answers to (a) to express $\dfrac{dy}{dx}$ in terms of x and y.

6 (a) Find $\dfrac{dy}{dx}$ if $3xy - 2x^2 = 8$ and so show that the graph of

$3xy - 2x^2 = 8$ has stationary points at $(2, 2\frac{2}{3})$ and $(-2, -2\frac{2}{3})$.

(b) Rewrite $3xy - 2x^2 = 8$ in the form $y = f(x)$ and use the quotient rule to check the coordinates of the stationary points.

(c) Do you prefer implicit differentiation or rearrangement and use of the quotient rule for checking the coordinates of stationary points? Which would you use if you had to *find* the coordinates of stationary points?

Exercise E (answers p. 122)

1 Use implicit differentiation to find $\dfrac{dy}{dx}$ when

(a) $2y^2 - 3y + 4x^2 = 2$ (b) $x^3 + \frac{1}{2}y^2 - 7x + 3y = 3$

2 The graph of $9x^2 + 4y^2 = 45$ is as shown.

(a) Use implicit differentiation to find $\dfrac{dy}{dx}$.

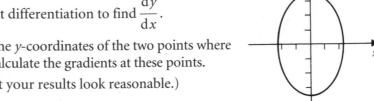

(b) Work out the y-coordinates of the two points where $x = 1$ and calculate the gradients at these points.

(Check that your results look reasonable.)

3 Work out $\dfrac{dy}{dx}$ for the following functions.

(a) $2x^2 + 3xy - 4y + y^2 = 5$ (b) $y^2 - 2xy + 3x - x^2 = 1$
(c) $x^2 + 4y^2 - 4x + 8y = 28$ (d) $y^3 + x^3 + xy^2 = 4$

4 For $xy = 12$,

(a) differentiate implicitly to find $\dfrac{dy}{dx}$

(b) express y as an explicit function of x and differentiate to find $\dfrac{dy}{dx}$

(c) show that your answers to (a) and (b) are the same.

5 For $x^2y + x^3 = 4$,
(a) use implicit differentiation to find $\dfrac{dy}{dx}$ and so show that $(-2, 3)$ is a stationary point on the curve

(b) rewrite the equation as a function of y and use the quotient rule to find $\dfrac{dy}{dx}$. Show that this also indicates a stationary point $x = -2$.

6 The circle with centre $(-3, 1)$ and radius 5 units has equation

$$(x+3)^2 + (y-1)^2 = 25$$

i.e. $x^2 + 6x + y^2 - 2y = 15$

(a) Work out an expression for $\dfrac{dy}{dx}$ and use it to find the equation of the tangent to the circle at the point $(1, 4)$.

(b) The point $(1, -2)$ lies on the circumference of the circle. Work out the gradient of the tangent at this point and the gradient of the radius of the circle to this point. Check that your results are in agreement with the property of circles that a tangent is always perpendicular to the radius at that point.

(c) Repeat (b) for any other point on the circumference of the circle.

7 The curve $\dfrac{x^2}{4} + \dfrac{y^2}{9} = 1$ can also be described by the parametric

equations $x = 2\cos\theta$, $y = 3\sin\theta$.

Use (a) implicit differentiation and (b) parametric differentiation to find the gradient at the point $\left(\sqrt{2}, \dfrac{3}{\sqrt{2}}\right)$.

8 In *Pure 1* you obtained the following results by numerical methods.

$$\frac{d}{dx}(2^x) = 0.69 \times 2^x$$

$$\frac{d}{dx}(3^x) = 1.10 \times 3^x$$

You can now obtain these results using implicit differentiation and the fact that

$$y = 2^x$$
$$\Rightarrow \quad \ln y = \ln 2^x$$
$$\Rightarrow \quad \ln y = x \ln 2$$

(a) Explain why $\dfrac{d}{dx}(\ln y) = \dfrac{1}{y}\dfrac{dy}{dx}$ and hence find $\dfrac{dy}{dx}$ (i.e. the derivative of 2^x).

Show that your answer agrees with the numerical result.

(b) Work out the derivative of 3^x using implicit differentiation.

(c) What is the derivative of a^x, where a is any constant?

(d) Explain why the derivative of e^x is e^x.

9E (a) Explain why the derivative of $\left(\dfrac{dy}{dx}\right)^2$ is $2\dfrac{dy}{dx}\dfrac{d^2y}{dx^2}$.

(b) Explain why the derivative of $\left(\dfrac{dy}{dx}\right)^3$ is $3\left(\dfrac{dy}{dx}\right)^2\dfrac{d^2y}{dx^2}$.

After working through this chapter you should

1   understand the word 'parameter' and recognise equations expressed in parametric form

2   be able to plot graphs from parametric equations

3   recognise the parametric and Cartesian forms for the circle, ellipse, parabola and rectangular hyperbola

4   be able to convert equations from parametric form to Cartesian form

5   be able to find the gradient of a curve expressed in parametric form

6   know how to use implicit differentiation and be aware that this will involve use of the chain rule and sometimes also the product rule.

S1.1 **Further differentiation practice** (answers p. 123)

1   Find $\dfrac{\mathrm{d}y}{\mathrm{d}x}$, using parametric or implicit differentiation as appropriate.

(a) $x^2 y = 36$

(b) $x = 4 \cos \theta$, $y = 3 \sin \theta$

(c) $x = \sin 2\theta$, $y = 2 \cos 3\theta$

(d) $x^2 + y^2 = 25$

(e) $x = \dfrac{1}{t}$, $y = t^3$

(f) $x^2 + 3xy + 2y^2 = 8$

(g) $e^{3x} y = x^2$

2   Find the equation of the tangent to the ellipse $3x^2 + 4y^2 = 12$ at the point $(-1, 1\tfrac{1}{2})$.

3   Differentiate both sides of the equation $x^2 + y^2 = 4x + 6y + 3$ with respect to x, and hence express $\dfrac{\mathrm{d}y}{\mathrm{d}x}$ in terms of x and y.

4   Find $\dfrac{\mathrm{d}y}{\mathrm{d}x}$ in terms of x and y.

(a) $6x^2 + 5y^2 = 7$ (b) $x^2(y+1) = 4$ (c) $3x = \cos y$

2 Binomial theorem

A Binomial expansions (answers p. 124)

Algebraic expressions which have two terms, for example $a + b$, $2x - 3y$ and $p^2 + 2p$, are known as **binomials**. In the same way, an expression like $a + b + c$, with three terms, is referred to as **trinomial**.

If you expand the brackets for $(a + b)(a + b)$, you obtain the identity
$$(a + b)^2 = a^2 + 2ab + b^2$$

1   Expand $(a + b)(a^2 + 2ab + b^2)$ to show that
$$(a + b)^3 = a^3 + 3a^2 b + 3ab^2 + b^3$$

2   Find a similar expansion for $(a + b)^4$.

If you include the obvious results that $(a + b)^0 = 1$ and $(a + b)^1 = a + b$ and also include the (usually unnecessary) coefficient of 1, you can tabulate your results as follows.

$$
\begin{aligned}
(a + b)^0 &= \qquad\qquad\qquad\qquad 1 \\
(a + b)^1 &= \qquad\qquad\qquad 1a \;+\; 1b \\
(a + b)^2 &= \qquad\quad 1a^2 \;+\; 2ab \;+\; 1b^2 \\
(a + b)^3 &= 1a^3 \;+\; 3a^2 b \;+\; 3ab^2 \;+\; 1b^3
\end{aligned}
$$

3D   (a) Can you spot the pattern produced by the coefficients of the various terms?

(b) Check whether your answer for $(a + b)^4$ fits the pattern.

(c) Assuming the pattern continues, write down what you would expect for the expansion of $(a + b)^5$.
(The answer should have six terms, involving a^5, $a^4 b$, $a^3 b^2$, $a^2 b^3$, ab^4 and b^5.)

You should have spotted that the coefficients of the various terms are the binomial coefficients you may already have met in Pascal's triangle. The pattern continues for *all* positive integer powers of $a + b$.

4E   Find $(a + 2b)^4$.

> The binomial expression $(a + b)^n$ can be expanded using the nth line of Pascal's triangle.

To expand $(a+b)^4$, use Pascal's triangle.

$$(a+b)^4 = a^4 + 4a^3b + 6a^2b^2 + 4ab^3 + b^4$$

$$\begin{array}{ccccccccc} & & & & 1 & & & & \\ & & & 1 & & 1 & & & \\ & & 1 & & 2 & & 1 & & \\ & 1 & & 3 & & 3 & & 1 & \\ 1 & & 4 & & 6 & & 4 & & 1 \end{array}$$

The coefficients of a particular power of $a+b$ are formed by adding pairs of coefficients of the previous power, just as in Pascal's triangle. This is illustrated below.

$$(a+b)(1a^3 + 3a^2b + 3ab^2 + 1b^3)$$
$$= a^4 + 3a^3b \boxed{+3} a^2b^2 + ab^3 +$$
$$a^3b \boxed{+3} a^2b^2 + 3ab^3 + b^4$$

$$\Rightarrow \qquad (a+b)^4 = \quad \dots \boxed{+6} \; a^2b^2 \dots$$

5D $(a+b)^5 = (a+b)(a^4 + 4a^3b + 6a^2b^2 + 4ab^3 + b^4)$

What is the coefficient of a^3b^2 in the expansion of $(a+b)^5$?

The result for $(a+b)^n$ can be extended to any binomial expression.

Example 1

Expand $(2x-3y)^3$.

Solution

$$((2x)+(-3y))^3 = 1(2x)^3 + 3(2x)^2(-3y) + 3(2x)(-3y)^2 + 1(-3y)^3$$
$$= 8x^3 - 36x^2y + 54xy^2 - 27y^3$$

Exercise A (answers p. 124)

1   Expand the following expressions.
   (a) $(a+b)^6$ (b) $(p-q)^5$ (c) $(3x+y)^4$ (d) $(1+z)^6$

2   (a) Expand $(a+b)^3$ and $(a-b)^3$.
   (b) Show that $(a+b)^3 + (a-b)^3 = 2a(a^2+3b^2)$.
   (c) Find a corresponding result for $(a+b)^3 - (a-b)^3$.

3E   (a) By putting $p=a+b$ and $q=a-b$ in question 2(b), find the factors of p^3+q^3.
   (b) Hence, or otherwise, factorise p^3-q^3.

4E   By writing 11 as $10+1$, explain the pattern of digits in the powers of 11.

B   Binomial coefficients (answers p. 124)

If a binomial expansion such as $(a+b)^3$ is expanded to give $1a^3 + 3a^2b + 3ab^2 + 1b^3$, then the coefficients are referred to as **binomial coefficients**. (For example, the binomial coefficient of a^2b is 3.)

The notation $\binom{n}{r}$ is used for binomial coefficients, where n and r are the rows and columns of Pascal's triangle as indicated below. The notation $_nC_r$ is also sometimes used.

			r			
n	0	1	2	3	4	5
0	1					
1	1	1				
2	1	2	1			
3	1	3	3	1		
4	1	4	6	4	1	
5	1	5	10	10	5	1

So, for example, $\binom{5}{0} = 1$ and $\binom{5}{3} = 10$.

It is also useful to notice the symmetry of the table:

for example, $\binom{4}{1} = \binom{4}{3}$ and $\binom{5}{2} = \binom{5}{3}$.

It is sensible to link n to the power of the binomial expansion as follows.

			1
line number 1	$(a+b)^1$		1 1
line number 2	$(a+b)^2$		1 2 1
line number 3	$(a+b)^3$		1 3 3 1
line number 4	$(a+b)^4$		1 4 6 4 1

The top line therefore corresponds to $n = 0$.

Similarly, the first term in each row corresponds to the coefficient of $a^n b^0$ and is therefore the term corresponding to $r = 0$.

It is easy enough to write down the first few lines of Pascal's triangle. However, if you want the 20th line it is a hard task to write down the preceding 19 lines! The following questions develop a general formula for the binomial coefficients.

You can always write down the first two terms of any line of Pascal's triangle. The 10th line certainly starts 1   10 , but it is not immediately obvious how to write down the next term unless you already know the 9th line.

1 The 4th line is 1   4   6   4   1 . Each number is related to the previous number as shown below.

How are the multipliers 4 and $\frac{3}{2}$ related to the multipliers $\frac{2}{3}$ and $\frac{1}{4}$?

2 (a) Find multipliers in a similar form for the 5th line of Pascal's triangle. (Express the multipliers with denominators 1, 2, 3, 4 and 5 .)

   (b) What patterns do you notice?

3 (a) Use the pattern you have found to generate the 6th line.

   (b) Check that your result is correct by using the 5th line to generate the 6th line in the usual way.

4 Use the pattern of multipliers to generate the 10th line of Pascal's triangle.

5E Add up the terms you have generated in question 4. How does the sum act as a check that the terms are correct?

6 Find the first four terms of the 80th line of Pascal's triangle.

The next step is to consider how any individual binomial coefficient can be found independently of any others.

Consider how the method of multipliers is used to generate the 12th line.

$$\times \tfrac{12}{1} \qquad\qquad \times \tfrac{11}{2} \qquad\qquad \times \tfrac{10}{3} \qquad\qquad\qquad \times \tfrac{9}{4}$$

$$1 \longrightarrow \frac{12}{1} \longrightarrow \frac{12 \times 11}{1 \times 2} \longrightarrow \frac{12 \times 11 \times 10}{1 \times 2 \times 3} \longrightarrow \frac{12 \times 11 \times 10 \times 9}{1 \times 2 \times 3 \times 4} \quad \text{etc.}$$

$$= 12 \qquad\qquad = 66 \qquad\qquad = 220 \qquad\qquad = 495$$

Using $\binom{n}{r}$ notation, $\binom{12}{1} = \frac{12}{1}$, $\binom{12}{2} = \frac{12 \times 11}{1 \times 2}$, $\binom{12}{3} = \frac{12 \times 11 \times 10}{1 \times 2 \times 3}$, ...

7 In a similar way, write down $\binom{12}{5}$.

Results such as these can be simplified using **factorials**. For example $4 \times 3 \times 2 \times 1$ is written 4!, which is read as '4 factorial'. Most calculators have keys labelled $x!$

8 (a) By writing out the factorials and cancelling, explain why

$$\frac{12!}{7!} = 12 \times 11 \times 10 \times 9 \times 8 .$$

   (b) Show that $\binom{12}{5} = \frac{12!}{5!7!}$.

   (c) Use your calculator to evaluate $\binom{12}{5}$.

9 Use factorial notation to explain why $\binom{12}{4} = \binom{12}{8}$.

10 Evaluate these binomial coefficients.

(a) $\binom{12}{9}$ (b) $\binom{12}{7}$ (c) $\binom{12}{11}$

11 Suggest a formula, using factorial notation, for $\binom{n}{r}$ in terms of n and r.

12 (a) What are the values of $\binom{12}{0}$ and $\binom{12}{12}$?

(b) How are these expressed in factorial notation, assuming that 0! has a meaning?

(c) How should 0! be defined?

The notation $n!$ (called n factorial) is used to denote
$$n(n-1)(n-2) \times \ldots \times 2 \times 1$$
0! is defined to be equal to 1 .

The binomial coefficients are then $\binom{n}{r} = \dfrac{n!}{r!(n-r)!}$

For example,

$$\binom{7}{2} = \frac{7!}{2!5!} = \frac{7 \times 6 \times 5 \times 4 \times 3 \times 2 \times 1}{2 \times 1 \times 5 \times 4 \times 3 \times 2 \times 1} = \frac{7 \times 6}{2 \times 1} = 21$$

The binomial expansion can now be summarised in terms of binomial coefficients. The result is known as the **binomial theorem**.

For n a positive integer,

$$(a+b)^n = \binom{n}{0}a^n b^0 + \binom{n}{1}a^{n-1}b^1 + \binom{n}{2}a^{n-2}b^2 + \ldots$$
$$+ \binom{n}{r}a^{n-r}b^r + \ldots + \binom{n}{n}a^0 b^n$$

where

$$\binom{n}{r} = {}_nC_r = \frac{n!}{r!(n-r)!}$$

The series is valid for all values of a and b .

Binomial coefficients may be found directly using some scientific and graphical calculators.

Exercise B (answers p. 125)

1   Evaluate these binomial coefficients.

(a) $\begin{pmatrix} 8 \\ 3 \end{pmatrix}$ (b) $\begin{pmatrix} 5 \\ 2 \end{pmatrix}$ (c) $\begin{pmatrix} 9 \\ 6 \end{pmatrix}$ (d) $\begin{pmatrix} 100 \\ 98 \end{pmatrix}$

2   Expand $(a + b)^7$ using the binomial theorem.

3   Find the first four terms of the expansions of these expressions.

(a) $(a - b)^8$ (b) $(2a - 3b)^{10}$ (c) $\left(x^2 - \dfrac{1}{x^2} \right)^6$

4   If $\begin{pmatrix} 15 \\ 4 \end{pmatrix} = \begin{pmatrix} 15 \\ a \end{pmatrix}$ find a.

5   Evaluate these expressions.

(a) $\dfrac{100!}{80!} \times \dfrac{78!}{99!}$ (b) $\begin{pmatrix} 80 \\ 20 \end{pmatrix} \div \begin{pmatrix} 80 \\ 19 \end{pmatrix}$

6E   (a) Show that $\begin{pmatrix} 10 \\ 4 \end{pmatrix} = \begin{pmatrix} 9 \\ 3 \end{pmatrix} + \begin{pmatrix} 9 \\ 4 \end{pmatrix}$.

(b) Generalise the result in (a) and prove your result.

C   Binomial series (answers p. 126)

When the binomial theorem is applied to the function $(1 + x)^n$, the resulting series is particularly useful and important. Sir Isaac Newton saw that this result could be extended to powers other than positive integers. The binomial series was Newton's first major discovery, which he published in 1676 in a letter to the Royal Society.

You can use the binomial theorem to obtain the expansion of $(1 + x)^n$ as follows.

$$(1 + x)^n = 1^n + \begin{pmatrix} n \\ 1 \end{pmatrix} 1^{n-1} x + \begin{pmatrix} n \\ 2 \end{pmatrix} 1^{n-2} x^2 + \begin{pmatrix} n \\ 3 \end{pmatrix} 1^{n-3} x^3 + \dots + x^n$$

$$= 1 + \frac{n!}{1!(n-1)!} x + \frac{n!}{2!(n-2)!} x^2 + \frac{n!}{3!(n-3)!} x^3 + \dots + x^n$$

$$= 1 + nx + \frac{n(n-1)}{2!} x^2 + \frac{n(n-1)(n-2)}{3!} x^3 + \dots + x^n$$

There are $n + 1$ terms in the expansion.

A number of possibilities arise which you can now explore. Can you use the binomial theorem when the value of n is not an integer (for example, $(1 + x)^{\frac{1}{2}}$) or when n is negative (for example, $(1 + x)^{-2}$)?

1D $(1 + x)^3 = 1 + 3x + 3x^2 + x^3$

(a) Use a graph plotter to plot the graph of the function $(1 + x)^3$.

(b) Plot the function $1 + 3x$, taken from the first two terms of the expansion. What do you notice about the line that is produced?

(c) Calculate the values of $1 + 3x$ and $(1 + x)^3$ for x from 0.05 to 0.25 at intervals of 0.05. What do you notice about the results?

$1 + 3x$ is a *linear* approximation to $(1 + x)^3$ and you will notice from your graphs and your numerical calculations that the approximation is good for small values of x.

2D (a) Compare the graphs of the functions $(1 + x)^3$ and $1 + 3x + 3x^2$.

(b) Calculate values of $1 + 3x + 3x^2$ for the same values of x as before and compare them with the values obtained for $(1 + x)^3$ and $1 + 3x$.

$1 + 3x + 3x^2$ is a *quadratic* approximation to $(1 + x)^3$. This is a better approximation than $1 + 3x$ for small values of x.

3 (a) Find a quadratic approximation to $(1 + x)^8$.

(b) Use a graph plotter to compare the graph of your quadratic approximation with that of $y = (1 + x)^8$.

The binomial expansion of $(1 + x)^n$ can be written in the form

$$(1 + x)^n = 1 + nx + \frac{n(n-1)}{2!}x^2 + \frac{n(n-1)(n-2)}{3!}x^3 + \dots$$

4 (a) By putting $n = -1$ in the series above, show that a possible quadratic approximation to $(1 + x)^{-1}$ is $1 - x + x^2$.

(b) Use a graph plotter to compare the graphs of $y = (1 + x)^{-1}$ and $1 - x + x^2$ using a domain of $-2 < x < 2$ (and $-5 < y < 5$).

For what range of values of x is the comparison a good one?

5 (a) By putting $n = \frac{1}{2}$ into the binomial expansion, show that a possible quadratic approximation to $\sqrt{1 + x}$ is $1 + \frac{1}{2}x - \frac{1}{8}x^2$.

(b) Use a graph plotter to compare the graphs of $\sqrt{1 + x}$ and $1 + \frac{1}{2}x - \frac{1}{8}x^2$. For what range of values of x is the comparison a good one?

6 Use the binomial series to show that $1 + \frac{1}{2}x - \frac{1}{8}x^2 + \frac{1}{16}x^3$ is a possible cubic approximation to $\sqrt{1 + x}$. Check your result using a graph plotter.

Questions 4 to 6 suggest that the following is true for *all* values of n, provided x is small.

$$(1 + x)^n = 1 + nx + \frac{n(n-1)x^2}{2!} + \frac{n(n-1)(n-2)x^3}{3!} + \dots$$

The result is known as the **binomial series**.

7E Further evidence to support the use of the binomial series may be found by summing a geometric series.

(a) Find the sum to infinity of the geometric series $1 - x + x^2 - x^3 + \dots$

(b) Expand $(1 + x)^{-1}$ from the binomial series. How does your answer relate to the sum in (a)?

8E Work out $(1 + \frac{1}{2}x - \frac{1}{8}x^2)^2$ and comment on your answer.

You have seen that the binomial expansion appears to generalise to values of n which are rational and/or negative, though with the restriction that the result only works for $-1 < x < 1$.

The following result, although *not proved here*, is always true. You will meet a proof in Chapter 3.

Binomial series

For $-1 < x < 1$ and *any* value of n

$$(1 + x)^n = 1 + nx + \frac{n(n-1)}{2!}x^2 + \frac{n(n-1)(n-2)}{3!}x^3 + \dots$$

Example 2

Show that, for small values of x, $\dfrac{1}{(1 + x)^2} \approx 1 - 2x$.

Solution

$$\frac{1}{(1 + x)^2} = (1 + x)^{-2} = 1 + (-2)x + \frac{(-2)(-3)}{2!}x^2 + \dots$$

$$\approx 1 - 2x \quad \text{where } x^2 \text{ and higher powers of } x \text{ are ignored}$$

Example 3

Show that $\sqrt[3]{1-2x} = 1 - \frac{2}{3}x - \frac{4}{9}x^2 - \frac{40}{81}x^3 + \ldots$

Solution

$$(1-2x)^{\frac{1}{3}} = 1 + \frac{1}{3}(-2x) + \frac{(\frac{1}{3})(-\frac{2}{3})}{2!}(-2x)^2 + \frac{(\frac{1}{3})(-\frac{2}{3})(-\frac{5}{3})}{3!}(-2x)^3 + \ldots$$

$$= 1 - \frac{2}{3}x - \frac{4}{9}x^2 - \frac{40}{81}x^3 + \ldots$$

The result is valid for $-1 < -2x < 1$

$\Rightarrow$ $-\frac{1}{2} < -x < \frac{1}{2}$

$\Rightarrow$ $-\frac{1}{2} < x < \frac{1}{2}$

9D   (a)   Use the fact that $(a+x)^n = a^n \left(1 + \dfrac{x}{a}\right)^n$ to expand $(a+x)^n$ as far as

the term in x^3.

(b)   Explain why this expansion is valid for $|x| < |a|$.

For $-a < x < a$ and any value of n,

$$(a+x)^n = a^n + na^{n-1}x + \frac{n(n-1)}{2!}a^{n-2}x^2 + \frac{n(n-1)(n-2)}{3!}a^{n-3}x^3 + \ldots$$

Exercise C (answers p. 127)

1   Use the formula for the binomial series to expand the following as far as the term in x^3.

(a) $(1+x)^{\frac{1}{3}}$ (b) $(1+x)^{-3}$

2   Use the laws of indices to write the following in the form $(1+x)^n$. (There is no need to expand the functions.)

(a) $\sqrt{1+x}$ (b) $\dfrac{1}{(1+x)^3}$ (c) $\sqrt[5]{1+x}$ (d) $\dfrac{1}{\sqrt[3]{1+x}}$

3   Expand the following as far as the term in x^3.

(a) $\dfrac{1}{(1+x)^4}$ (b) $\sqrt{1-2x}$ (c) $\dfrac{1}{\sqrt{1+x^2}}$

4   (a)   Show that $\sqrt{9-18x} = 3\sqrt{1-2x}$.

(b)   Hence show that

$\sqrt{9-18x} \approx 3 - 3x - \frac{3}{2}x^2 - \frac{3}{2}x^3 - \frac{15}{8}x^4$, for $-\frac{1}{2} < x < \frac{1}{2}$.

5 Find the first three terms of the binomial expansion of the following.

(a) $\dfrac{1}{\sqrt{4+4x}}$ (b) $\dfrac{1}{(3+3x)^2}$

6 The binomial expansion for $\sqrt{1+x} = 1 + \dfrac{x}{2} - \dfrac{x^2}{8} + \dfrac{x^3}{16} - \dots$

(a) Why would it be incorrect to conclude that
$$\sqrt{50} = \sqrt{1+49} = 1 + \frac{49}{2} - \frac{49^2}{8} + \frac{49^3}{16} - \dots?$$

(b) Show that $\sqrt{50} = 7\sqrt{1+\frac{1}{49}}$ and hence find an approximate value for $\sqrt{50}$ using the binomial expansion for $\sqrt{1+x}$.

7E Einstein's theory of relativity predicts that if a stick of length l moves with velocity v in the direction of its length it will shrink by a factor $\left(1 - \dfrac{v^2}{c^2}\right)^{\frac{1}{2}}$ where c is the speed of light.

(a) Show that for low speeds this factor is approximately $1 - \dfrac{v^2}{2c^2}$.

(b) Hence show that if $v = \dfrac{c}{3}$, the stick shrinks to approximately 94% of its original length.

After working through this chapter you should

1 be able to use Pascal's triangle to find $(a+b)^n$ for small integral values of n

2 know that $n! = n \times (n-1) \times \dots \times 2 \times 1$

3 understand and be able to use the notation for binomial coefficients
$$\binom{n}{r} = \frac{n!}{r!(n-r)!}$$

4 be able to expand $(a+b)^n$ using the binomial theorem

5 know how to use the binomial series and be aware of its limitations.

3 Maclaurin's series

A Introduction (answers p. 127)

In the last chapter, you used the binomial expansion to turn some functions of x into power series. For example, you found that, for $-1 < x < 1$,

$$(1 + x)^{\frac{1}{3}} = 1 + \tfrac{1}{3}x - \tfrac{1}{9}x^2 + \tfrac{5}{81}x^3 + \ldots$$

You would need an infinite number of terms in order to evaluate $(1 + x)^{\frac{1}{3}}$ for a particular value of x. However, if x is very small, the first few terms will give a reasonably accurate answer. In this chapter, you will learn about power series which can be used to approximate a range of functions. These can be used by computers and calculators to give values which, although not exact, are accurate enough for all practical purposes.

1D | Use a graph plotter to draw the graphs $y = (1 + x)^{\frac{1}{3}}$ and $y = 1 + \tfrac{1}{3}x$ for $-3 \leqslant x \leqslant 3$. What do you notice?

The **first-order approximation** to a function at a point is the linear function which passes through that point with the same gradient as the function. So, the first-order approximation to $(1 + x)^{\frac{1}{3}}$ at $x = 0$ is $1 + \tfrac{1}{3}x$.

As you can see from the graphs, this is a reasonable approximation for small values of x.

2D | Use a graph plotter to compare $y = (1 + x)^{\frac{1}{3}}$ and $y = 1 + \tfrac{1}{3}x - \tfrac{1}{9}x^2$.
Is this a better approximation than $y = 1 + \tfrac{1}{3}x$
(a) for small x?
(b) for large x?

This is an example of a quadratic, or **second-order**, approximation.

The symbol $f''(x)$ is used when the function f is differentiated twice, $f^{(3)}(x)$ is used when the function is differentiated three times, $f^{(4)}(x)$ when the function is differentiated four times, and so on.

For example,

$$f(x) = a + bx + cx^2$$
$$\implies \quad f'(x) = b + 2cx$$
$$\implies \quad f''(x) = 2c$$

The Leibnitz notation for $f^{(n)}(x)$ is $\dfrac{d^n y}{dx^n}$ $\left(\text{i.e. } f''(x) = \dfrac{d}{dx}\left(\dfrac{dy}{dx}\right) = \dfrac{d^2 y}{dx^2}\right).$

3 (a) For $f(x) = (1 + x)^{\frac{1}{3}}$, find $f'(x)$ and $f''(x)$. Calculate $f(0)$, $f'(0)$ and $f''(0)$.

(b) For $g(x) = 1 + \frac{1}{3}x - \frac{1}{9}x^2$, find $g'(x)$ and $g''(x)$. Calculate $g(0)$, $g'(0)$ and $g''(0)$.

(c) Comment on your results.

4E (a) For $f(x)$ in question 3, differentiate $f''(x)$ to get $f^{(3)}(x)$. Calculate $f^{(3)}(0)$.

(b) Explain how your answer relates to the coefficient of x^3 in the expansion of $(1 + x)^{\frac{1}{3}}$.

5 (a) Given that the graph of a function passes through the point $(0, 10)$ with gradient 4, find the first-order approximation to the function.

(b) Suppose that the function can be approximated by $f(x) = a + bx + cx^2$. You know that $f(0) = 10$, and $f'(0) = 4$. Use this information to find out what you can about a, b and c.

You should have found out that $a = 10$ and $b = 4$, but more information is needed to find a value for c.

6D Using a graph plotter, plot $y = 10 + 4x + cx^2$ for several different values of c. What do you notice?

You will see that the curves all pass through $(0, 10)$ with gradient 4. What is different is the rate at which the gradient is changing, i.e.

$$\frac{d}{dx}(f'(x)) = f''(x).$$

You needed two pieces of information to find a linear approximation, and so it is not surprising that you need three pieces of information to define a quadratic. It is convenient to use the values for $f(0)$, $f'(0)$ and $f''(0)$.

7 If in question 5 above, $f''(0) = 2$, find the quadratic approximation to $f(x)$.

8 If $p(x) = a + bx + cx^2 + dx^3$ and $p(0) = 12$, $p'(0) = 11$, $p''(0) = 10$ and $p^{(3)}(0) = 6$, find $p'(x)$, $p''(x)$ and $p^{(3)}(x)$. Hence find the values of a, b, c and d.

9 (a) If $p(x) = a + bx + cx^2 + dx^3$ express a, b, c and d in terms of $p(0)$, $p'(0)$, $p''(0)$ and $p^{(3)}(0)$ and hence show that

$$p(x) = p(0) + p'(0)x + p''(0)\frac{x^2}{2} + p^{(3)}(0)\frac{x^3}{6}$$

(b) Explain where the 2 and 6 come from in the equation above.

10 Explain why, if $p(x)$ is a polynomial of degree 4, then

$$p(x) = p(0) + p'(0)x + p''(0)\frac{x^2}{2!} + p^{(3)}(0)\frac{x^2}{3!} + p^{(4)}(0)\frac{x^4}{4!}$$

11 (a) In a similar way, if $p(x)$ is a polynomial of degree 5 write down $p(x)$ in terms of its derivatives at $x = 0$.

(b) Generalise this result to a polynomial of degree n.

12 If $f(x) = e^{2x}$, find $f(0)$, $f'(0)$, $f''(0)$, $f^{(3)}(0)$, $f^{(4)}(0)$.

Hence explain why $1 + 2x + 2x^2 + \dfrac{4x^3}{3} + \dfrac{2x^4}{3}$ is a good approximation to e^{2x} for values of x near $x = 0$.

Plot both of these functions on a graph plotter and suggest a range of x values for which the approximation is good.

If a function $f(x)$ can be differentiated n times at $x = 0$, then a polynomial of degree n which has the same derivatives as the function will be a good approximation to the function for values of x near zero.

The result developed in questions 7 to 11 was published by Colin Maclaurin (1698–1746). Maclaurin graduated from the University of Glasgow at the age of 14, and was later appointed to a Professorship at Edinburgh University at the instigation of Isaac Newton. In 1742, Maclaurin published his book *Treatise of Fluxions*, an exposition of Newton's work. It is in this work that he used what are now called **Maclaurin's series**, although he did acknowledge that their discovery was largely down to the work of another man, Brook Taylor (1685–1731).

Maclaurin's series

If $f(x)$ can be differentiated n times at $x = 0$, then the approximation

$$f(x) = f(0) + f'(0)x + \frac{f''(0)x^2}{2!} + \frac{f^{(3)}(0)x^3}{3!} + \frac{f^{(4)}(0)x^4}{4!} + \dots$$

$$+ \frac{f^{(n)}(0)x^n}{n!}$$

will be good for values of x close to $x = 0$.

Example 1

Find the Maclaurin's series for $\sin x$.

Solution

If $\quad$ $f(x) = \sin x$ $\qquad$ then $\qquad$ $f(0) = 0$
$\qquad\quad$ $f'(x) = \cos x$ $\qquad \Longrightarrow \qquad$ $f'(0) = 1$
$\qquad\quad$ $f''(x) = -\sin x$ $\qquad \Longrightarrow \qquad$ $f''(0) = 0$
$\qquad\quad$ $f^{(3)}(x) = -\cos x$ $\qquad \Longrightarrow \qquad$ $f^{(3)}(0) = -1$
$\qquad\quad$ $f^{(4)}(x) = \sin x$ $\qquad \Longrightarrow \qquad$ $f^{(4)}(0) = 0$
$\qquad\quad$ $f^{(5)}(x) = \cos x$ $\qquad \Longrightarrow \qquad$ $f^{(5)}(0) = 1$ $\qquad$ and the cycle repeats itself.

Thus, using these values for $f(0)$, $f'(0)$, $f''(0)$, ... , the Maclaurin's series will be

$$f(0) + f'(0)x + \frac{f''(0)x^2}{2!} + \frac{f^{(3)}(0)x^3}{3!} + \frac{f^{(4)}(0)x^4}{4!} + \dots + \frac{f^{(7)}(0)x^7}{7!} + \dots$$

$$= 0 + 1x + \frac{0x^2}{2!} - \frac{1x^3}{3!} + \frac{0x^4}{4!} + \frac{1x^5}{5!} + \frac{0x^6}{6!} - \frac{1x^7}{7!} + \dots$$

$$\Longrightarrow \qquad \sin x = x - \frac{x^3}{3!} + \frac{x^5}{5!} - \frac{x^7}{7!} + \frac{x^9}{9!} - \dots$$

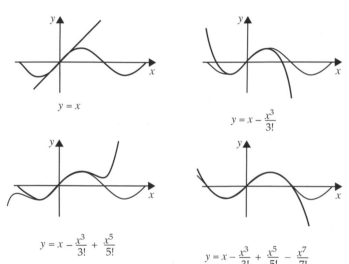

$y = x$

$y = x - \dfrac{x^3}{3!}$

$y = x - \dfrac{x^3}{3!} + \dfrac{x^5}{5!}$

$y = x - \dfrac{x^3}{3!} + \dfrac{x^5}{5!} - \dfrac{x^7}{7!}$

You can see from these graphs how the approximation becomes more accurate as terms are added.

In this case, not only does the accuracy improve for small x, the range of values for which the approximation can be used increases. You will see later that, for some other functions, the series can only ever be used for a limited range of values of x.

Exercise A (answers p. 128)

1 (a) Show that $\cos x = 1 - \dfrac{x^2}{2!} + \dfrac{x^4}{4!} - \dfrac{x^6}{6!} + \dots$

$\quad$ (b) Find the Maclaurin's series for e^x.

$\quad$ (c) Find the Maclaurin's series for (i) $\sin 2x$ (ii) e^{3x}

2 (a) If $f(x) = \ln x$, explain what happens if you attempt to evaluate $f(0)$.

   (b) Explain why it is not possible to find a Maclaurin's series for $\ln x$.

For the reason given in question 2, $\ln x$ does not have a series expansion. The series for $\ln(1 + x)$ is found instead.

3 (a) If $f(x) = \ln(1 + x)$, write down $f'(x)$.

   (b) By writing $\dfrac{1}{1 + x}$ as $(1 + x)^{-1}$, write down $f''(x)$.

   (c) Show that $f^{(3)}(x) = 2(1 + x)^{-3}$ and find $f^{(4)}(x)$ and $f^{(5)}(x)$.

   (d) Find $f(0)$, $f'(0)$, $f''(0)$, $f^{(3)}(0)$, $f^{(4)}(0)$ and $f^{(5)}(0)$.

   (e) Show that the Maclaurin's series for $\ln(1 + x)$ is

$$x - \frac{x^2}{2} + \frac{x^3}{3} - \frac{x^4}{4} + \frac{x^5}{5} - \dots$$

4 Using the series expansions, show that

   (a) $\dfrac{d}{dx}(\sin x) = \cos x$

   (b) $\dfrac{d}{dx}(\cos x) = -\sin x$

(Of course, this is not a proof of these results, as we used the results themselves in obtaining the series expansions!)

5E (a) If $f(x) = (1 + x)^n$, write down $f'(x)$.

   (b) Write down $f''(x)$ and show that
$$f^{(3)}(x) = n(n - 1)(n - 2)(1 + x)^{n-3}.$$

   (c) Use the results from (a) and (b) to show that the first four terms of $(1 + x)^n$ are

$$1 + nx + \frac{n(n - 1)}{2!} x^2 + \frac{n(n - 1)(n - 2)}{3!} x^3$$

This is, of course, the start of the binomial series: this method of finding it does not assume that n is a positive integer, so you now know it to be true for all rational and negative values of n.

6 Differentiate the Maclaurin's series for e^x. Does this give the result you would expect?

B Using Maclaurin's series (answers p. 129)

You have now derived a number of Maclaurin's series, which we know to give valid approximations for values of x close to $x = 0$.

In fact, some series, like the one for e^x, are valid for all x, and the value of the function can be calculated to any required degree of accuracy by taking enough terms of the series.

Others, like the series for $\dfrac{1}{1+x}$, **diverge** for values of x outside a

certain range. For instance, putting $x = 2$ gives

$$\frac{1}{1+2} = 1 - 2 + 4 - 8 + 16 - \ldots$$

which is clearly untrue.

Sometimes it is easy to tell from the graph of the
function that its series will be limited in range. For

example, $f(x) = \dfrac{1}{1+x}$ cannot be differentiated at

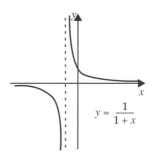

$y = \dfrac{1}{1+x}$

$x = -1$, and it is clear that the series cannot work
for $x \leqslant -1$.

The series is also invalid for $x > 1$, which is not
obvious from the graph.

Sometimes the graph gives no clues to the
validity of the Maclaurin's series; the graph on
the right does not suggest any problems, but

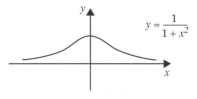

$y = \dfrac{1}{1+x^2}$

the Maclaurin's series for $y = \dfrac{1}{1+x^2}$ is valid

only for $|x| \leqslant -1$.

Determining the validity of series expansions is well beyond the scope
of this course, but you must be aware that the standard results below
have limitations.

$$\sin x = x - \frac{x^3}{3!} + \frac{x^5}{5!} - \frac{x^7}{7!} + \ldots \quad \text{(all } x\text{)}$$

$$\cos x = 1 - \frac{x^2}{2!} + \frac{x^4}{4!} - \frac{x^6}{6!} + \ldots \quad \text{(all } x\text{)}$$

$$e^x = 1 + x + \frac{x^2}{2!} + \frac{x^3}{3!} + \frac{x^4}{4!} + \ldots \quad \text{(all } x\text{)}$$

$$\ln(1 + x) = x - \frac{x^2}{2!} + \frac{x^3}{3!} - \frac{x^4}{4!} + \ldots \quad (-1 < x \leqslant 1)$$

$$(1 + x)^n = 1 + nx + \frac{n(n-1)}{2!}x^2 + \frac{n(n-1)(n-2)}{3!}x^3 + \ldots \quad (-1 < x < 1)$$

The standard results above can be used to establish series expansions
for more complicated functions.

Example 2

Use the Maclaurin's series for $\sin x$ to find the series for $\sin x^2$.

Solution

$$\sin x = x - \frac{x^3}{3!} + \frac{x^5}{5!} - \frac{x^7}{7!} + \dots$$

Replace x by x^2.

$$\sin(x^2) = (x^2) - \frac{(x^2)^3}{3!} + \frac{(x^2)^5}{5!} - \frac{(x^2)^7}{7!} + \dots$$

$$= x^2 - \frac{x^6}{3!} + \frac{x^{10}}{5!} - \frac{x^{14}}{7!} + \dots$$

1   Using the standard results proved in section A, find the first four terms of the series expansions for the following functions, giving the range of values of x for which the expansion is valid.
    (a) e^{2x} (b) $\ln(1-x)$ (c) $(1+2x)^{\frac{1}{2}}$.

We can also combine two or more series expansions.

Example 3

Find the series expansion for $\ln\left(\frac{1+x}{1-x}\right)$.

Solution

$$\ln\left(\frac{1+x}{1-x}\right) = \ln(1+x) - \ln(1-x)$$

$$= \left(x - \frac{x^2}{2} + \frac{x^3}{3} - \frac{x^4}{4} + \dots\right) - \left(-x - \frac{x^2}{2} - \frac{x^3}{3} - \frac{x^4}{4} - \dots\right)$$

$$= 2x + \frac{2x^3}{3} + \frac{2x^5}{5} + \dots$$

2   (a) Find the series expansion for $\ln(1+x) + \ln(1-x)$.
    (b) By substituting $-x^2$ for x in the expansion for $\ln(1+x)$, find the series expansion for $\ln(1-x^2)$.
    (c) Explain why your answers to (a) and (b) are the same.

3   Find the series expansion for $\sin x + \cos x$.

4   Show that the series expansion of $\sin x \cos x$ up to the term in x^5 is $x - \frac{2}{3}x^3 + \frac{2}{15}x^5$.

5D | In what circumstances is it reasonable to ignore higher powers of x?

Exercise B (answers p. 130)

In this exercise, you may use the standard series expansions on page 35.

1 (a) Find the series expansion of $\sin 2x$ up to the term in x^5.
   (b) Explain the connection between this and the expansion of $\sin x \cos x$ found earlier.

2 Find the first four terms of the series expansions for the following functions.
   (a) e^{3x} (b) e^{x^2} (c) e^{-x}

3 Write down the nth term of the series expansions for the following functions.
   (a) e^x (b) $\cos x$ (c) e^{x^2}

4 Stating the values of x for which they are valid, find the first four terms of the series expansions of the following.
   (a) $(1 + 3x)^{\frac{1}{3}}$ (b) $\ln(1 - x)$ (c) $\ln(1 + \tfrac{1}{2}x)$ (d) $(1 - 2x)^{\frac{1}{2}}$.

5 Find the series expansions of the following, up to the term in x^6.
   (a) $e^x + e^{-x}$ (b) $\cos 2x - \cos x$

6 Find the series expansion of $e^x \cos x$ up to the term in x^4.

7 Find the series expansion of $e^x(1 + x)^2$ up to the term in x^4.

8 Find the series expansion of $e^{2x} \cos x$ up to the term in x^6.

9 (a) Find the series expansion of $\cos 2x$ up to the term in x^6.
   (b) Find the series expansion of $(\cos x)^2$ up to the term in x^6.
   (c) Verify that the identity $\cos 2x = 2\cos^2 x - 1$ holds up to the term in x^6.

10E (a) Explain why it is difficult to find the series expansion of e^{x+1} by substituting $x + 1$ for x in the series for e^x.
   (b) Suggest an alternative method.

11E If you have met complex numbers, find the series expansion of e^{ix}.
   What do you notice about the real part?
   What do you notice about the imaginary part?

C Accuracy of approximations (answers p. 130)

For the Maclaurin's series of a function to be exactly equivalent to the function, an infinite number of terms would be required. Since, in any calculations from Maclaurin's series, you will use only a finite number of terms, it is important to be aware of the effect on accuracy.

1D
(a) With your calculator working in radians, find cos 0.2.

(b) How many terms of the cosine series are needed to give an answer that is accurate to ±0.001 ?

(c) How many terms are needed to give cos 0.5 to an accuracy of ±0.001 ?

(d) What about cos 1.0 ?

(e) What about cos 5.0 ?

It should be clear that for larger values of x, more terms are required to get a given degree of accuracy.

2
(a) How many terms of the e^x series are required to find $e^{0.2}$, accurate to ±0.001 ?

(b) What about $e^{0.5}$?

(c) What about e ?

(d) What about e^2 ?

3
(a) How many terms of the series for $\ln(1 + x)$ are required to find $\ln 1.2$ accurate to ±0.001 ?

(b) What about $\ln 1.9$?

(c) What happens if you use the power series for $x = 5$?

4
(a) Show that $e^{-x} \approx 1 - x$.

(b) Use this result to show that $\sqrt{1 - e^{-x}} \approx \sqrt{x}$.

(c) What is the percentage error in using $\sqrt{x}$ as an approximation to $\sqrt{1 - e^{-x}}$ when $x = 0.1$?

5
(a) For $x = 1$, find each of the first four terms of the power series for $\sin x$.

(b) Do the same for $x = 0.1$.

(c) Do the same for $x = 0.01$.

(d) Suppose you want to know $\sin x$ to 4 decimal places. Use your answers above to say how many terms are likely to be needed

(i)   for values of x up to 1

(ii) for values of x up to 0.1

(iii) for values of x up to 0.01 .

Exercise C (answers p. 130)

1 Using the Maclaurin's series, evaluate each of the following to 4 decimal places.

(a) $\sin 0.8$ (b) $\cos 0.1$ (c) e^2 (d) $1.3^{\frac{1}{3}}$

2 Calculate the percentage error in using $x - \dfrac{x^2}{2} + \dfrac{x^3}{3}$ as an approximation for $\ln(1 + x)$, when $x = \frac{1}{2}$.

3 The approximation $\sin x \approx x$ is often used. Find the percentage error in doing this for the following values.

(a) $x = 0.5$ (b) $x = 0.1$ (c) $x = 0.01$

After working through this chapter you should

1 be able to find second and higher derivatives and be familiar with the notations

$$f'(x), \quad f''(x), \quad f^{(3)}(x), \quad f^{(4)}(x), \quad ..., \quad f^{(n)}(x)$$

and

$$\frac{d^2 y}{dx^2}, \quad \frac{d^3 y}{dx^3}, \quad ..., \quad \frac{d^n y}{dx^n}$$

2 be able to derive from first principles the Maclaurin's series for simple functions

3 know the Maclaurin's series of particular functions such as $\sin x$, $\cos x$, e^x, $\ln(1 + x)$ and $(1 + x)^n$ and know the range of x for which these series are valid

4 be able to find sums and products of these series

5 be aware of the accuracy of approximations obtained from these series.

4 Algebraic fractions

A Partial fractions (answers p. 131)

This section covers an important technique for handling certain polynomial fractions. In Chapter 3, you learned to expand expressions using series. Sometimes before you can do this, it is necessary to split single polynomial fractions into simpler fractions. This process can also be useful for expressing some integrals in a form which you know how to integrate.

Example 1

Express $\dfrac{3x-8}{(x+6)(2x-1)}$ in the form $\dfrac{A}{x+6} + \dfrac{B}{2x-1}$.

Solution

Start from the required form,

$$\frac{A}{x+6} + \frac{B}{2x-1} = \frac{A(2x-1) + B(x+6)}{(x+6)(2x-1)}$$

(You may encounter the use of the 'identically equals' symbol, $\equiv$, in this situation, where the equality holds for all values of x.)

If $\dfrac{A(2x-1) + B(x+6)}{(x+6)(2x-1)} = \dfrac{3x-8}{(x+6)(2x-1)}$

then $A(2x-1) + B(x+6) = 3x-8$ \quad (1)

Putting $x = -6$ in (1) to eliminate B gives

$$-13A = -26 \Rightarrow A = 2$$

Putting $x = \frac{1}{2}$ in (1) to eliminate A gives

$$6\tfrac{1}{2}B = -6\tfrac{1}{2} \Rightarrow B = -1$$

1 Use a similar method to express $\dfrac{5x+4}{(x+3)(3x-2)}$ in the form $\dfrac{A}{x+3} + \dfrac{B}{3x-2}$.

The following example illustrates how to deal with the situation where the denominator includes a repeated linear factor.

2 (a) By trying to find A and B such that $\dfrac{5+x}{(x-2)(x+1)^2} = \dfrac{A}{x-2} + \dfrac{B}{(x+1)^2}$ explain why it is not possible to do so.

(b) Find A, B and C such that

$$\frac{5+x}{(x-2)(x+1)^2} = \frac{A}{x-2} + \frac{Bx+C}{(x+1)^2} \quad (1)$$

(c) Find A, D and E such that

$$\frac{5+x}{(x-2)(x+1)^2} = \frac{A}{x-2} + \frac{D}{x+1} + \frac{E}{(x+1)^2} \quad (2)$$

(d) Show that the expressions in (b) and (c) are the same.

You now have two equivalent sets of partial fractions. You may find (1) simpler to calculate, but (2) will be easier to use when you look at integration later in the chapter.

When resolving a fraction into partial fractions,

- each linear factor in the denominator has a partial fraction of the form $\dfrac{A}{ax+b}$

- each repeated linear factor, such as $\dfrac{1}{(ax+b)^2}$, has partial fractions of the form $\dfrac{A}{ax+b} + \dfrac{B}{(ax+b)^2} = \dfrac{Cx+D}{(ax+b)^2}$

In the example and questions above, the degree of the numerator was less than the degree of the denominator. You will now look at algebraic fractions where this is not the case.

Example 2

Express $\dfrac{3x+1}{x+2}$ in the form $A + \dfrac{B}{x+2}$.

Solution

$$\frac{3x+1}{x+2} = \frac{3x+6-5}{x+2} = \frac{3x+6}{x+2} - \frac{5}{x+2} = 3 - \frac{5}{x+2}$$

3 Use a similar method to express $\dfrac{4x-3}{2x+1}$ in the form $A + \dfrac{B}{2x+1}$.

In these examples, the numerator of the fraction is split into two parts, one being a multiple of the denominator, and the other being a 'remainder' whose degree is less than the denominator.

Division of polynomials was covered in Chapter 7 of *Pure 2*. For more complicated examples, you may find it easier to use the long division method described there.

Example 3

Express $\dfrac{3x^2 - x}{x^2 - 1}$ in partial fractions.

Solution

Method 1

Begin by looking at the term of highest degree in the numerator. In this case it is $3x^2$.

$$\frac{3x^2 - x}{x^2 - 1} = \frac{3x^2 - 3 + 3 - x}{x^2 - 1}$$

$$= \frac{3x^2 - 3}{x^2 - 1} + \frac{3 - x}{x^2 - 1}$$

$$= \frac{3(x^2 - 1)}{x^2 - 1} + \frac{3 - x}{x^2 - 1}$$

$$= 3 + \frac{3 - x}{x^2 - 1}$$

Method 2

$$x^2 - 1 \overline{)\begin{array}{l} 3 \\ 3x^2 - x \end{array}}$$

$$\begin{array}{l} 3x^2 \qquad -3 \\ \hline \quad -x + 3 \end{array}$$

$$\frac{3x^2 - x}{x^2 - 1} = 3 + \frac{-x + 3}{x^2 - 1}$$

$$= 3 + \frac{3 - x}{x^2 - 1}$$

You now must express $\dfrac{3 - x}{x^2 - 1}$ in partial fractions.

$$x^2 - 1 = (x + 1)(x - 1)$$

$$\Rightarrow \qquad \frac{3 - x}{x^2 - 1} = \frac{A}{x - 1} + \frac{B}{x + 1} = \frac{A(x + 1) + B(x - 1)}{(x - 1)(x + 1)}$$

$$\Rightarrow \qquad 3 - x = A(x + 1) + B(x - 1)$$

Substitute $x = 1$ to give $A = 1$, and substitute $x = -1$ to give $B = -2$. So, finally,

$$\frac{3x^2 - x}{x^2 - 1} = 3 + \left(\frac{1}{x - 1} + \frac{-2}{x + 1} \right)$$

$$= 3 + \frac{1}{x - 1} - \frac{2}{x + 1}$$

Exercise A (answers p. 131)

1 Split the following into partial fractions.

(a) $\dfrac{x}{(x+2)(x+3)}$ (b) $\dfrac{3}{(2x+1)(x+1)}$ (c) $\dfrac{x+7}{2x^2+3x-2}$

(d) $\dfrac{7x-12}{(x-1)(x-2)}$ (e) $\dfrac{5x+4}{(2x+1)(3x+2)}$ (f) $\dfrac{x-1}{x(x+1)}$

2 Express $\dfrac{8x-72}{(x+1)(x-3)^2}$ in the form $\dfrac{A}{x+1}+\dfrac{B}{x-3}+\dfrac{C}{(x-3)^2}$.

3 Resolve the following into partial fractions.

(a) $\dfrac{x^2}{x^2-9}$ (b) $\dfrac{3x^2}{x^2-5x+4}$

4 Resolve the following into partial fractions.

(a) $\dfrac{2x^3-5x+2}{x^2-4}$ (b) $\dfrac{x^3+1}{x^2+2x-15}$

B Using the binomial series to expand algebraic fractions (answers p. 131)

1D Expand the following, using the binomial series. Give the values of x for which your expansion is valid.

(a) $\dfrac{1}{(1+x)^n}$ (b) $\dfrac{3}{(1+x)^2}$ (c) $\dfrac{1}{(a+x)^n}$

(d) $\dfrac{1+2x}{1+x}$ (e) $\dfrac{1}{(1+2x)(x-1)}$

Some of the above are straightforward binomial expansions or multiples and sums of such expansions. The fraction in (e), however, needed to be expressed as two simpler fractions before you could apply the binomial expansion to each and add the results together.

Example 4

Expand $\dfrac{5-x}{(1+x)(1-2x)}$ up to the term in x^3.

Solution

$$\frac{5-x}{(1+x)(1-2x)} = \frac{A}{1+x} + \frac{B}{1-2x} = \frac{A(1-2x)+B(1+x)}{(1+x)(1-2x)}$$

$$\Rightarrow \qquad 5-x = A(1-2x)+B(1+x)$$

$$x=-1 \qquad \Rightarrow 6=3A \Rightarrow A=2$$
$$x=0 \qquad \Rightarrow 5=A+B \Rightarrow B=3$$

$$\frac{5-x}{(1+x)(1-2x)} = \frac{2}{1+x} + \frac{3}{1-2x}$$

$$= 2(1+x)^{-1} + 3(1-2x)^{-1}$$
$$= 2(1-x+x^2-x^3+...)$$
$$\quad + 3(1+2x+(2x)^2+(2x)^3+...)$$
$$= 5+4x+14x^2+22x^3+...$$

This expansion is valid for $|2x| < 1$, i.e. $|x| < \frac{1}{2}$.

Exercise B (answers p. 131)

Use the binomial series to expand these as far as the term in x^3. Give the values of x for which your expansion is valid.

1 (a) $\dfrac{x+1}{x-1}$ (b) $\dfrac{x+1}{x-4}$ (c) $\dfrac{x+9}{(x-1)(x-4)}$

2 (a) $\dfrac{x^2+3}{2x+1}$ (b) $\dfrac{4x^3+2x+1}{(2x-1)^2}$

3 (a) $\dfrac{3x^2-x-2}{(x+1)(x-1)^2}$ (b) $\dfrac{9+2x^2}{(2x+1)(x-3)^2}$

C Revision of integration techniques already met (answers p. 132)

1D What functions give algebraic fractions when differentiated?

2D Discuss which of these integrals you are able to do.

$$\int \frac{1}{x}\,dx \qquad \int \frac{1}{2x+5}\,dx \qquad \int \frac{2x}{x^2+3}\,dx$$

$$\int \frac{3}{x^6}\,dx \qquad \int \frac{x+1}{x^2+1}\,dx \qquad \int \frac{2}{\sqrt{1-x^2}}\,dx$$

$$\int \frac{1}{1+x^2}\,dx \qquad \int \frac{x^2}{(1-x^3)^2}\,dx \qquad \int \frac{1}{x^2+9}\,dx$$

$$\int \frac{1}{(x+3)^2}\,dx \qquad \int \frac{x^2}{x^2+4}\,dx \qquad \int \frac{x+2}{x^2+4x}\,dx$$

If you have little difficulty in integrating the functions above, it may be appropriate for you to go straight to the exercise on p. 49.

3 Differentiate the following functions with respect to x, writing your answers as algebraic fractions rather than with negative indices.

(a) $(x+1)^{-4}$ (b) $\dfrac{1}{(2x+1)^3}\,(=(2x+1)^{-3})$ (c) $(ax+b)^{-6}$

Note that in each case, you obtain an algebraic fraction whose numerator is a constant, and whose denominator is a linear function of x raised to a power. This suggests that you should be able to integrate algebraic fractions of this form fairly easily. You may want to use substitution.

Example 5

Find

$$\int \frac{1}{(2x+3)^4}\,\mathrm{d}x$$

Solution

Let $u = 2x+3$. Then $\dfrac{\mathrm{d}u}{\mathrm{d}x} = 2$.

$$\int \frac{1}{(2x+3)^4}\,\mathrm{d}x = \int \frac{1}{u^4} \times 2 \,\mathrm{d}u$$

$$= \int 2u^{-4}\,\mathrm{d}u$$

$$= 2 \times -\tfrac{1}{3}u^{-3} + c$$

$$= \frac{-2}{3(2x+3)^3} + c$$

4 Use a similar method for the following integrations.

(a) $\displaystyle\int \frac{1}{(x+3)^7}\,\mathrm{d}x$ (b) $\displaystyle\int \frac{1}{(3x-1)^5}\,\mathrm{d}x$

Some algebraic fractions need to be recognised as standard results, following from differentiation of particular functions. Recall the following results, met in *Pure 2*.

$$\frac{\mathrm{d}}{\mathrm{d}x}(\sin^{-1} x) = \frac{1}{\sqrt{1-x^2}}, \qquad \frac{\mathrm{d}}{\mathrm{d}x}(\tan^{-1} x) = \frac{1}{1+x^2}$$

By extending these results you can integrate a wider range of similar functions.

5 Use the chain rule to show the following.

(a) $\dfrac{d}{dx}\left(\sin^{-1}\dfrac{x}{a}\right) = \dfrac{1}{\sqrt{a^2 - x^2}}$
  (b) $\dfrac{d}{dx}\left(\dfrac{1}{a}\tan^{-1}\dfrac{x}{a}\right) = \dfrac{1}{a^2 + x^2}$

6 Write down the answers to these integrals.

(a) $\displaystyle\int \dfrac{1}{x^2 + 9}\,dx$
  (b) $\displaystyle\int \dfrac{1}{\sqrt{4 - x^2}}\,dx$

(c) $\displaystyle\int \dfrac{1}{1 + 4x^2}\,dx$ (Hint: divide through by 4 first.)

Another function which yields a fraction when differentiated is the logarithmic function. Recall the following.

$$\frac{d}{dx}(\ln|x|) = \frac{1}{x}$$

Using the chain rule, we also see that

$$\frac{d}{dx}(\ln|ax + b|) = \frac{d}{dx}(\ln|u|), \qquad \text{where } u = ax + b$$

$$= \frac{d}{du}(\ln|u|) \times \frac{du}{dx}$$

$$= \frac{1}{u} \times a$$

$$= \frac{a}{ax + b}$$

Hence

$$\int \frac{1}{ax + b}\,dx = \frac{1}{a}\ln|ax + b| + c$$

More generally,

$$\frac{d}{dx}(\ln|f(x)|) = \frac{d}{dx}(\ln|u|), \qquad \text{where } u = f(x)$$

$$= \frac{d}{du}(\ln|u|) \times \frac{du}{dx}$$

$$= \frac{1}{u} \times f'(x)$$

$$= \frac{f'(x)}{f(x)}$$

This enables you to integrate functions of the form $\dfrac{f'(x)}{f(x)}$, using the result

$$\int \frac{f'(x)}{f(x)}\,dx = \ln|f(x)| + c$$

Remember, though, that this result is only valid if the graph of $f(x)$ is continuous over the range of the integration.

Example 6

Find

$$\int \frac{\cos x}{\sin x}\,dx$$

Solution

Observe that if you differentiate $\sin x$, you get $\cos x$.
Therefore

$$\int \frac{\cos x}{\sin x}\,dx = \ln|\sin x| + c$$

Example 7

Find

$$\int \frac{x^2}{x^3 + 2}\,dx$$

Solution

Observe that if you differentiate $x^3 + 2$, you get $3x^2$.

Although this is not exactly the same as the numerator, it differs only by a constant multiple.

Therefore

$$\int \frac{x^2}{x^3 + 2}\,dx = \frac{1}{3}\ln|x^3 + 2| + c$$

7 Integrate the following, using the result

$$\int \frac{f'(x)}{f(x)}\,dx = \ln|f(x)| + c$$

(a) $\displaystyle\int \frac{6x}{3x^2 - 2}\,dx$ (b) $\displaystyle\int \frac{\sin x}{\cos x}\,dx$ (c) $\displaystyle\int \frac{x - 1}{x^2 - 2x + 3}\,dx$

(d) $\displaystyle\int \frac{2x^5 - 1}{x^6 - 3x}\,dx$ (e) $\displaystyle\int \frac{6x - 3}{x^2 - x}\,dx$ (f) $\displaystyle\int \frac{2x + 1}{x^2 + x + 1}\,dx$

8E (a) Show, using the substitution $u = f(x)$, that $\displaystyle\int \frac{f'(x)}{(f(x))^n}\,dx = \int u^{-n}\,du$.

(b) Use this substitution to integrate these.

(i) $\displaystyle\int \frac{2}{(2x + 1)^4}\,dx$ (ii) $\displaystyle\int \frac{3x^2}{(x^3 + 1)^3}\,dx$

Sometimes splitting the numerator enables you to form simpler fractions, as in the next question.

9   Complete this integration.

$$\int \frac{x+3}{x^2+1}\, dx = \int \left(\frac{x}{x^2+1} + \frac{3}{x^2+1} \right) dx$$

10D   (a) Evaluate $\displaystyle\int_1^2 \frac{5}{(x-3)(x+2)}\, dx$ using a numerical method.

(b) Evaluate $\displaystyle\int_1^2 \left(\frac{1}{x-3} - \frac{1}{x+2} \right) dx$ algebraically.

(c) Explain why the two integrals have the same answer.

Partial fractions are a very useful technique for integration, as the separate fraction terms are straightforward to integrate.

11   (a) Express $\dfrac{5x+1}{x^2-x-12}$ in the form $\dfrac{A}{x+3} + \dfrac{B}{x-4}$.

(b) Hence find $\displaystyle\int \frac{5x+1}{x^2-x-12}\, dx$.

Techniques for integrating algebraic fractions

Standard integrals:
$$\int \frac{1}{a^2+x^2}\, dx = \frac{1}{a}\tan^{-1}\frac{x}{a} + c$$

$$\int \frac{1}{\sqrt{a^2-x^2}}\, dx = \sin^{-1}\frac{x}{a} + c$$

Logs:
$$\int \frac{1}{ax+b}\, dx = \frac{1}{a}\ln|ax+b| + c$$

$$\int \frac{kf'(x)}{f(x)}\, dx = k\ln|f(x)| + c$$

Substitution:
$$\int \frac{1}{(ax+b)^n}\, dx \qquad \text{Use } u = ax+b$$

Splitting the numerator:
$$\int \frac{2x-1}{x^2+1}\, dx = \int \left(\frac{2x}{x^2+1} - \frac{1}{x^2+1} \right) dx$$

Partial fractions:
$$\int \frac{5}{(x-3)(x+2)}\, dx = \int \left(\frac{1}{x-3} - \frac{1}{x+2} \right) dx$$

Don't forget the constant of integration!

Exercise C (answers p. 132)

1 Find the following indefinite integrals.

(a) $\displaystyle\int \frac{2}{3x+1}\,dx$ (b) $\displaystyle\int \frac{2x^2-1}{2x^3-3x}\,dx$ (c) $\displaystyle\int \frac{e^x+1}{e^x+x}\,dx$

(d) $\displaystyle\int \frac{2}{9+x^2}\,dx$ (e) $\displaystyle\int \frac{2}{3-x}\,dx$ (f) $\displaystyle\int \frac{2-x}{x^2+1}\,dx$

2 Evaluate the following definite integrals.

(a) $\displaystyle\int_1^5 \frac{1}{2x-1}\,dx$ (b) $\displaystyle\int_0^1 \frac{x}{x^2+3}\,dx$ (c) $\displaystyle\int_0^{0.25} \frac{2}{1+4x^2}\,dx$

(d) $\displaystyle\int_0^1 \frac{1}{x+1}\,dx$ (e) $\displaystyle\int_{\frac{\pi}{3}}^{\frac{\pi}{2}} \frac{\sin x}{1-\cos x}\,dx$ (f) $\displaystyle\int_{\frac{\pi}{3}}^{\frac{2\pi}{3}} \frac{\sin x}{1-\cos x}\,dx$

3 By first resolving into partial fractions, find the following indefinite integrals.

(a) $\displaystyle\int \frac{x+1}{(x-1)(x-2)}\,dx$ (b) $\displaystyle\int \frac{1}{x^2-4}\,dx$ (c) $\displaystyle\int \frac{x+1}{x^2+5x+6}\,dx$

4 (a) Express $\dfrac{1}{(x+1)(x-1)^2}$ in partial fractions and hence find $\displaystyle\int \frac{dx}{(x+1)(x-1)^2}$.

(b) Evaluate $\displaystyle\int_2^3 \frac{x}{(x+1)(x-1)^2}\,dx$.

5 Rewrite $\dfrac{x^2+8x+9}{x^2+3x+2}$ in the form $A + \dfrac{px+q}{x^2+3x+2}$ and then in the form

$A + \dfrac{B}{x+1} + \dfrac{C}{x+2}$. Hence evaluate $\displaystyle\int_0^1 \frac{x^2+8x+9}{x^2+3x+2}\,dx$.

6 Express $\dfrac{2x^2+5x+1}{x^2+2x}$ in partial fractions, and hence find $\displaystyle\int \frac{2x^2+5x+1}{x^2+2x}\,dx$.

7E Find $\displaystyle\int \frac{3x^3-2x^2-3x+1}{x^2-x}$.

After working through this chapter you should

1 know how to split an algebraic fraction into partial fractions

2 be able to use partial fractions in the series expansion of algebraic fractions

3 be familiar with techniques for integrating algebraic fractions covered throughout the course

4 be aware of how to deal with cases where the degree of the numerator is equal to or greater than the degree of the denominator.

5 Differential equations

A Introduction (answers p. 113)

1D A murder victim was discovered by the police at 6.00 a.m. The body temperature of the victim was measured and found to be 25 °C. A doctor arrived on the scene of the crime 30 minutes later and measured the body temperature again. It was found to be 22 °C. The temperature of the room had remained constant at 15 °C. The doctor, knowing normal body temperature to be 37 °C, was able to estimate the time of death of the victim.

What would be your estimate for the time of death? What assumptions have you made?

The cooling of an object which is hotter than it surroundings is described by Newton's law of cooling.

> The rate of cooling at any instant is *directly proportional to the difference in temperature between the object and its surroundings*

Newton's law of cooling can be verified by experiment.

2D Some coffee was made and its temperature was monitored continually as it was allowed to cool down over a 2-hour period.

The graph at the top of page 51 shows a plot of the temperature difference between the coffee and the room, y °C, and the time in minutes.

(a) Estimate the gradient of the cooling curve at 10, 30, 50, 70 and 90 minutes. You may find it helpful to draw tangents on an enlarged copy of the graph.

(b) Plot the gradient from (a) against the temperature difference at the time.

(c) What sort of relationship appears to exist between the gradient and the temperature difference?

(d) Explain in physical terms what the gradient represents.

(e) Express the gradient using calculus notation.

(f) Express the relationship found in (c) in a fully symbolised form.

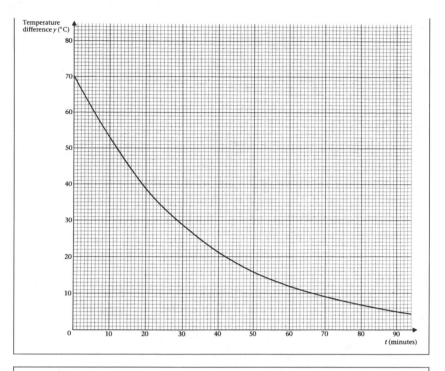

3D   Firm conclusions should not be drawn on the basis of a single experiment.

This graph shows three cooling curves, each for a different cup of coffee.

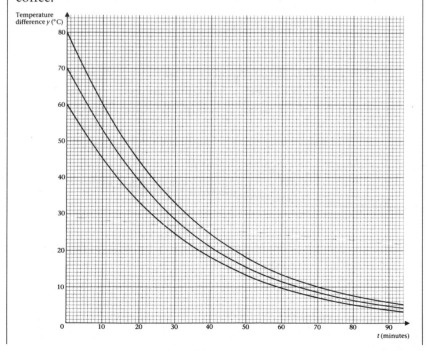

(a) Explain why the three cups of coffee can have different temperatures at the time $t = 0$.

(b) Estimate the gradient of each curve at the temperature difference $y = 40\,°C$. Comment on your result.

(c) Pick another temperature difference and find the gradient on each curve for this value of y.

(d) Make a general statement regarding what appears to be true from (b) and (c).

(e) All three curves represent the cooling of cups of coffee. In particular, one of these curves is for the cup of coffee from question 2. Which one?

(f) Write down an equation, with the gradient represented as a derivative, that can represent any one, or all, of these cooling curves.

Using calculus notation, Newton's law of cooling can expressed as

$$\frac{dy}{dt} = -ky$$

4   Explain the meaning of each of the symbols used in the formulation of the law given above.

The equation for Newton's law of cooling is an example of an equation involving a derivative. Any equation involving a derivative, such as $\frac{dy}{dx}$ or $\frac{dy}{dt}$, is called a **differential equation**.

Because differential equations occur frequently in mathematics and science, understanding and solving them is a substantial element in any course in mathematics. In this chapter we consider some of the situations which give rise to these equations, and consider ways to solve them.

Finding a solution to a differential equation means expressing the relation between the variables in a form which does not contain any derivatives. In the case of the equation for Newton's law,

$$\frac{dy}{dt} = -ky$$

it means expressing y as a function of t. We shall return to the murder story and this equation in section C.

Some differential equations can be solved algebraically by inspection. For example, if you know that $\frac{dy}{dx} = x^2$, then integrating the function gives $y = \frac{1}{3}x^3 + c$.

This equation gives a whole family of solution curves which all satisfy the differential equation. You will recall that in questions 2 and 3, several curves gave rise to the same differential equation.

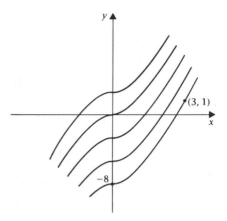

To get a single solution to the differential equation, an additional piece of information is required.

If, for example, you know that the graph passes through the point $(3, 1)$, then you can specify the **particular solution** as $y = \frac{1}{3}x^3 - 8$.

Example 1

Find the solution to the following differential equation, for which $y = 1$ when $x = 0$.

$$\frac{\mathrm{d}y}{\mathrm{d}x} = 3x + 2$$

Solution

The equation may be solved directly by integration with respect to the variable x.

$$y = \int (3x + 2)\,\mathrm{d}x$$

$$\Rightarrow \quad y = \frac{3x^2}{2} + 2x + c$$

$$y = 1 \text{ when } x = 0 \Rightarrow c = 1$$

So $y = \dfrac{3x^2}{2} + 2x + 1$ is the particular solution required.

Notice that in this case the solution involves integration once only, and that this yields a single constant of integration. In the solution of differential equations, the constants of integration are a most important part of the solution process, and *must not be overlooked.*

5 Consider the differential equation $\dfrac{\mathrm{d}y}{\mathrm{d}x} = 3x^2 - 5$.

    (a) Integrate to find an expression for y.

    (b) Find the solution to the differential equation for which $y = 3$ when $x = 2$.

6 Find the solution to the differential equation $\dfrac{\mathrm{d}y}{\mathrm{d}x} = 3x + 2$ which passes through the point $(1, 4)$.

Example 2

For the differential equation $\dfrac{dy}{dx} = 2x + \sin x$, find the value of y when $x = 2$ for the particular solution through $(3, 4)$.

Solution

$$y = \int (2x + \sin x)\,dx$$

$\Longrightarrow \qquad y = x^2 - \cos x + c$

$\qquad\qquad y = 4$ when $x = 3$

$\Longrightarrow \qquad 4 = 3^2 - \cos 3 + c$

$\Longrightarrow \qquad 4 = 9 + 0.99 + c$

$\Longrightarrow \qquad c = -5.99 \qquad$ (to 2 d.p.)

$\Longrightarrow \qquad y = x^2 - \cos x - 5.99$

So when $x = 2$, $y = -1.57$ (to 2 d.p.).

7   If $\dfrac{dy}{dx} = e^x - \cos x$, and the curve passes through the origin, find the value of y when $x = 2$.

Exercise A (answers p. 133)

1   Solve the following differential equations and in each case make a sketch showing some particular solutions.

(a) $\dfrac{dy}{dx} = e^x$ (b) $\dfrac{dy}{dx} = \cos 2x$ (c) $x^2\dfrac{dy}{dx} + 1 = 0$

2   For each of the differential equations given below, find y when $x = 3$ for the particular solutions which pass through the point $(1, 0)$.

(a) $\dfrac{dy}{dx} = 4x^3$ (b) $\dfrac{dy}{dx} = 3x^2 - 2x + 2$

(c) $\dfrac{dy}{dx} = \dfrac{1}{x^3}$ (d) $\dfrac{dy}{dx} = 2e^{2x}$

3   A can of water is heated at a rate which decreases steadily with time. The temperature $y\,°C$ after t minutes satisfies the differential equation

$$\frac{dy}{dt} = 8 - \frac{4t}{3}$$

(a) Find y when $t = 4$ if $y = 32$ initially.

(b) Do you think the model will still be valid at time $t = 10$?

4E   For each of the differential equations given below, find y when $x = 2$
for the particular solutions which pass through the origin.

(a) $\dfrac{dy}{dx} = \sin(3x + 2)$ (b) $\dfrac{dy}{dx} = x^2 e^{x^3}$ (c) $\dfrac{dy}{dx} = x \cos(x^2 + 1)$

B   Numerical methods (answers p. 134)

1D   Where possible write down the equation of the particular solution
curve which passes through the point $(0, 1)$ for each of the
following differential equations.

(a) $\dfrac{dy}{dx} = 3x + 2$ (b) $\dfrac{dy}{dx} = 3x^2 - 2x - 1$ (c) $\dfrac{dy}{dx} = x \cos x$

(d) $\dfrac{dy}{dx} = x \cos x^2$ (e) $\dfrac{dy}{dx} = \cos x^2$ (f) $\dfrac{dy}{dx} = \dfrac{y + x}{y - x}$

Discuss why you are not able to solve all of the equations.

Numerical methods are often the only way to solve differential
equations.

The method described in this chapter starts from a point known to be
on the graph. You can use the differential equation to calculate the
gradient at that point, and this tells you the direction that the graph is
taking at that point. You move a small distance in that direction, and
then calculate the gradient at the new point. You can then continue
the process. Of course the gradient is continuously changing, but if
you only every move small distances, your answers should be
reasonably accurate.

More formally, if (x, y) is a point on a graph, and the point
$(x + \delta x, y + \delta y)$ is on the tangent, then for a locally straight graph, and
for small δx, the point $(x + \delta x, y + \delta y)$ is close to the graph.

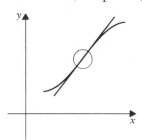
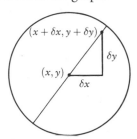

An approximate numerical solution can therefore be obtained by
fixing a small numerical value for δx, then calculating a point further
along the curve as $(x + \delta x, y + \delta y)$ and taking this as a new starting
point. Consider a particular situation for the simple differential
equation $\dfrac{dy}{dx} = 2x$ and starting from the point $(1, 4)$.

At $(1, 4)$ the gradient is 2, so a step along of $\delta x = 0.1$ will give a step up of $\delta y = 0.2$. The move along the tangent is from $(1, 4)$ to $(1.1, 4.2)$.

The gradient at $(1.1, 4.2)$ is $2 \times 1.1 = 2.2$.

Since $\delta x = 0.1$, then $\delta y = 0.22$ $\left(\delta y = \dfrac{\mathrm{d}y}{\mathrm{d}x} \times \delta x\right)$

So the next point will be $x + \delta x = 1.2$

$$y + \delta y = 4.42$$

2 (a) Calculate $\dfrac{\mathrm{d}y}{\mathrm{d}x}$ at $(1.2, 4.42)$

(b) Using $\delta x = 0.1$, calculate δy.

(c) Find $x + \delta x$ and $y + \delta y$.

(d) Using these new values for x and y, run through one more iteration of the process.

It may help to set the calculation out in a table, working down column by column.

	x	y	$\dfrac{\mathrm{d}y}{\mathrm{d}x}$	δx	δy	$x + \delta x$	$y + \delta y$
First step	1	4	2	0.1	0.2	1.1	4.2
Second step	1.1	4.2	2.2	0.1	0.22	1.2	4.42
⋮	⋮	⋮	⋮	⋮	⋮	⋮	⋮

A spreadsheet is an ideal tool for performing these calculations.

The spreadsheet below shows the next few steps in the numerical solution.

	A	B	C	D	E	F	G
	x	y	$\mathrm{d}y/\mathrm{d}x$	δx	δy	$x + \delta x$	$y + \delta y$
1	1	4	2	0.1	0.2	1.1	4.2
2	1.1	4.2	2.2	0.1	0.22	1.2	4.42
3	1.2	4.42	2.4	0.1	0.24	1.3	4.66
4	1.3	4.66	2.6	0.1	0.26	1.4	4.92
5	1.4	4.92	2.8	0.1	0.28	1.5	5.2
6	1.5	5.2	3	0.1	0.3	1.6	5.5
7	1.6	5.5	3.2	0.1	0.32	1.7	5.82
8	1.7	5.82	3.4	0.1	0.34	1.8	6.16
9	1.8	6.16	3.6	0.1	0.36	1.9	6.52
10	1.9	6.52	3.8	0.1	0.38	2.0	6.9

3D   (a) What formula is needed in the dy/dx column?

(b) What formula is needed in the δy column?

(c) Describe what would happen if you changed the values for δx from 0.1 to 0.01 .

(d) Discuss which columns would need to be changed in order to use this spreadsheet to solve a different differential equation.

4   (a) Use integration to solve $\dfrac{dy}{dx} = 2x$ for the particular solution passing through $(1, 4)$.

(b) Find the value for y when $x = 2$.

(c) Compare your answer with the value obtained from the table above.

The accuracy of the step-by-step method could be improved by using smaller step sizes for δx .

Example 3

For the differential equation

$$\frac{dy}{dx} = \frac{y}{1 + x^4}$$

find the value of y when $x = 2$ for the particular solution passing through $(1, 6)$.

Solution

The table below shows the start of the calculation, using steps of $\delta x = 0.2$ and working to 3 significant figures.

x	y	$\dfrac{dy}{dx}$	δx	δy	$x + \delta x$	$y + \delta y$
1	6	3	0.2	0.6	1.2	6.6
1.2	6.6	2.15	0.2	0.43	1.4	7.03
1.4	7.03	1.45	0.2	0.29	1.6	7.32
1.6	7.32	0.97	0.2	0.19	1.8	7.51
1.8	7.51	0.65	0.2	0.13	2.0	7.64
2.0	7.64					

5   Continue the table above to find the value of y when $x = 3$.

6   Using a spreadsheet, solve example 3 using 20 steps of $\delta x = 0.1$. Which answer would you expect to be more accurate?

7 (a) What is the equation of the solution curve for $\dfrac{dy}{dx} = \sin 2x$ which passes through $(0, -0.5)$?

   (b) Using a step size of 0.1, find the percentage error in the numerical solution for y at $x = 1$.

Exercise B (answers p. 134)

1 (a) What is the equation of the solution curve for $\dfrac{dy}{dx} = \cos x$ which passes through $(0, 0)$?

   (b) Using a spreadsheet, calculate the numerical solution of the differential equation $\dfrac{dy}{dx} = \cos x$ starting at $x = 0$, $y = 0$ with step 0.1. Record the values of x and y for $x = 0, 0.5, 1$ and so on, giving y values to 1 decimal place. How accurate is the numerical solution for different values of x?

2 (a) What is the equation of the solution curve for $\dfrac{dy}{dx} = 4x^3$ which passes through $(1, 0)$? Find the value of y when $x = 2$.

   (b) Use a numerical method, with a step size of 0.2, to find the value of y when $x = 2$.

3 For the differential equation $\dfrac{dy}{dx} = 2xy - x^2$, use a numerical method with a step size of 0.1 to find the value of y when $x = 2$, given that the curve passes through $(1, 1)$.

4 The differential equation $\dfrac{dy}{dx} = 2^y - x$ has a particular solution which passes through the point $(4, 1)$.

   (a) Use a numerical method with a step size of 0.1 to find the value of y when $x = 5$.

   (b) Using a spreadsheet, answer (a) using a step size of 0.05.

   (c) What is the value of x when the curve crosses the x-axis?

5 (a) $\dfrac{dy}{dx} = 2x \Longrightarrow y = x^2 + c$

   For $\dfrac{dy}{dx} = 2x$, what is the particular solution curve through $(1, 2)$?

   Plot this solution curve on graph paper for $-1 \leqslant x \leqslant 3$.

(b) Calculate a numerical solution of $\dfrac{\mathrm{d}y}{\mathrm{d}x} = 2x$ starting at $x = 1, y = 2$.

Using steps of size 0.2, record the values from $x = 1$ to 3 and round off the y values to 1 decimal place. Record also the values from $x = 1$ to -1. Plot the numerical solutions for $-1 \leqslant x \leqslant 3$ on the same diagram as your graph of the solution curve and comment on the accuracy of the numerical method.

(c) Repeat (b) with step size 0.1. Comment on the improvement in accuracy obtained with the smaller step value.

6E For equations where you can find a solution curve by integration, it is possible to use a spreadsheet to check the accuracy of the numerical method for different-sized steps. Use an extra column of the spreadsheet to display the correct value of y as obtained by integration, and plot both the numerical and calculated values on a single graph. Use this method to investigate the accuracy of numerical solutions

for $\dfrac{\mathrm{d}y}{\mathrm{d}x} = e^x$ for different step values, starting at $x = 0, y = 1$.

C Growth and decay (answers p. 135)

In *Pure 1*, you learnt that when certain drugs are injected into the body, the amount remaining in the bloodstream decays exponentially. For one particular drug, the amount remaining was modelled by the equation

$$y = 5e^{-0.2t}$$

where y is the amount remaining, in milligrams, and t is the time in hours.

1 (a) What is the initial value of y?

(b) What is the value of y when $t = 5$?

(c) Complete the working to find the value of t when $y = 2.5$.

$$5e^{-0.2t} = 2.5$$
$$e^{-0.2t} = ?$$
$$-0.2t = \ln ?$$
$$= ?$$
$$t = ?$$

(d) Find the value of t when $y = 1.25$.

(e) Compare your answers to (c) and (d), and comment.

(f) Differentiate the equation and show that $\dfrac{\mathrm{d}y}{\mathrm{d}t} = -0.2y$.

The differential equation $\dfrac{dy}{dx} = -y$ is a type that until now you have only been able to solve using a numerical method.

2 (a) Differentiate $y = 3e^{2x}$ and show that $\dfrac{dy}{dx} = 2y$.

(b) If $y = 5e^{-3x}$, find $\dfrac{dy}{dx}$ in terms of y.

(c) If $y = 2e^{-3x}$, find $\dfrac{dy}{dx}$ in terms of y.

(d) If $y = Ae^{\lambda x}$, find $\dfrac{dy}{dx}$ in terms of y.

Situations involving exponential growth or decay can be described by differential equations of the form $\dfrac{dy}{dx} = \lambda y$. You have already met one such equation, in the example of cooling coffee at the start of this chapter.

You will have observed in (b) and (c) above that two different situations can give the same differential equation. But as you have already seen, solving a differential equation gives rise to a family of curves, and substituting known values will establish which is required.

The equation $\dfrac{dy}{dx} = y$ cannot be solved by algebraic integration as it stands. However, a simple rearrangement is helpful.

$$\frac{dy}{dx} = y \implies \frac{dx}{dy} = \frac{1}{y}$$

$$\implies x = \int \frac{1}{y}\,dy$$

$$\implies x = \ln|y| + c$$

$$\implies x - c = \ln|y|$$

$$\implies y = \pm e^{x-c}$$

$$\implies y = \pm e^{-c}e^{x}$$

$$\implies y = Ae^{x}, \qquad \text{where } A = \pm e^{-c}$$

The last step above is perhaps the least easy to understand. If c is some constant (a number), then e^{-c} and $-e^{-c}$ are also just numbers. So, rather than use a somewhat cumbersome expression, you can simply rename the constant A, equal to $\pm e^{-c}$.

The solution may be generalised easily to solve $\dfrac{dy}{dx} = \lambda y$ as follows.

$$\frac{dy}{dx} = \lambda y \implies \frac{dx}{dy} = \frac{1}{\lambda y}$$

$$\implies x = \frac{1}{\lambda} \int \frac{1}{y}\, dy$$

$$\implies \lambda x = \ln|y| + c$$

$$\implies \lambda x - c = \ln|y|$$

$$\implies y = \pm e^{\lambda x - c}$$

$$\implies y = \pm e^{-c} e^{\lambda x}$$

$$\implies y = Ae^{\lambda x}, \qquad \text{where } A = \pm e^{-c}$$

This makes sense, when you look back at question 2: you can see that each of these particular solutions was of the form $Ae^{\lambda x}$.

$$\frac{dy}{dx} = \lambda y \implies y = Ae^{\lambda x}$$

For a particular solution, the value of A can be calculated by substituting in a known point on the curve.

Example 4

Wilhelm's law states that, in a chemical reaction, the rate of change of mass is proportional to the mass, m, of the reacting substance present at any instant. In a particular reaction, this is modelled by the differential equation $\dfrac{dm}{dt} = -0.5m$, where m kg was the mass of the reacting chemical present t hours after the start of the reaction. Initially there was 8 kg of the substance. Find the mass of the substance after 1 hour.

Solution

$$\frac{dm}{dt} = -0.5m \implies \frac{dt}{dm} = \frac{1}{-0.5m}$$

$$\implies -0.5t = \int \frac{1}{m}\, dm$$

$$\implies -0.5t = \ln|m| + c$$

$$\implies -0.5t - c = \ln|m|$$

$$\implies m = \pm e^{-0.5t - c}$$

$$\implies m = \pm e^{-c} e^{-0.5t}$$

$$\implies m = Ae^{-0.5t}, \qquad \text{where } A = \pm e^{-c}$$

When $t = 0$, $m = 8 \Rightarrow A = 8$. Then $m = 8e^{-0.5t}$ and, after 1 hour, $m = 8e^{-0.5} \approx 4.85$.

After 1 hour there is approximately 4.85 kg of the substance remaining.

3 The number of bacteria in a population is modelled by the differential equation $\dfrac{dy}{dt} = 2y$, where y is the number of bacteria after t hours.

Initially there are 100 bacteria.

(a) Find an expression for y in terms of t.

(b) Find the number of bacteria after 5 hours.

Example 5

A murder victim was discovered by the police at 6:00 a.m. The body temperature of the victim was measured and found to be 25 °C. A doctor arrived on the scene of the crime 30 minutes later and measured the body temperature again. It was found to be 22 °C. The temperature of the room had remained constant at 15 °C. The doctor, knowing normal body temperature to be 37 °C, was able to estimate the time of death of the victim.

What would be your estimate for the time of death?

Solution

Assume Newton's law of cooling.

The rate of cooling at any instant is directly proportional to the difference in temperature between the object and its surroundings.

At t hours after 6 a.m., let the body temperature be y °C above the temperature of the surroundings.

$$\frac{dy}{dt} = \lambda y \Rightarrow \frac{dt}{dy} = \frac{1}{\lambda y}$$

$$\Rightarrow \lambda t = \int \frac{1}{y}\, dy$$

$$\Rightarrow \lambda t = \ln|y| + c$$

$$\Rightarrow \lambda t - c = \ln|y|$$

$$\Rightarrow y = \pm e^{\lambda t - c}$$

$$\Rightarrow y = \pm e^{-c} e^{\lambda t}$$

$$\Rightarrow y = A e^{\lambda t}$$

When $t = 0$ and $y = 10$,

$$10 = A e^0 \Rightarrow A = 10$$

When $t = 0.5$ and $y = 7$,

$$7 = 10e^{0.5\lambda} \implies 0.5\lambda = \ln 0.7$$

$$\implies \lambda = -0.713 \qquad \text{(to 3 s.f.)}$$

So $y = 10e^{-0.713t}$.

You can find the time, t, when the temperature was 22 degrees above room temperature.

$$y = 22 \implies 22 = 10e^{-0.713t}$$

$$\implies \ln 2.2 = -0.713t$$

$$\implies t = -1.106$$

1.106 hours is 1 hour 6 minutes. The time of death was about 1 hour 6 minutes before 6:00 a.m., or 4:54 a.m.

4   A patient admitted to hospital has injected 6 mg of a particular drug, but it is not known when. At 3 p.m., a test indicates that there is 3 mg of the drug present in the bloodstream. At 4 p.m. this has fallen to 2 mg. When is it likely that the drug was injected?

5   The radioactivity of the carbon-14 found in live organisms decays exponentially after death, according to the differential equation
$\dfrac{dR}{dt} = -\dfrac{1}{8300} R$, where R is the radioactivity in pico-curies per gram
t years after death. The radioactivity of live material is 6.68 pico-curies per gram. Pete Marsh is the name popularly given to the remains of a man whose body was found in a bog in Lindow Moss in Cheshire. When it was found, the radioactivity levels were about 5.3 pico-curies per gram. The man had apparently been murdered by garrotting before being thrown in the bog; but how long ago had this happened?

Exercise C (answers p. 135)

1   Find the equation of the solution curve of
$$\frac{dy}{dx} = -y$$
which passes through the point $(0, 2)$.

2   The mass, m kg, of a substance satisfies the differential equation
$$\frac{dm}{dt} = -0.1m$$
where t is the time in hours after the start of a chemical reaction.
(a)   Initially there was 2 kg of the substance. Find a formula for m in terms of t.
(b)   Hence calculate the time taken for the mass of the substance to be halved.

3   Boiling water is left in a room and cools to 90 °C in 5 minutes. If the room temperature is 20 °C, how long will the water take to cool to 60 °C?

4   A colony of insects initially has a population of 100 and is growing at the rate of 50 insects per day. If the rate of growth at any time is proportional to the population size at that time, how many insects will there be after 10 days?

5   A radioactive substance decays at a rate proportional to its mass. When the mass of a sample of the substance is 0.020 g it is decaying at a rate of 0.001 g per day. There are m grams left after t days.

   (a) Formulate a differential equation connecting m and t.

   (b) How long does the sample take to decay to 0.010 g?

6   Historical records indicate that the Egyptian king Sneferu died some time between 2700 BC and 2550 BC. Radioactivity levels from carbon-containing artefacts in his tomb gave a reading of about 3.8 pico-curies per gram.

   Does this reading agree with the historical records?

7   For a long time, historians believed that the origins of agriculture were in the Near East around 4500 BC. Archaeological investigations at the ancient city of Jericho (in modern-day Israel) found farming implements that gave a radiocarbon reading of 2.8 pico-curies per gram.

   Why did this lead to a storm in historical circles?

8E   Find the half-life of carbon-14. (The **half-life** is the time taken for a substance to decay to half its original mass. As the radioactivity is proportional to the mass of the substance present, you can use the differential equation given in question 5 on p. 63.)

D   Separating the variables (answers p. 136)

With the differential equations that you have so far solved by algebraic means, it has always been possible to do so with a single direct integration. Many other differential equations may be rearranged so that they are in a form suitable for direct integration. One important procedure for doing this for certain forms of differential equation is examined here.

Consider the problem of finding the general solution to the equation

$$\frac{dy}{dx} = xy$$

The solution requires one integration with respect to the variable x. However, on the right-hand side this leads to the integral

$$\int xy \, dx$$

1D	Why can't this be integrated?

However, you can proceed as follows.

$$\frac{dy}{dx} = xy \implies \frac{1}{y}\frac{dy}{dx} = x$$

Integrating with respect to x,

$$\int \left(\frac{1}{y}\frac{dy}{dx}\right) dx = \int x\, dx$$

$$\int \frac{1}{y}\, dy = \int x\, dx$$

2 (a) Integrate the left-hand side of the above equation.

(b) Integrate the right-hand side of the above equation.

You have probably included a constant of integration in your answers to both (a) and (b). Of course it is unlikely that both constants would be the same, so you might call them c_1 and c_2. However, there is no need to use two constants: you can subtract c_1 from both sides, and then you would have $c_2 - c_1$ on just one side. You might as well call this constant c. So, when you integrate both sides of a differential equation, you would usually put a constant of integration on just one side.

Hence the equation above becomes

$$\ln |y| = \frac{x^2}{2} + c$$

$$y = \pm e^{\frac{1}{2}x^2 + c} = \pm e^c e^{\frac{1}{2}x^2}$$

or $\qquad y = Ae^{\frac{1}{2}x^2}$, $\qquad$ where A is a constant

The technique illustrated above depends on your being able to 'separate' the two variables (here x and y) so that one side of the equation consists of a function of x alone and the other side has a product of $\dfrac{dy}{dx}$ and a function of y.

In other words, you must have an equation which can be rearranged in the form

$$f(y)\frac{dy}{dx} = g(x) \qquad\qquad (1)$$

Then, integrating with respect to x, you obtain

$$\int f(y)\frac{dy}{dx}\, dx = \int g(x)\, dx \qquad (2)$$

or

$$\int f(y)\,dy = \int g(x)\,dx \quad (3)$$

Provided the two integrations can be performed, the differential equation has then been solved. The method is called **separating the variables**.

In practice, (2) is usually omitted and you can proceed directly from (1) to (3). However, you should bear in mind that it is integrating *both* sides of (1) with respect to x which leads to (3), in which one integral is with respect to x and the other with respect to y.

3D | Which of these equations can be solved by separating the variables?

(a) $\dfrac{dy}{dx} = xy^2$ (b) $\dfrac{dy}{dx} = y^2$ (c) $\dfrac{dy}{dx} = x^2 + 3y$

(d) $\dfrac{dy}{dt} = ye^t$ (e) $\dfrac{dy}{dx} = x + yx$ (f) $\dfrac{dy}{dx} = \dfrac{y+3}{2x}$

(g) $\dfrac{dx}{dt} = x^2 + 2x$ (h) $\dfrac{dy}{dx} = e^{x+y}$ (i) $\dfrac{dy}{dx} = 3ye^x - y^2$

Example 6

Find the solution to the differential equation $\dfrac{dy}{dx} = x(y+1)$, given that $y = 2$ when $x = 0$.

Solution

$$\frac{dy}{dx} = x(y+1) \implies \frac{1}{y+1}\frac{dy}{dx} = x$$

Integrating with respect to x,

$$\int \frac{1}{y+1}\frac{dy}{dx}\,dx = \int x\,dx$$

$$\int \frac{1}{y+1}\,dy = \int x\,dx$$

$$\ln|y+1| = \frac{x^2}{2} + c$$

When $x = 0$, $y = 2 \implies \ln 3 = c$.

So

$$\ln|y+1| - \ln 3 = \frac{x^2}{2}$$

$$\ln\left|\frac{y+1}{3}\right| = \frac{x^2}{2}$$

$$\frac{y+1}{3} = e^{\frac{1}{2}x^2} \qquad \text{(l.h.s. must be positive)}$$

$$\Rightarrow \qquad y = 3e^{\frac{1}{2}x^2} - 1$$

If a differential equation can be written in the form $g(y)\dfrac{dy}{dx} = f(x)$, then the solution can be obtained from

$$\int g(y)\,dy = \int f(x)\,dx$$

This procedure is known as the **separation of variables**.

Only one constant of integration is necessary in the general solution. As with other differential equations, a particular solution may be found by substituting in a known point on the curve.

---

4   Find the general solution of $\dfrac{dy}{dx} = \dfrac{\cos x}{y^2}$.

5   Find the particular solution of $\dfrac{dy}{dx} = x^2 e^y$ for which the curve passes through $(3, 0)$.

Example 7

For a particular body falling vertically subject to gravity and air resistance, $\dfrac{dv}{dt} = 10 - 0.1v$, where v is the downward vertical speed in metres per second and t is the time in seconds. Solve the differential equation, given that the body starts from rest, and comment on the answer.

Solution

$$\frac{dv}{dt} = 10 - 0.1v$$

$$\Rightarrow \quad \int \frac{1}{10 - 0.1v}\, dv = \int 1 \, dt$$

$$\Rightarrow \quad \frac{1}{-0.1} \ln|10 - 0.1v| = t + c$$

$$\Rightarrow \quad -10 \ln|10 - 0.1v| = t + c$$

$$\Rightarrow \quad \ln|10 - 0.1v| = -0.1t - 0.1c$$

$$\Rightarrow \quad 10 - 0.1v = \pm e^{-0.1t - 0.1c}$$

$$\Rightarrow \quad 100 - v = \pm 10e^{-0.1c}e^{-0.1t}$$

$$\Rightarrow \quad 100 - v = Ae^{-0.1t}, \qquad \text{where } A = \pm 10e^{-0.1c}$$

$$\Rightarrow \quad v = 100 - Ae^{-0.1t}$$

When $t = 0$, $v = 0$, so $A = 100$. Therefore $v = 100(1 - e^{-0.1t})$.

As $t \to \infty$, $e^{-0.1t} \to 0$, and so the velocity tends to 100 m s^{-1}, which is called the terminal velocity.

6   An object is projected horizontally with speed 10 m s^{-1}. It is acted on by air resistance, so that its horizontal speed is modelled by the differential equation $\dfrac{dv}{dt} = -\dfrac{v^2}{10}$, with v in metres per second and t in seconds.

Solve the differential equation to find v in terms of t. What is the horizontal speed after 4 seconds?

Exercise D (answers p. 136)

1   Find the general solution to the following differential equations.

(a) $\dfrac{dy}{dx} = xy$ (b) $\dfrac{dp}{dt} = \dfrac{t}{p}$ (c) $\dfrac{dm}{dt} = 2m$

(d) $\dfrac{dy}{dx} = \dfrac{e^x}{y}$ (e) $\dfrac{dy}{dx} = \dfrac{y+1}{x+1}$

2   Find the solution to the differential equation

$$\frac{dy}{dx} = 3 - 2y$$

for which $y = 0$ when $x = 0$.

3 Solve the following differential equations; in each example, use the information given to find y as a function of x.

(a) $\dfrac{dy}{dx} = y$ and $y = 10$ when $x = 0$

(b) $\dfrac{dy}{dx} = -xy$ and $y = 2$ when $x = 1$

(c) $\dfrac{dy}{dx} = -y^2$ and $y = 1$ when $x = \frac{1}{2}$

4 Find the particular solutions to the following differential equations.

(a) $\dfrac{dy}{dx} = e^{-y} \cos 2x$ and $y = 0$ when $x = 0$

(b) $\dfrac{dy}{dx} = 4x^3 e^y$ and $y = 0$ when $x = 1$

E Formulating differential equations (answers p. 136)

You have studied some of the numerical and analytical methods for solving differential equations. The geometrical picture of the family of solution curves is also valuable. In particular, it indicates the effect of different initial conditions.

The relative advantages and disadvantages of solving a differential equation by algebraic integration or by a numerical method can be summarised as follows.

> Solving a differential equation by algebraic integration has the advantage that precise solutions are obtained.
>
> The power of a numerical method is that it can be applied to calculate a solution however complicated the gradient function may be.

To be able to apply either of these methods you must be able to formulate the differential equation correctly. This section considers a few examples of formulation.

You can follow the usual procedure for solving any problem.

Set up a model

You will need to identify the variables involved, and you may need to make some simplifying assumptions. The word **rate** usually indicates the derivative, although some rates (speed, acceleration) have special names.

Analyse the problem

You now solve the differential equation, and substitute any known values to get a particular solution. Whether you use a numerical or an analytical method will depend on the complexity of the differential equation, and whether the variables can be separated.

Interpret/validate

Does your answer look sensible? What happens in the long term? Are there any data you could use to verify what your model says?

Example 8

A child makes his way to school at a speed which is proportional to the distance he still has to cover. He leaves home, 2 km from school, running at $10\ \mathrm{km\ h^{-1}}$. How long will it be before he has gone nine-tenths of the way?

Solution

Set up a model

The rate involved is the speed, the rate of change of distance from home. You are told that this is proportional to the distance left to go. Use x for the distance from **home** in km after t hours; then

$$\frac{\mathrm{d}x}{\mathrm{d}t} = k(2 - x)$$

You also know that when $t = 0$, $x = 0$ and $\dfrac{\mathrm{d}x}{\mathrm{d}t} = 10$.

Analyse the problem

You can get rid of the constant k at this point, by using the initial conditions.

$$10 = 2k \implies k = 5$$

So $\dfrac{\mathrm{d}x}{\mathrm{d}t} = 5(2 - x)$

Rearranging,

$$\int \frac{1}{2 - x}\,\mathrm{d}x = \int 5\,\mathrm{d}t$$

$$\implies \quad -\ln|2 - x| = 5t + c$$

Substituting,

$$-\ln 2 = c$$

So

$$t = \frac{1}{5}(\ln 2 - \ln|2-x|) = \frac{1}{5}\ln\left|\frac{2}{2-x}\right|$$

When the child has travelled nine-tenths of the way to school, $x = 1.8$ and $t = \frac{1}{5}\ln 10 \approx 0.46$ hours.

Interpret/validate

The child has gone nine-tenths of the way after about 28 minutes.

The speed of the child is getting less and less. If you think about when the child will get to school, you will realise that your formula for t is not valid for $x = 2$, as the fraction's denominator would be zero. The model you were told to use may give a reasonable approximation for the question asked, but is inappropriate for the whole journey.

1D An animal disease spreads so that the rate at which animals are infected is proportional to the square root of the number already infected. In a particular outbreak, after 8 days, 100 cases have been reported, and new cases are being reported at the rate of 30 per day.

(a) Form a differential equation to model this situation.

(b) Solve your differential equation, and use the information given to find the particular solution.

(c) Sketch the graph of the number of animals infected against time.

(d) What does the graph tell you about the long term? Is this realistic?

(e) It is decided to cull animals as soon as they are diagnosed with the disease. This will result in about half the infected animals being culled each day; others will not yet have shown visible signs of the disease. Explain why an appropriate differential equation is now

$$\frac{dN}{dt} = 3\sqrt{N} - 0.5N$$

(f) Starting from $t = 0$, $N = 100$, and using increments of 1 day, use a numerical method to find the number of infected animals after another 20 days, if the cull is implemented.

(g) It can be shown, by analytical techniques, that the number of infected animals, according to this model, will never reach zero.

Find the value of N for which $\frac{dN}{dt} = 0$.

This shows that if N ever reaches this value, it will neither increase nor decrease. In fact, the graph of the solution curve has a horizontal asymptote at this value, and so never actually attains it.

So far, you have been given information about how the rate is related to the other quantities. A scientist who is seeking to establish a model must make some intelligent guesses about how things might be related. The model can then be analysed and compared with real data.

Example 9

High on the moors, perched on a rocky crag, lies a most curious boulder. It has fascinated the locals and tourists alike for years, for it is almost perfectly spherical in shape. Over the years it has gradually been eroded by the action of the winds, but it has retained its basic shape. In fact, according to the locals, it now has half the diameter it had 100 years ago. 'Be gone in another 100 years,' they say. Are they right?

Solution

Set up a model

The locals will be right only if there is a linear relationship between the radius of the boulder and time. To decide if this is the case you need to make some assumptions about the rate of erosion and decide upon the variables and units to be used.

Volume of boulder $V \, \text{cm}^3$	Radius of boulder $r \, \text{cm}$	Time from 100 years ago t years

It is reasonable to assume that the rate of erosion is proportional to the surface area, $A = 4\pi r^2$. Since the rate of erosion is $-\dfrac{\mathrm{d}V}{\mathrm{d}t}$, the important differential equation is

$$-\frac{\mathrm{d}V}{\mathrm{d}t} = kA \qquad \text{i.e.} \ \frac{\mathrm{d}V}{\mathrm{d}t} = -4k\pi r^2$$

Analyse the problem

Since $V = \frac{4}{3}\pi r^3$,

$$\frac{dV}{dt} = \frac{4}{3}\pi \times 3r^2 \frac{dr}{dt} \qquad \text{(by the chain rule)}$$

$$= 4\pi r^2 \frac{dr}{dt}$$

So $4\pi r^2 \frac{dr}{dt} = -4k\pi r^2$

$$\Rightarrow \qquad \frac{dr}{dt} = -k$$

Interpret/validate

The radius decreases at a constant rate and so the boulder *will* be gone in another 100 years. You cannot validate this conclusion directly although you could find out known facts about erosion rates. In fact, it is unlikely that the boulder will retain its shape as it is eroded.

2D Consider a lock in a river being filled by opening the top gates. Discuss how the rate of increase might be related to the depth of water.

As you have seen in question 1(e) in this section, and example 7 in section D, some differential equations have more than two terms because the rate of change is the sum or difference of two effects.

3 Bacteria in a tank of water increase at a rate proportional to the number present. Water is drained from the tank, initially containing 100 litres, at a steady rate of 2 litres per hour.

(a) If the water were not draining from the tank, find a differential equation involving N, the number of bacteria, t, the time in hours, and k, a constant.

(b) Write down an expression for the amount of water in the tank at time t.

(c) Write down an expression for the number of bacteria in each litre of water at time t. (Remember that N was defined to be the number of bacteria in the tank at time t.)

(d) Write down an expression for the number of bacteria in the water drained from the tank each hour.

(e) Your final differential equation will be of the form

$$\frac{dN}{dt} = (\text{rate of growth of bacteria}) - (\text{bacteria drained each hour})$$

Write down this equation.

(f) Given that $k = 0.7$, and that the number of bacteria at the start was 100, find the number of bacteria after 5 hours. (Hint: you will probably want to take a factor of N out of the right-hand side of your equation.)

Exercise E (answers p. 137)

1   In an electrical circuit, the current is reducing at a rate proportional to the current itself. Initially, the current is 25 mA, and is falling at 1 mA per second. Find the current flowing after 5 seconds, and after 10 seconds.

2   The linear growth rate of a sapling is thought to be proportional to the square root of its height. When it is planted, it measures 25 cm, and is growing at 2 cm per week.

(a) Form a differential equation and solve it.

(b) Find how long it will take the sapling to reach
   (i) 1 m   (ii) 4 m

(c) Comment on whether the model is realistic in the long term.

3   A tank with a base measuring 3 by 4 metres has vertical sides. The base and sides are made of a porous material, and water in the tank seeps out at a rate proportional to the area of the base and sides in contact with the water. Initially, the tank is full to a depth of 2 m and the water is falling at 0.1 metres per hour.

(a) Form a differential equation, and solve it to find an equation connecting the depth and the time.

(b) Find the time it will take for the tank to empty.

4   The area covered by an oil spillage in the North Sea is increasing at a rate proportional to its half-diameter, r. Assuming the slick to be roughly circular,

(a) find $\dfrac{dA}{dt}$ in terms of r

(b) find $\dfrac{dA}{dr}$ in terms of r.

(c) Use the chain rule to find a differential equation involving r and t. Comment on your answer.

5 Water is leaking from a hole in the bottom of a tank at a rate proportional to the square root of the depth of water in the tank. The tank's base area is 2 square metres, and initially the depth is 4 m, and the water is leaking out at 0.2 cubic metres per minute.

(a) Find an expression for $\dfrac{dV}{dt}$ in terms of the depth, h, and use the initial conditions to eliminate any constant.

(b) Find an expression for $\dfrac{dV}{dh}$ in terms of h.

(c) Use the chain rule to find a differential equation involving h and t.

(d) Solve your differential equation and use it to find the time it takes for the tank to empty.

6 A tank contains a solution of a chemical which needs to be diluted. The tank holds 1000 litres, which is made up of 900 litres of water and 100 litres of the chemical. It is necessary to reduce the strength of the solution to half this level. This is to be done by pumping in water at 5 litres per minute, and pumping the solution out at the same rate. Constant stirring means that you may assume that the solution has the same strength everywhere.

(a) How many litres of water do you need to end up with in the tank?

(b) How many litres of water are pumped in every minute?

(c) If W is the number of litres of water in the tank at time t, find an expression for the proportion of the solution which is water at time t.

(d) Find an expression in terms of W for the amount of water removed per minute.

(e) Form an expression for $\dfrac{dW}{dt}$.

(f) How long will it take to dilute the solution to half the initial strength?

7 The volume of a large spherical snowball decreases as it melts at a rate proportional to its surface area at any instant.

(a) Express this statement in symbols.

(b) Given that a snowball of radius 30 cm takes 10 days to melt, find an expression for the radius r in terms of the time t.

(c) After how many days will
(i) the radius be halved? (ii) the volume be halved?

8   In a lake, about 2000 newly hatched fish survive each year. However, about 10% of the fish in the lake die each year as the result of disease, predators or old age. These observations lead to the hypothesis that

$$\frac{dy}{dt} = \alpha + \beta y, \qquad \text{where } y \text{ is the number of fish present}$$

(a) Explain why $\beta = -0.1$ and state the value of α.

(b) In what units are y and $\dfrac{dy}{dt}$ measured?

(c) The lake had a stable population of 20 000 fish before a careless discharge of chemicals killed 5000 fish. Estimate how long it will take for the population to reach 19 000.

(d) Write down the differential equation which will apply if 12% of the fish die each year and 2500 newly hatched fish survive.

9   It is estimated that the rate of growth of an island population of mice, P, is 4% per day. A new type of predator is introduced to the island, which kills rabbits at a rate of about $0.2\sqrt{P}$ per day. Given that at the time of the arrival of the predators the population of rabbits was 2500, find the number of rabbits remaining after 100 days. (When you integrate, you will find it helpful to make the substitution $s = 0.2\sqrt{P}$.)

10E Look at the differential equation formed in question 9. For some initial values of P, the population will increase, and for others it will decrease. Find the critical value for which the population remains stable.

11E A more complicated model of disease spread says that the rate of spread is directly proportional to the product of the number of people already infected and the number of people not yet infected. Form a differential equation for the rate of infection on an island of 2000 people, assuming that just one person brings the infection to the island, and that he infects one other person in the first day. Solve the differential equation to find out when half the island will be infected.

After working through this chapter you should

1   be able to interpret and formulate simple differential equations

2   know that each differential equation is associated with a family of curves

3   know how to use initial conditions or a known point on the curve to find a particular solution to a differential equation

4   be able to find solutions by straightforward integration when appropriate

5   be able to solve differential equations by separating variables when appropriate

6   be able to calculate approximate solutions using a numerical method where necessary.

6 Vector geometry

A Vectors and position vectors (answers p. 138)

The work in this section may have been met already, in *Mechanics 1*.

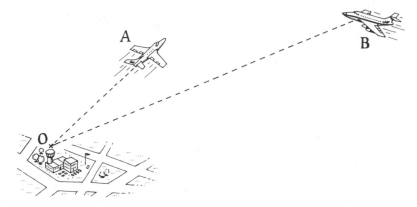

An aircraft A takes off from an airport O. After 1 minute it is 1 km east and 5 km north of O at a height of 0.8 km.

A second aircraft B is then 5 km east and 5 km north of O at a height of 4 km.

A situation of this kind, concerning the relative position of two aircraft and how this may change with time, is handled most conveniently using the notation and mathematics of vectors. Many problems in mathematics, and in the application of mathematics, are best handled using vectors – you may have already done vector work in mechanics, for example. In this section we extend this work to consider the vector equations of lines and planes.

Taking the vector $\begin{bmatrix} a \\ b \\ c \end{bmatrix}$ to represent a position a km east and b km north of O, at a height of c km, aircraft A has position vector $\overrightarrow{OA} = \begin{bmatrix} 1 \\ 5 \\ 0.8 \end{bmatrix}$ and B has position vector $\overrightarrow{OB} = \begin{bmatrix} 5 \\ 5 \\ 4 \end{bmatrix}$.

$\overrightarrow{OA}$ and $\overrightarrow{OB}$ are the position vectors from the point O of the points A and B respectively.

They are given in **column vector** form above. The position vector $\overrightarrow{OA}$ of a point is often denoted by $\underline{a}$ or $\mathbf{a}$.

The notation $\mathbf{a}$ is used in printed texts, and underlining is used in handwritten work. Although $\mathbf{a}$ is used to indicate the vector from O to A, the start-point can be anywhere.

Later in the chapter, you will work with three-dimensional vectors as in the example above. However, it is helpful to develop some ideas in two dimensions first.

Vectors can be added. Adding vectors is equivalent to going along one vector and then along the other.

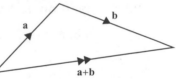

1   Use squared paper for this question.

For each part of the question, draw **a** and **b** and then find **a** + **b** as a column vector.

(a) $\mathbf{a} = \begin{bmatrix} 3 \\ -1 \end{bmatrix}, \mathbf{b} = \begin{bmatrix} 2 \\ 5 \end{bmatrix}$ (b) $\mathbf{a} = \begin{bmatrix} 2 \\ -3 \end{bmatrix}, \mathbf{b} = \begin{bmatrix} -4 \\ 1 \end{bmatrix}$

(c) $\mathbf{a} = \begin{bmatrix} 4 \\ 1 \end{bmatrix}, \mathbf{b} = \begin{bmatrix} -3 \\ 0 \end{bmatrix}$

(d) Explain how **a** + **b** can be calculated without drawing.

(e) For (a), find **b** + **a** and comment on your answer.

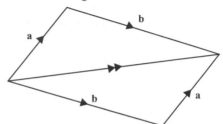

The parallelogram illustrates that

$\mathbf{a} + \mathbf{b} = \mathbf{b} + \mathbf{a}$

2   Use squared paper for this question.

For each part of the question, draw $\overrightarrow{OA} = \mathbf{a}$ and $\overrightarrow{OB} = \mathbf{b}$ as position vectors, both starting from the origin, and then find the vector $\overrightarrow{AB}$ in each case.

(a) $\mathbf{a} = \begin{bmatrix} 4 \\ 5 \end{bmatrix}, \mathbf{b} = \begin{bmatrix} 2 \\ 3 \end{bmatrix}$ (b) $\mathbf{a} = \begin{bmatrix} 1 \\ 3 \end{bmatrix}, \mathbf{b} = \begin{bmatrix} 4 \\ -1 \end{bmatrix}$

(c) $\mathbf{a} = \begin{bmatrix} 3 \\ 0 \end{bmatrix}, \mathbf{b} = \begin{bmatrix} 2 \\ 4 \end{bmatrix}$

(d) Explain how $\overrightarrow{AB}$ could be calculated without drawing.

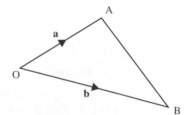

$\overrightarrow{AB} = \mathbf{b} - \mathbf{a}$

You can see that if you go from A to O to B, you have gone along **a** backwards, i.e. −**a**, and then along **b** .

Hence $\overrightarrow{AB} = -\mathbf{a} + \mathbf{b} = \mathbf{b} - \mathbf{a}$.

3 If $p = \overrightarrow{OP}$ and $q = \overrightarrow{OQ}$, write down $\overrightarrow{PQ}$ and $\overrightarrow{QP}$ in terms of p and q.

Vectors can be multiplied by numbers. For instance $3a = a + a + a$.

If $a = \begin{bmatrix} a_1 \\ a_2 \end{bmatrix}$, then $3a = \begin{bmatrix} 3a_1 \\ 3a_2 \end{bmatrix}$.

4 If $a = \begin{bmatrix} 2 \\ 1 \end{bmatrix}$ and $b = \begin{bmatrix} 3 \\ 0 \end{bmatrix}$, find

(a) $a + b$ (b) $a - b$ (c) $b + a$

(d) $2a + b$ (e) $3a - 2b$ (f) $3a - 3b$

(g) $3(a - b)$ (h) $\frac{1}{3}b$

5 It is not always necessary to use a square grid for vectors. Vectors a and b are as shown on this isometric grid.

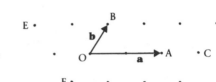

(a) Write down the position vectors of C, D, E and F in terms of a and b.

(b) Find the vectors $\overrightarrow{AB}$, $\overrightarrow{CD}$, $\overrightarrow{DE}$, $\overrightarrow{EF}$ and $\overrightarrow{FC}$ in terms of a and b.

(c) Check that $\overrightarrow{CD} + \overrightarrow{DE} + \overrightarrow{EF} + \overrightarrow{FC} = 0$. Why is this so?

(d) Compare $\overrightarrow{AD}$ and $\overrightarrow{EF}$. Explain what you notice.

6 Draw the following sets of vectors and comment on your findings.

(a) $\begin{bmatrix} 2 \\ 1 \end{bmatrix}, \begin{bmatrix} 4 \\ 2 \end{bmatrix}, \begin{bmatrix} -2 \\ -1 \end{bmatrix}, \begin{bmatrix} -6 \\ -3 \end{bmatrix}$ (b) $\begin{bmatrix} 3 \\ -2 \end{bmatrix}, \begin{bmatrix} -6 \\ 4 \end{bmatrix}, \begin{bmatrix} 6 \\ -4 \end{bmatrix}, \begin{bmatrix} -9 \\ 6 \end{bmatrix}$

A point may be described in terms of its **coordinates** (x, y) or in terms of its **position vector** $\begin{bmatrix} x \\ y \end{bmatrix}$, which describes a translation from the origin to the point.

For two points P and Q, with position vectors p and q, the vector describing a translation from P to Q is given by $\overrightarrow{PQ} = q - p$.

Vectors may be added and subtracted by adding and subtracting the corresponding components. They may be multiplied by a **scalar** (number), in which case each component is multiplied by this amount.

Vectors are parallel if their components are in the same ratio, i.e. if one is a multiple of the other.

The ideas above extend to three dimensions in the obvious way.

7 If $\mathbf{p} = \begin{bmatrix} 3 \\ 1 \\ 2 \end{bmatrix}$ and $\mathbf{q} = \begin{bmatrix} 2 \\ 0 \\ -2 \end{bmatrix}$, find

(a) $\mathbf{p} + \mathbf{q}$ (b) $\mathbf{p} - \mathbf{q}$ (c) $\mathbf{q} - \mathbf{p}$

(d) $3\mathbf{q} - \mathbf{p}$ (e) $\frac{1}{2}\mathbf{q}$ (f) $4\mathbf{p} + \frac{1}{2}\mathbf{q}$

8 OABCDEFG is a cube with edges of length 6 and axes as shown.

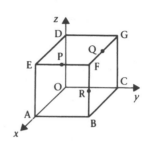

P, Q, R are the mid-points of the edges EF, FG, FB.

(a) Find the position vectors of the points A, B, C, D, E, F and G.

(b) Find the position vectors of the points P, Q and R.

(c) Demonstrate that $\overrightarrow{PQ} + \overrightarrow{QR} + \overrightarrow{RP} = \mathbf{0}$.

In some contexts, a different notation is used for vectors.

If $\mathbf{i}$ is a unit vector in the x direction, or $\begin{bmatrix} 1 \\ 0 \\ 0 \end{bmatrix}$,

$\mathbf{j}$ is a unit vector in the y direction, or $\begin{bmatrix} 0 \\ 1 \\ 0 \end{bmatrix}$, and

$\mathbf{k}$ is a unit vector in the z direction, or $\begin{bmatrix} 0 \\ 0 \\ 1 \end{bmatrix}$,

then the vector $\begin{bmatrix} 3 \\ 1 \\ 2 \end{bmatrix}$ can be written as $3\mathbf{i} + \mathbf{j} + 2\mathbf{k}$. This notation can be useful when sophisticated typesetting tools are not available.

In this book, however, column vectors are used throughout.

It is often important to know the **magnitude**, or length, of a vector. For example, the distance between two points A and B is given by the magnitude of the vector $\overrightarrow{AB}$.

> The magnitude or length of the vector $\mathbf{c}$ is denoted by $|\mathbf{c}|$ or simply c. Similarly the magnitude of the vector $\overrightarrow{AB}$ is denoted by $|AB|$ or AB.

This is why it is important to underline handwritten vectors, so that $\mathbf{c}$ and c are distinguished.

In two dimensions, the magnitude is easy to calculate, using Pythagoras' theorem.

It is usual to leave the value in surd form. For example,

$$\mathbf{a} = \begin{bmatrix} -2 \\ 4 \end{bmatrix}$$

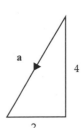

$$|\mathbf{a}| = \sqrt{(-2)^2 + 4^2}$$
$$= \sqrt{4 + 16} = \sqrt{20} = 2\sqrt{5}$$

9 Find the magnitudes of these vectors.

(a) $\begin{bmatrix} 2 \\ 1 \end{bmatrix}$ (b) $\begin{bmatrix} 3 \\ -4 \end{bmatrix}$ (c) $\begin{bmatrix} -3 \\ 1 \end{bmatrix}$

Three dimensions are not a great deal harder.

10 Consider the vector $\overrightarrow{OQ} = \begin{bmatrix} 2 \\ 1 \\ 5 \end{bmatrix}$.

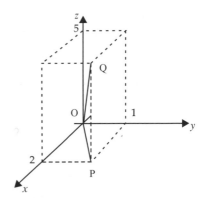

(a) Use Pythagoras' theorem to find the length OP.

(b) Use Pythagoras' theorem on triangle OPQ to find the length OQ.

11 Consider the vector $\overrightarrow{OQ} = \begin{bmatrix} a \\ b \\ c \end{bmatrix}$.

(a) Find the length OP.

(b) Find the length OQ.

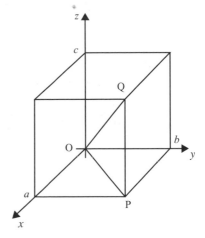

The magnitude of $\begin{bmatrix} a \\ b \end{bmatrix}$ is $\sqrt{a^2 + b^2}$.

The magnitude of $\begin{bmatrix} a \\ b \\ c \end{bmatrix}$ is $\sqrt{a^2 + b^2 + c^2}$.

Exercise A (answers p. 139)

1 $\overrightarrow{OA} = \mathbf{a} = \begin{bmatrix} 3 \\ 1 \\ 2 \end{bmatrix}$, $\overrightarrow{OB} = \mathbf{b} = \begin{bmatrix} 4 \\ 3 \\ 0 \end{bmatrix}$, $\overrightarrow{OC} = \mathbf{c} = \begin{bmatrix} 2 \\ -1 \\ 4 \end{bmatrix}$

Find the following.

(a) $\mathbf{a} + 2\mathbf{b}$ (b) $\mathbf{c} - 3\mathbf{b}$ (c) $\mathbf{b} + \mathbf{c}$

(d) $|\mathbf{a}|$ (e) $|\mathbf{a} + \mathbf{b}|$ (f) $\overrightarrow{AB}$

(g) $\overrightarrow{BC}$ (h) $\overrightarrow{OA} + \overrightarrow{AB} + \overrightarrow{BC}$

2 Look at your answers to question 1.

(a) Comment on your answer to (h).

(b) Show that $\mathbf{b} + \mathbf{c}$ is parallel to $\mathbf{a}$.

3 The position vectors of four points P, Q, R and S are

$$\begin{bmatrix} 3 \\ 1 \end{bmatrix}, \begin{bmatrix} 5 \\ -2 \end{bmatrix}, \begin{bmatrix} 2 \\ -4 \end{bmatrix} \quad \text{and} \quad \begin{bmatrix} 0 \\ -1 \end{bmatrix}$$

(a) Find the vectors $\overrightarrow{PQ}$ and $\overrightarrow{SR}$.

What does this tell you about the quadrilateral PQRS?

(b) What can you say about the vectors $\overrightarrow{PS}$ and $\overrightarrow{QR}$?

4 OABCDE is a triangular prism with

$$\overrightarrow{OA} = \begin{bmatrix} 6 \\ 0 \\ 0 \end{bmatrix}, \quad \overrightarrow{OB} = \begin{bmatrix} 0 \\ 8 \\ 0 \end{bmatrix}, \quad \overrightarrow{OC} = \begin{bmatrix} 0 \\ 0 \\ 10 \end{bmatrix}$$

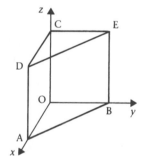

(a) (i) Find the position vectors of D and E.

(ii) Find the vectors $\overrightarrow{AB}$, $\overrightarrow{AD}$, $\overrightarrow{AC}$, $\overrightarrow{AE}$ and $\overrightarrow{DE}$.

(b) M is the mid-point of AB and N is the mid-point of DE.

(i) Find the position vectors of M and N.

(ii) Find the vectors $\overrightarrow{AN}$ and $\overrightarrow{ME}$.

(iii) Explain what you notice about the results.

5 OABCDE is the roof of a house. OABC is a
rectangle with OA of length 8 m and OC of length
10 m. The ridge DE of length 6 m is positioned
symmetrically, 3 m above the rectangle.

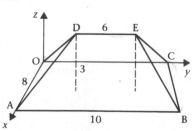

(a) With axes as shown, find the position
vectors of A, B, C, D and E.

(b) Find the vectors $\overrightarrow{AD}$, $\overrightarrow{OD}$, $\overrightarrow{BE}$ and $\overrightarrow{CE}$,
representing the slant edges of the roof.

(c) What is the length of a slant edge?

B Vector equations of lines (answers p. 140)

1D On squared paper plot the the points (x, y) whose position vectors are given by the following vector equations. Take $0, \pm 1, \pm 2$ and ± 3 as values of the parameter t.

(a) $\begin{bmatrix} x \\ y \end{bmatrix} = t \begin{bmatrix} 2 \\ 3 \end{bmatrix}$

(b) $\begin{bmatrix} x \\ y \end{bmatrix} = \begin{bmatrix} 3 \\ -1 \end{bmatrix} + t \begin{bmatrix} 2 \\ 3 \end{bmatrix}$

(c) $\begin{bmatrix} x \\ y \end{bmatrix} = \begin{bmatrix} 2 \\ 4 \end{bmatrix} + t \begin{bmatrix} 2 \\ 3 \end{bmatrix}$

(d) What do you notice about each set of points?

(e) What is the significance of the vector $\begin{bmatrix} 2 \\ 3 \end{bmatrix}$?

Any straight line can be described in terms of the position vector of a point on the line and a direction vector.

Any point P on this line has position vector $\mathbf{r} = \mathbf{a} + t\mathbf{b}$, for some value of t.

We can write a **vector equation** for the line as

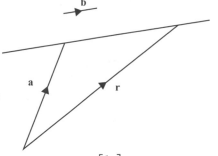

$$\begin{bmatrix} x \\ y \end{bmatrix} = \begin{bmatrix} a_1 \\ a_2 \end{bmatrix} + t \begin{bmatrix} b_1 \\ b_2 \end{bmatrix}$$

where (a_1, a_2) is a particular point on the line and the vector $\begin{bmatrix} b_1 \\ b_2 \end{bmatrix}$ determines the direction of the line.

2 On squared paper, plot the following lines.

(a) $\begin{bmatrix} x \\ y \end{bmatrix} = \begin{bmatrix} 2 \\ 3 \end{bmatrix} + t \begin{bmatrix} -1 \\ 2 \end{bmatrix}$

(b) $\begin{bmatrix} x \\ y \end{bmatrix} = \begin{bmatrix} 3 \\ 1 \end{bmatrix} + t \begin{bmatrix} -2 \\ 4 \end{bmatrix}$

(c) $\begin{bmatrix} x \\ y \end{bmatrix} = \begin{bmatrix} 1 \\ 5 \end{bmatrix} + t \begin{bmatrix} 1 \\ -2 \end{bmatrix}$

The vector equation of a line is not unique: any point on the line can be used for the position vector, and any vector in the right direction can be used as the direction vector.

Example 1

Find a vector equation of the line joining the points A $(2, 3)$ and B $(5, 4)$.

Solution

The position vector of a point on the line is $\begin{bmatrix} 2 \\ 3 \end{bmatrix}$ and

the direction of the line is given by the vector

$\overrightarrow{AB} = \begin{bmatrix} 3 \\ 1 \end{bmatrix}$. Thus the equation of the line AB is

$$\begin{bmatrix} x \\ y \end{bmatrix} = \begin{bmatrix} 2 \\ 3 \end{bmatrix} + t \begin{bmatrix} 3 \\ 1 \end{bmatrix}$$

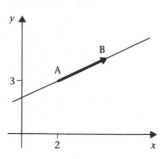

3   Find a vector equation of the line joining $\begin{bmatrix} -2 \\ 1 \end{bmatrix}$ and $\begin{bmatrix} 3 \\ -4 \end{bmatrix}$.

4   The vector equation $\begin{bmatrix} x \\ y \end{bmatrix} = \begin{bmatrix} 3 \\ -1 \end{bmatrix} + t \begin{bmatrix} 2 \\ 3 \end{bmatrix}$ can be written in terms of its components as

$$x = 3 + 2t \qquad (1)$$
$$y = -1 + 3t \qquad (2)$$

(a) Express t in terms of x from equation (1).

(b) Substitute this for t in equation (2) to find the Cartesian equation of the line in the form $y = mx + c$.

(c) What is the gradient of the line? How is this related to the vector $\begin{bmatrix} 2 \\ 3 \end{bmatrix}$?

5   Find Cartesian equations for these lines.

(a) $\begin{bmatrix} x \\ y \end{bmatrix} = \begin{bmatrix} 3 \\ -2 \end{bmatrix} + s \begin{bmatrix} -2 \\ 1 \end{bmatrix}$ (b) $\begin{bmatrix} x \\ y \end{bmatrix} = \begin{bmatrix} 1 \\ -1 \end{bmatrix} + t \begin{bmatrix} 2 \\ -1 \end{bmatrix}$

Again, the idea of a vector equation can easily be extended to three dimensions.

Consider the motion of the two aircraft described earlier.

The position of aircraft A, t minutes after take-off, is given by the equation

$$\begin{bmatrix} x \\ y \\ z \end{bmatrix} = t \begin{bmatrix} 1 \\ 5 \\ 0.8 \end{bmatrix}$$

The position of aircraft B at the same time, t minutes, is given by the vector equation

$$\begin{bmatrix} x \\ y \\ z \end{bmatrix} = \begin{bmatrix} 5 \\ 0 \\ 4 \end{bmatrix} + t \begin{bmatrix} 0 \\ 5 \\ 0 \end{bmatrix}$$

Aircraft B is flying in the direction of the vector $\begin{bmatrix} 0 \\ 5 \\ 0 \end{bmatrix}$.

The position vector of each aircraft after 2 minutes is

$$\overrightarrow{OA} = \begin{bmatrix} 2 \\ 10 \\ 1.6 \end{bmatrix} \quad \text{and} \quad \overrightarrow{OB} = \begin{bmatrix} 5 \\ 10 \\ 4 \end{bmatrix}$$

The displacement vector $\overrightarrow{AB}$ at this moment is given by $\overrightarrow{OB} - \overrightarrow{OA}$,

$$\text{i.e.} \quad \overrightarrow{AB} = \begin{bmatrix} 3 \\ 0 \\ 2.4 \end{bmatrix}$$

Notice that when $t = 5$ the aircraft have the same position vectors – a collision occurs!

Each aircraft is moving in a straight line. The following examples examine in more detail the vector equations of lines.

Questions 6 to 10 refer to the cuboid CFGEOADB with OA = 4, OB = 6 and OC = 3.

$$\overrightarrow{OA} = \begin{bmatrix} 4 \\ 0 \\ 0 \end{bmatrix}$$

$$\overrightarrow{OB} = \begin{bmatrix} 0 \\ 6 \\ 0 \end{bmatrix}$$

$$\overrightarrow{OC} = \begin{bmatrix} 0 \\ 0 \\ 3 \end{bmatrix}$$

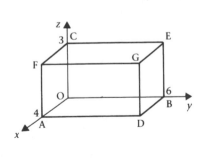

6 Find the position vectors of the points D, E, F and G.

7 Points are given by the vector equation

$$\begin{bmatrix} x \\ y \\ z \end{bmatrix} = \lambda \begin{bmatrix} 4 \\ 6 \\ 0 \end{bmatrix}, \qquad \text{where } \lambda \text{ is a parameter}$$

(a) Which points correspond to $\lambda = 0$ and $\lambda = 1$?

(b) On a large copy of the diagram, mark points corresponding to $\lambda = \frac{1}{4}, \frac{1}{2}$ and $\frac{3}{4}$. What do you notice about them?

(c) What can you say about the positions of the points where $\lambda = 2$ and $\lambda = -1$?

8 $\begin{bmatrix} x \\ y \\ z \end{bmatrix} = \lambda \begin{bmatrix} 4 \\ 6 \\ 0 \end{bmatrix}$ is the vector equation of the line OD .

Identify the lines with the following vector equations.

(a) $\begin{bmatrix} x \\ y \\ z \end{bmatrix} = \lambda \begin{bmatrix} 0 \\ 0 \\ 3 \end{bmatrix}$ 　　　(b) $\begin{bmatrix} x \\ y \\ z \end{bmatrix} = \lambda \begin{bmatrix} 0 \\ 6 \\ 3 \end{bmatrix}$

Give vector equations for these lines.

(c) OB 　　　　(d) OF 　　　　(e) OG

9 Identify the lines with the following vector equations.

(a) $\begin{bmatrix} x \\ y \\ z \end{bmatrix} = \begin{bmatrix} 0 \\ 6 \\ 0 \end{bmatrix} + \lambda \begin{bmatrix} 0 \\ 0 \\ 3 \end{bmatrix}$ 　　(b) $\begin{bmatrix} x \\ y \\ z \end{bmatrix} = \begin{bmatrix} 4 \\ 0 \\ 3 \end{bmatrix} + \lambda \begin{bmatrix} -4 \\ 6 \\ 0 \end{bmatrix}$

What is the significance of the vectors $\begin{bmatrix} 0 \\ 0 \\ 3 \end{bmatrix}$ in (a) and $\begin{bmatrix} -4 \\ 6 \\ 0 \end{bmatrix}$ in (b)?

10 Give vector equations for these lines.

(a) AD 　　　　(b) AG 　　　　(c) AE

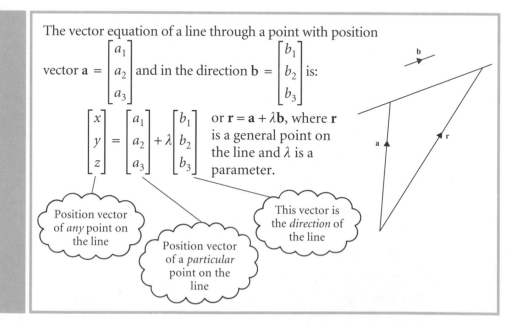

The vector equation of a line through a point with position

vector $\mathbf{a} = \begin{bmatrix} a_1 \\ a_2 \\ a_3 \end{bmatrix}$ and in the direction $\mathbf{b} = \begin{bmatrix} b_1 \\ b_2 \\ b_3 \end{bmatrix}$ is:

$\begin{bmatrix} x \\ y \\ z \end{bmatrix} = \begin{bmatrix} a_1 \\ a_2 \\ a_3 \end{bmatrix} + \lambda \begin{bmatrix} b_1 \\ b_2 \\ b_3 \end{bmatrix}$ or $\mathbf{r} = \mathbf{a} + \lambda \mathbf{b}$, where $\mathbf{r}$ is a general point on the line and λ is a parameter.

Position vector of *any* point on the line

Position vector of a *particular* point on the line

This vector is the *direction* of the line

Example 2

Find a vector equation of the line joining the points A $(3, 1, 0)$ and B $(1, 5, -2)$.

Solution

The position vector of a point on the line is $\begin{bmatrix} 3 \\ 1 \\ 0 \end{bmatrix}$, and the direction of

the line is given by the vector $\overrightarrow{AB} = \begin{bmatrix} -2 \\ 4 \\ -2 \end{bmatrix}$, or the simpler parallel

vector $\begin{bmatrix} 1 \\ -2 \\ 1 \end{bmatrix}$.

Thus an equation of the line AB is

$$\begin{bmatrix} x \\ y \\ z \end{bmatrix} = \begin{bmatrix} 3 \\ 1 \\ 0 \end{bmatrix} + t \begin{bmatrix} 1 \\ -2 \\ 1 \end{bmatrix}$$

11 Find a vector equation of the line joining the points C $(0, 2, -3)$ and D $(1, 4, 0)$.

Exercise B (answers p. 141)

1 Find vector equations for
  (a) the line joining the points $(4, 1)$ and $(7, 7)$
  (b) the line joining the points $(2, 1)$ and $(-1, 5)$
  (c) the line through the point $(5, 1)$ parallel to the vector $\begin{bmatrix} -2 \\ 4 \end{bmatrix}$
  (d) the line $y = x$
  (e) the y-axis

2 Find vector equations in three dimensions for
  (a) the line joining the points $(2, 1, 0)$ and $(3, 4, 4)$
  (b) the line joining the points $(-1, 0, 3)$ and $(2, 2, 3)$
  (c) the line through the point $(1, 2, 2)$ parallel to the vector $(3, -1, 2)$
  (d) the x-axis

3 OABCDEFG is a cuboid with edges OA, OC and OD of lengths 4, 5 and 3 respectively.

Which lines have the following vector equations?

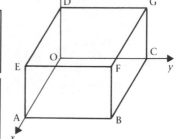

(a) $\begin{bmatrix} x \\ y \\ z \end{bmatrix} = \lambda \begin{bmatrix} 0 \\ 5 \\ 3 \end{bmatrix}$ (b) $\begin{bmatrix} x \\ y \\ z \end{bmatrix} = \begin{bmatrix} 4 \\ 0 \\ 3 \end{bmatrix} + \lambda \begin{bmatrix} -4 \\ 5 \\ 0 \end{bmatrix}$

(c) $\begin{bmatrix} x \\ y \\ z \end{bmatrix} = \begin{bmatrix} 0 \\ 5 \\ 0 \end{bmatrix} + \lambda \begin{bmatrix} 4 \\ -5 \\ 3 \end{bmatrix}$ (d) $\begin{bmatrix} x \\ y \\ z \end{bmatrix} = \begin{bmatrix} 4 \\ 5 \\ 0 \end{bmatrix} + \lambda \begin{bmatrix} -4 \\ -5 \\ 3 \end{bmatrix}$

4 For the cuboid in question 3, find vector equations for these lines.

(a) AB   (b) AC   (c) AF   (d) AG

C Intersections of lines (answers p. 142)

1D

(a) On squared paper, draw the straight lines whose vector equations are given below, by plotting points, taking 0, ±1, ±2 as the values of the parameters λ and μ.

$$\begin{bmatrix} x \\ y \end{bmatrix} = \begin{bmatrix} 1 \\ 0 \end{bmatrix} + \lambda \begin{bmatrix} 1 \\ 1 \end{bmatrix}, \qquad \begin{bmatrix} x \\ y \end{bmatrix} = \begin{bmatrix} 1 \\ 3 \end{bmatrix} + \mu \begin{bmatrix} 2 \\ -1 \end{bmatrix}$$

(b) Where do the lines intersect?

(c) What are the values of λ and μ at this point?

(d) By equating components, write down the two simultaneous equations given by

$$\begin{bmatrix} 1 \\ 0 \end{bmatrix} + \lambda \begin{bmatrix} 1 \\ 1 \end{bmatrix} = \begin{bmatrix} 1 \\ 3 \end{bmatrix} + \mu \begin{bmatrix} 2 \\ -1 \end{bmatrix}$$

(e) Solve the simultaneous equations and confirm your values of λ and μ.

Example 3

Find the point of intersection of the lines with equations

$$\begin{bmatrix} x \\ y \end{bmatrix} = \begin{bmatrix} -3 \\ 5 \end{bmatrix} + \lambda \begin{bmatrix} 2 \\ 1 \end{bmatrix} \quad \text{and} \quad \begin{bmatrix} x \\ y \end{bmatrix} = \begin{bmatrix} 4 \\ 1 \end{bmatrix} + \mu \begin{bmatrix} 1 \\ -2 \end{bmatrix}$$

Notice that it is necessary to have *different* parameters, λ and μ, for the two lines as it would otherwise be impossible to generate points independently.

Solution

At the point of intersection, the two position vectors will be equal. Equating the x components, $-3 + 2\lambda = 4 + \mu$, and equating the y components, $5 + \lambda = 1 - 2\mu$.

Solving these two equations simultaneously gives $\lambda = 2$ and $\mu = -3$.

Substituting these values into either of the vector equations gives the position vector of the point of intersection as $\begin{bmatrix} 1 \\ 7 \end{bmatrix}$.

2 Use simultaneous equations to find the intersection of

$$\begin{bmatrix} x \\ y \end{bmatrix} = \begin{bmatrix} 2 \\ 2 \end{bmatrix} + \lambda \begin{bmatrix} 1 \\ 2 \end{bmatrix} \quad \text{and} \quad \begin{bmatrix} x \\ y \end{bmatrix} = \begin{bmatrix} 1 \\ 3 \end{bmatrix} + \mu \begin{bmatrix} 2 \\ -1 \end{bmatrix}$$

In two dimensions there are three possible relationships between two lines.

(i) They are parallel.   (ii) They intersect.   (iii) They are coincident (the same line).

3D (a) How would you identify when two lines are parallel?

(b) How would you identify when two lines are coincident?

4D In this cuboid, describe the relationships between the lines

(a) AB and AD

(b) AB and DC

(c) AB and EG

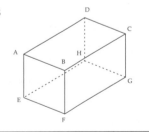

When you move into three dimensions, you have to be aware of a new possible relationship between lines, illustrated by AB and EG. In this case, the lines are not parallel, and do not intersect. They are called **skew lines**.

You can still identify parallel lines by checking whether the direction vectors are multiples of one another.

You can, as before, equate the x and y components to find values of λ and μ which make the x- and y-coordinates the same. When you substitute these values of λ and μ into the z components, two possibilities exist.

- The z-coordinates are equal, as with AB and AD in the example above.

- The z-coordinates are unequal and so the lines do not intersect. In this case the lines are skew.

If you imagine looking at the lines AB and EG from above the cuboid, they appear to meet at a point when, in fact, one crosses over the other: the x- and y-coordinates are equal, but the z-coordinates show that the lines are at different heights at that point.

Example 4

Show that the lines $\mathbf{r} = \begin{bmatrix} 2 \\ 3 \\ 5 \end{bmatrix} + t \begin{bmatrix} 4 \\ -1 \\ 3 \end{bmatrix}$ and $\mathbf{r} = \begin{bmatrix} 4 \\ 7 \\ 2 \end{bmatrix} + s \begin{bmatrix} 2 \\ -2 \\ 3 \end{bmatrix}$ meet, and find the point of intersection.

Solution

If the point (x, y, z) lies on both lines, then

$$\begin{bmatrix} x \\ y \\ z \end{bmatrix} = \begin{bmatrix} 2 \\ 3 \\ 5 \end{bmatrix} + t \begin{bmatrix} 4 \\ -1 \\ 3 \end{bmatrix} = \begin{bmatrix} 4 \\ 7 \\ 2 \end{bmatrix} + s \begin{bmatrix} 2 \\ -2 \\ 3 \end{bmatrix}$$

for suitable values of s and t, which must satisfy the three equations

$$2 + 4t = 4 + 2s$$
$$3 - t = 7 - 2s$$
$$5 + 3t = 2 + 3s$$

Adding the first two of these equations gives

$$5 + 3t = 11 \quad \Longrightarrow \quad t = 2 \quad \text{and} \quad s = 3$$

The third equation is also satisfied by $t = 2$, $s = 3$, which means that there *is* a point common to the two lines. Substituting $t = 2$ in the equation of the first line gives the coordinates of the point, $(10, 1, 11)$.

Example 5

Show that the lines $\mathbf{r} = \begin{bmatrix} 2 \\ 3 \\ 6 \end{bmatrix} + t \begin{bmatrix} 4 \\ -1 \\ 5 \end{bmatrix}$ and $\mathbf{r} = \begin{bmatrix} 4 \\ 7 \\ 8 \end{bmatrix} + s \begin{bmatrix} 2 \\ -2 \\ 1 \end{bmatrix}$ are skew lines.

Solution

Following the method of example 4 to find a point of intersection gives the equations

$$2 + 4t = 4 + 2s$$
$$3 - t = 7 - 2s$$
$$6 + 5t = 8 + s$$

As before, the first two equations are satisfied simultaneously by $t = 2$ and $s = 3$. But these values do not satisfy the third equation so there is no point common to the two lines. The lines are not parallel, since the directions of $\begin{bmatrix} 4 \\ -1 \\ 5 \end{bmatrix}$ and $\begin{bmatrix} 2 \\ -2 \\ 1 \end{bmatrix}$ are different. The lines are therefore skew.

5 Show that the lines $\mathbf{r} = \begin{bmatrix} 5 \\ 4 \\ 3 \end{bmatrix} + \lambda \begin{bmatrix} 1 \\ 0 \\ -3 \end{bmatrix}$ and $\mathbf{r} = \begin{bmatrix} 7 \\ 10 \\ 9 \end{bmatrix} + \mu \begin{bmatrix} 0 \\ 2 \\ 4 \end{bmatrix}$ meet, and find the point of intersection.

6 Show that the lines $\mathbf{r} = \begin{bmatrix} 2 \\ 0 \\ -1 \end{bmatrix} + s \begin{bmatrix} 0 \\ 2 \\ 3 \end{bmatrix}$ and $\mathbf{r} = \begin{bmatrix} -3 \\ 0 \\ 2 \end{bmatrix} + t \begin{bmatrix} 5 \\ 4 \\ -1 \end{bmatrix}$ are skew lines.

In two dimensions, a pair of lines may be parallel, coincident or intersecting.

In three dimensions, a pair of lines may be parallel, coincident, intersecting or skew.

Parallel lines have direction vectors which are multiples of one another.

In two dimensions, the intersection of two lines can be found by equating components and solving the simultaneous equations to find the values of the parameters.

In three dimensions, if the values found by equating two pairs of components do not fit the third pair of components, the lines are skew.

Exercise C (answers p. 142)

1 For each pair of equations, decide whether the two lines are parallel, coincident or intersecting, and find the point of intersection if they intersect.

(a) $\begin{bmatrix} x \\ y \end{bmatrix} = \begin{bmatrix} 1 \\ 3 \end{bmatrix} + s \begin{bmatrix} 2 \\ 4 \end{bmatrix}$, $\begin{bmatrix} x \\ y \end{bmatrix} = \begin{bmatrix} 2 \\ 0 \end{bmatrix} + t \begin{bmatrix} 1 \\ 3 \end{bmatrix}$

(b) $\begin{bmatrix} x \\ y \end{bmatrix} = \begin{bmatrix} 3 \\ 0 \end{bmatrix} + \lambda \begin{bmatrix} -1 \\ 2 \end{bmatrix}$, $\begin{bmatrix} x \\ y \end{bmatrix} = \begin{bmatrix} 4 \\ 1 \end{bmatrix} + \mu \begin{bmatrix} 3 \\ -6 \end{bmatrix}$

(c) $\begin{bmatrix} x \\ y \end{bmatrix} = \begin{bmatrix} 3 \\ 4 \end{bmatrix} + \lambda \begin{bmatrix} 2 \\ -1 \end{bmatrix}$, $\begin{bmatrix} x \\ y \end{bmatrix} = \begin{bmatrix} 5 \\ 3 \end{bmatrix} + \mu \begin{bmatrix} -4 \\ 2 \end{bmatrix}$

(c) $\begin{bmatrix} x \\ y \end{bmatrix} = \begin{bmatrix} 0 \\ 2 \end{bmatrix} + s \begin{bmatrix} 3 \\ 1 \end{bmatrix}$, $\begin{bmatrix} x \\ y \end{bmatrix} = \begin{bmatrix} 8 \\ 8 \end{bmatrix} + t \begin{bmatrix} 2 \\ 0 \end{bmatrix}$

2 Two slant edges of a square-based pyramid, with its base on the (x, y) plane, have equations

$$\begin{bmatrix} x \\ y \\ z \end{bmatrix} = \begin{bmatrix} 4 \\ 3 \\ 0 \end{bmatrix} + \lambda \begin{bmatrix} -1 \\ -1 \\ 1 \end{bmatrix} \quad \text{and} \quad \begin{bmatrix} x \\ y \\ z \end{bmatrix} = \begin{bmatrix} 4 \\ -3 \\ 0 \end{bmatrix} + \mu \begin{bmatrix} -1 \\ 1 \\ 1 \end{bmatrix}$$

Find values of λ and μ such that the y and z components are equal.

Check that these values both give the same value for the x-coordinate. Hence write down the position vector of the vertex of the pyramid.

3 Find whether the following pairs of lines meet. If they meet, find the coordinates of the common point; if they do not, find whether they are parallel or skew lines.

(a) $\mathbf{r} = \begin{bmatrix} 2 \\ 3 \\ 5 \end{bmatrix} + t \begin{bmatrix} 1 \\ 0 \\ 2 \end{bmatrix}$, $\mathbf{r} = \begin{bmatrix} 5 \\ 0 \\ 4 \end{bmatrix} + s \begin{bmatrix} 0 \\ 3 \\ 7 \end{bmatrix}$

(b) $\mathbf{r} = \begin{bmatrix} 4 \\ 5 \\ 2 \end{bmatrix} + \lambda \begin{bmatrix} 1 \\ 2 \\ 3 \end{bmatrix}$, $\mathbf{r} = \begin{bmatrix} 1 \\ -3 \\ 4 \end{bmatrix} + \mu \begin{bmatrix} 2 \\ 4 \\ 6 \end{bmatrix}$

(c) $\mathbf{r} = \begin{bmatrix} 2 \\ 1 \\ 3 \end{bmatrix} + s \begin{bmatrix} 4 \\ 2 \\ -5 \end{bmatrix}$, $\mathbf{r} = \begin{bmatrix} -3 \\ 6 \\ -8 \end{bmatrix} + t \begin{bmatrix} 3 \\ -1 \\ 2 \end{bmatrix}$

(d) $\mathbf{r} = \begin{bmatrix} 4 \\ 3 \\ 1 \end{bmatrix} + \lambda \begin{bmatrix} 5 \\ -2 \\ 4 \end{bmatrix}$, $\mathbf{r} = \begin{bmatrix} 2 \\ 1 \\ 6 \end{bmatrix} + \mu \begin{bmatrix} 3 \\ 1 \\ 2 \end{bmatrix}$

4 Prove that the two lines with equations

$$\mathbf{r} = \begin{bmatrix} 0 \\ 2 \\ -3 \end{bmatrix} + s \begin{bmatrix} 6 \\ -1 \\ -1 \end{bmatrix} \quad \text{and} \quad \mathbf{r} = \begin{bmatrix} -4 \\ 6 \\ -4 \end{bmatrix} + t \begin{bmatrix} 2 \\ 1 \\ -1 \end{bmatrix}$$

have a common point.

5E Find p, given that the following two lines intersect.

$$\mathbf{r} = \begin{bmatrix} -4 \\ 3 \\ 2 \end{bmatrix} + s \begin{bmatrix} 2 \\ -1 \\ 0 \end{bmatrix}, \quad \mathbf{r} = \begin{bmatrix} 2 \\ 6 \\ 6 \end{bmatrix} + t \begin{bmatrix} 0 \\ 3 \\ p \end{bmatrix}$$

D Scalar product (answers p. 143)

You are familiar with the idea of adding and subtracting vectors, and with multiplying a vector by a scalar (number). Here you consider one way in which a meaning can be given to multiplication of vectors. This problem is closely related to finding the angle between two vectors.

Consider vectors **a** and **b** as shown.

$$\mathbf{a} = \begin{bmatrix} 3 \\ 1 \end{bmatrix}, \quad \mathbf{b} = \begin{bmatrix} 2 \\ 3 \end{bmatrix}$$

How could you find the angle, θ, between the two vectors?

One way would be to use the cosine rule on triangle OAB. The lengths OA and OB can be found using Pythagoras' theorem and since $\overrightarrow{AB} = \overrightarrow{OB} - \overrightarrow{OA}$ its length can also be found.

$$OA = \sqrt{3^2 + 1^2} = \sqrt{10}, \qquad OB = \sqrt{2^2 + 3^3} = \sqrt{13}$$

$$\overrightarrow{AB} = \mathbf{b} - \mathbf{a} = \begin{bmatrix} -1 \\ 2 \end{bmatrix}, \qquad AB = \sqrt{1^2 + 2^2} = \sqrt{5}$$

So, by the cosine rule $AB^2 = OA^2 + OB^2 - 2\,OA\,OB\cos\theta$

$$\Rightarrow \qquad\qquad 5 = 10 + 13 - 2\sqrt{10}\sqrt{13}\cos\theta$$

$$\Rightarrow \qquad\qquad \cos\theta = \frac{9}{\sqrt{130}} = 0.7894 \Rightarrow \theta = 37.9°$$

The aim of the following questions is to develop a more convenient method of finding the angle between two vectors.

1   For any triangle, $\mathbf{a} = \begin{bmatrix} a_1 \\ a_2 \end{bmatrix}$ and $\mathbf{b} = \begin{bmatrix} b_1 \\ b_2 \end{bmatrix}$.

(a) Explain why $a^2 = a_1^2 + a_2^2$ and write down a similar expression for b^2.

(b) The third side is $\mathbf{c} = \mathbf{b} - \mathbf{a} = \begin{bmatrix} b_1 - a_1 \\ b_2 - a_2 \end{bmatrix}$. Since the magnitude of $\mathbf{c}$ is c, you can write

$$c^2 = (b_1 - a_1)^2 + (b_2 - a_2)^2$$

By multiplying out the brackets and using the results of (a), show that

$$c^2 = a^2 + b^2 - 2(a_1 b_1 + a_2 b_2)$$

(c) By comparing with the cosine rule, explain why

$$a_1 b_1 + a_2 b_2 = ab \cos \theta$$

2   Use the result in 1(c) to calculate θ in the example above.

The **scalar product** of two vectors $\mathbf{a} = \begin{bmatrix} a_1 \\ a_2 \end{bmatrix}$ and $\mathbf{b} = \begin{bmatrix} b_1 \\ b_2 \end{bmatrix}$ is defined as $a_1 b_1 + a_2 b_2$ or $ab \cos \theta$ where a and b are the magnitudes of the two vectors and θ is the angle between them.

The scalar product is written as $\begin{bmatrix} a_1 \\ a_2 \end{bmatrix} \cdot \begin{bmatrix} b_1 \\ b_2 \end{bmatrix}$ or as $\mathbf{a} \cdot \mathbf{b}$ which is pronounced 'a dot b'. For obvious reasons some writers refer to it as the 'dot product'.

The word **scalar** is used to emphasise that the product is not a vector quantity.

In fact, a second product, known as the vector product, is also used. The notation used for the vector product is ×, and it is sometimes called the 'cross product'. The vector product is not covered in this book.

The angle between two vectors can be found by using

$$\cos \theta = \frac{\mathbf{a} \cdot \mathbf{b}}{ab}, \qquad \text{where } \mathbf{a} \cdot \mathbf{b} = a_1 b_1 + a_2 b_2$$

You need to be careful about which angle θ refers to. If you imagine $\mathbf{a}$ and $\mathbf{b}$ both starting from the origin, θ is the angle between them.

Consider the following three situations.

(i) 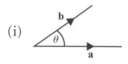 $\mathbf{a} \cdot \mathbf{b} = ab \cos \theta$

(ii) 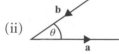   is equivalent to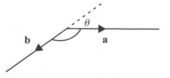

$\mathbf{a} \cdot \mathbf{b} = ab \cos(180 - \theta) = -ab \cos \theta$

(iii) 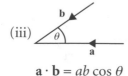   is equivalent to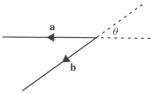

$\mathbf{a} \cdot \mathbf{b} = ab \cos \theta$

3   Find the acute angles between these pairs of vectors.

(a) $\begin{bmatrix} 4 \\ 7 \end{bmatrix}, \begin{bmatrix} 3 \\ 2 \end{bmatrix}$ (b) $\begin{bmatrix} -3 \\ 2 \end{bmatrix}, \begin{bmatrix} 4 \\ -1 \end{bmatrix}$ (c) $\begin{bmatrix} -2 \\ 1 \end{bmatrix}, \begin{bmatrix} 1 \\ 2 \end{bmatrix}$

The following questions explore some of the properties of the scalar product.

Consider the vectors

$$\mathbf{a} = \begin{bmatrix} 3 \\ 4 \end{bmatrix}, \quad \mathbf{b} = \begin{bmatrix} 5 \\ 5 \end{bmatrix}, \quad \mathbf{c} = \begin{bmatrix} 2 \\ 6 \end{bmatrix}, \quad \mathbf{d} = \begin{bmatrix} 4 \\ -3 \end{bmatrix}, \quad \mathbf{e} = \begin{bmatrix} -8 \\ 6 \end{bmatrix}$$

4   (a) Draw a diagram showing these five vectors.

   (b) Which pairs of vectors are parallel and which are perpendicular?

5   (a) Calculate the magnitude of each vector.

   (b) Calculate the scalar products

$$\mathbf{a} \cdot \mathbf{a}, \quad \mathbf{b} \cdot \mathbf{b}, \quad \mathbf{c} \cdot \mathbf{c}, \quad \mathbf{d} \cdot \mathbf{d}, \quad \mathbf{e} \cdot \mathbf{e}$$

   (c) What do you notice?

   (d) What can you say about $\cos \theta$ in these situations? How does this explain (c)?

6   (a) Calculate $\mathbf{a} \cdot \mathbf{b}$ and $\mathbf{b} \cdot \mathbf{a}$.

   (b) Calculate $\mathbf{a} \cdot \mathbf{c}$ and $\mathbf{c} \cdot \mathbf{a}$.

   (c) What do you notice? Explain why this occurs.

7   (a) Calculate $\mathbf{a} \cdot \mathbf{b} + \mathbf{a} \cdot \mathbf{c}$.

   (b) Calculate $\mathbf{a} \cdot (\mathbf{b} + \mathbf{c})$.

   (c) What do you notice?

8 (a) Calculate the scalar products

$$\mathbf{a} \cdot \mathbf{b}, \quad \mathbf{a} \cdot \mathbf{d}, \quad \mathbf{a} \cdot \mathbf{e}$$

(b) What can you say about two vectors which are perpendicular?

(c) What can you say about $\cos \theta$ when two lines are perpendicular? How does this explain (b)?

(d) Can you think of any other situation in which the scalar product will be zero?

9 A′A is the diameter of a circle centred at O and P is any point on the circumference.

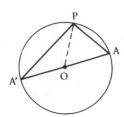

(a) With $\mathbf{a} = \overrightarrow{OA}$ and $\mathbf{p} = \overrightarrow{OP}$, express $\overrightarrow{OA'}$, $\overrightarrow{AP}$ and $\overrightarrow{A'P}$ in terms of $\mathbf{a}$ and $\mathbf{p}$.

(b) Calculate $\overrightarrow{AP} \cdot \overrightarrow{A'P}$.

(c) What is the geometrical significance of the value of this scalar product?

For the scalar product

$$\mathbf{a} \cdot \mathbf{b} = \mathbf{b} \cdot \mathbf{a}$$

$$\mathbf{a} \cdot (\mathbf{b} + \mathbf{c}) = \mathbf{a} \cdot \mathbf{b} + \mathbf{a} \cdot \mathbf{c}$$

$$\mathbf{a} \cdot \mathbf{b} = 0 \implies \mathbf{a} \text{ is perpendicular to } \mathbf{b} \text{ or } \mathbf{a} = \mathbf{0} \text{ or } \mathbf{b} = \mathbf{0}$$

$$\mathbf{a} \cdot \mathbf{a} = |\mathbf{a}|^2 = a^2$$

The scalar product can also be used in three dimensions, where it retains the properties listed above.

In three dimensions,

$$\mathbf{a} \cdot \mathbf{b} = \begin{bmatrix} a_1 \\ a_2 \\ a_3 \end{bmatrix} \cdot \begin{bmatrix} b_1 \\ b_2 \\ b_3 \end{bmatrix} = a_1 b_1 + a_2 b_2 + a_3 b_3 = ab \cos \theta$$

10 (a) Find the vectors $\overrightarrow{OA}$, $\overrightarrow{OB}$, $\overrightarrow{OD}$, $\overrightarrow{DE}$, $\overrightarrow{DF}$ and $\overrightarrow{DG}$.

(b) Using the scalar product, find the angles between

(i) $\overrightarrow{OA}$ and $\overrightarrow{OB}$

(ii) $\overrightarrow{OA}$ and $\overrightarrow{OD}$

(iii) $\overrightarrow{OA}$ and $\overrightarrow{DE}$

(iv) $\overrightarrow{OD}$ and $\overrightarrow{DF}$

(v) $\overrightarrow{OA}$ and $\overrightarrow{DF}$

(vi) $\overrightarrow{OA}$ and $\overrightarrow{DG}$

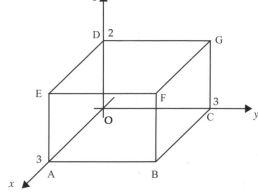

(c) Are these the answers that you would expect?

Exercise D (answers p. 143)

1 $a = \begin{bmatrix} 2 \\ 2 \\ 1 \end{bmatrix}$, $b = \begin{bmatrix} 1 \\ 0 \\ -2 \end{bmatrix}$, $c = \begin{bmatrix} 4 \\ -5 \\ 2 \end{bmatrix}$

(a) Calculate the scalar products $a \cdot b$, $b \cdot c$ and $c \cdot a$.

(b) Which pairs of vectors are perpendicular?

2 Find the angles between these pairs of vectors.

(a) $\begin{bmatrix} 5 \\ 2 \end{bmatrix}$, $\begin{bmatrix} 3 \\ 2 \end{bmatrix}$ (b) $\begin{bmatrix} 5 \\ 2 \end{bmatrix}$, $\begin{bmatrix} -3 \\ 2 \end{bmatrix}$

3 Triangle ABC is defined by the points A = (3, 2), B = (−1, 3) and C = (1, 7).

(a) Find the vectors $\overrightarrow{AB}$ and $\overrightarrow{AC}$.

(b) Explain why, to calculate angle A, you should find $\overrightarrow{AB} \cdot \overrightarrow{AC}$ and not $\overrightarrow{AB} \cdot \overrightarrow{CA}$. Hence calculate angle A.

4 Find the angles between these pairs of vectors.

(a) $\begin{bmatrix} 12 \\ 1 \\ -12 \end{bmatrix}$, $\begin{bmatrix} 8 \\ 4 \\ 1 \end{bmatrix}$ (b) $\begin{bmatrix} 4 \\ -1 \\ -8 \end{bmatrix}$, $\begin{bmatrix} 7 \\ 4 \\ -4 \end{bmatrix}$

5 Triangle PQR is defined by the points P = (5, −3, 1), Q = (−2, 1, 5) and R = (9, 5, 0). Find the angles of the triangle.

6 $a = \begin{bmatrix} 10 \\ 0 \end{bmatrix}$, $b = \begin{bmatrix} -6 \\ 8 \end{bmatrix}$

(a) Find the position vector c of the mid-point of AB.

(b) Find the vector $d = \overrightarrow{BA}$.

(c) Calculate the scalar product $c \cdot d$.

(d) Draw a diagram of the triangle OAB with the point C included. What can you deduce from the value of the scalar product $c \cdot d$?

7 Show that (0, 0, 0), (4, −2, 5), (3, 6, 0) and (7, 4, 5) are four vertices of a square.

8E OAB is a triangle with the altitudes from A and B intersecting at H as shown.

(The **altitude** of a triangle is the perpendicular from a vertex to the opposite side.)

$\overrightarrow{OA}$, $\overrightarrow{OB}$ and $\overrightarrow{OH}$ are denoted by a, b and h.

(a) Why is $a \cdot (b - h) = 0$?

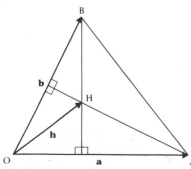

down a similar equation involving $\mathbf{a} - \mathbf{h}$.

racting the two equations, show that $(\mathbf{a} - \mathbf{b}) \cdot \mathbf{h} = 0$.

how this proves that the altitudes of a triangle are
...ent. (**Concurrent** lines all pass through a single point.)

9E (a) OPRQ is a parallelogram.
Write down the vectors $\overrightarrow{OR}$ and $\overrightarrow{QP}$ in terms of $\mathbf{p}$ and $\mathbf{q}$.

(b) Explain why
$(\mathbf{p} + \mathbf{q}) \cdot (\mathbf{p} - \mathbf{q}) = p^2 - q^2$.

(c) If $\overrightarrow{OR} \cdot \overrightarrow{QP} = 0$ what can you say about

(i) the lines OR and QP? (ii) the sides of the parallelogram?

10E Use the scalar product method to find the angle made by a longest diagonal of a cube with each of the following.

(a) An edge of the cube (b) A face diagonal

(c) Another longest diagonal

E Perpendicular lines (answers p. 145)

1D (a) On a copy of this diagram mark the point P on the line where the line is closest to O.

(b) Mark the point Q on the line where the line is closest to A.

(c) Comment on the lines OP and AQ.

(d) Explain why AR must be longer than AQ.

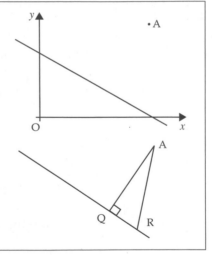

The shortest distance from a point to a line is always the distance along the perpendicular from the point to the line.

It is useful to be able to find this distance and the coordinates of the **foot** of the perpendicular, the point where it intersects the line.

Example 6

Find the shortest distance from the point A $(4, 7)$ to the line

$$\begin{bmatrix} x \\ y \end{bmatrix} = \begin{bmatrix} 1 \\ 0 \end{bmatrix} + \lambda \begin{bmatrix} 5 \\ 2 \end{bmatrix}$$

Solution

Let P be the point on the line which is closest to A.

You can express $\overrightarrow{OP}$ as $\begin{bmatrix} 1+5\lambda \\ 0+2\lambda \end{bmatrix}$ for some value of λ; call it λ_1.

So $\overrightarrow{OP} = \begin{bmatrix} 1+5\lambda_1 \\ 2\lambda_1 \end{bmatrix}$.

You know that the vector $\overrightarrow{AP}$ must be perpendicular to the line.

$\overrightarrow{AP} = \begin{bmatrix} 1+5\lambda_1 \\ 2\lambda_1 \end{bmatrix} - \begin{bmatrix} 4 \\ 7 \end{bmatrix} = \begin{bmatrix} 5\lambda_1 - 3 \\ 2\lambda_1 - 7 \end{bmatrix}$, and the direction of the line is given

by the vector $\begin{bmatrix} 5 \\ 2 \end{bmatrix}$.

So, since the scalar product of perpendicular vectors is zero,

$$\begin{bmatrix} 5\lambda_1 - 3 \\ 2\lambda_1 - 7 \end{bmatrix} \cdot \begin{bmatrix} 5 \\ 2 \end{bmatrix} = 0$$

$$5(5\lambda_1 - 3) + 2(2\lambda_1 - 7) = 0$$
$$25\lambda_1 - 15 + 4\lambda_1 - 14 = 0$$
$$29\lambda_1 = 29$$
$$\lambda_1 = 1$$

Hence $\overrightarrow{OP} = \begin{bmatrix} 6 \\ 2 \end{bmatrix}$, and $(6, 2)$ is the point on the line closest to A.

The distance AP can be calculated using Pythagoras' theorem to be $\sqrt{29}$.

2 Find the shortest distance from the point A $(7, 7)$ to the line

$$\begin{bmatrix} x \\ y \end{bmatrix} = \begin{bmatrix} 0 \\ 3 \end{bmatrix} + \lambda \begin{bmatrix} 2 \\ -1 \end{bmatrix}$$

This method can be extended to three dimensions.

3D Consider the point A $(10, 9, 11)$ and the line $\mathbf{r} = \begin{bmatrix} 1 \\ 0 \\ 2 \end{bmatrix} + \lambda \begin{bmatrix} 2 \\ 2 \\ -1 \end{bmatrix}$.

(a) If P is the point on the line which is closest to A, write $\overrightarrow{OP}$ as a column vector with components in terms of λ_1.

(b) Find $\overrightarrow{AP}$ in terms of λ_1.

(c) Find the scalar product $\overrightarrow{AP} \cdot \begin{bmatrix} 2 \\ 2 \\ -1 \end{bmatrix}$ in terms of λ_1.

(d) Use the fact that $\overrightarrow{AP}$ is perpendicular to the line to find λ_1.

(e) Find the coordinates of P.

(f) Find the length AP.

4   Find the distance from the point $(5, -5, -8)$ to the line $\mathbf{r} = \begin{bmatrix} 3 \\ 1 \\ 2 \end{bmatrix} + \lambda \begin{bmatrix} 0 \\ 4 \\ 1 \end{bmatrix}$.

Exercise E (answers p. 145)

1   Find the distance from the point $(11, 7)$ to the line $\mathbf{r} = \begin{bmatrix} x \\ y \end{bmatrix} = \begin{bmatrix} 2 \\ 0 \end{bmatrix} + s \begin{bmatrix} 1 \\ 3 \end{bmatrix}$.

2   Find the distance from the point $(9, 3, 12)$ to the line $\mathbf{r} = \begin{bmatrix} 3 \\ 0 \\ 1 \end{bmatrix} + t \begin{bmatrix} 0 \\ 3 \\ 1 \end{bmatrix}$.

3   A $(2, 0, -3)$, B $(5, 3, 3)$ and C $(3, 1, 2)$ are three vertices of a triangle.
   (a) Find a vector equation of the line joining A and B.
   (b) Find the length AB.
   (c) Find the distance from C to AB, and hence find the area of the triangle.

4   A quadrilateral has vertices A $(0, 3, 1)$, B $(6, 6, 7)$, C $(10, 11, 5)$ and D $(4, 8, -1)$.
   (a) Show that ABCD is a parallelogram.
   (b) Find the length AB.
   (c) Find the distance from D to AB and hence the area of the parallelogram.

F   Vector equations of planes (answers p. 146)

1D

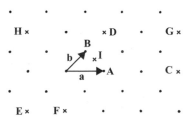

A and B are described by the position vectors **a** and **b** as shown.

(a) Express the position vectors of the points C, D, E, F, G, H, I in terms of vectors **a** and **b**.

(b) Can *any* point in the plane be found in terms of **a** and **b**?

The rest of this chapter will deal with situations in three dimensions, which may be difficult to visualise. You will find it helpful to make the following model, which will be referred to from time to time.

Make the framework of a cuboid measuring 10 cm by 15 cm by 25 cm. This can be done conveniently using five 40 cm paper straws and sellotape. Mark off the straws every 2.5 cm before sticking the cuboid together.

Cut a sheet of card 25 cm by 18 cm, which should be roughly the right size to fit diagonally across the cuboid. It may be necessary to trim it slightly to allow for the width of the straws.

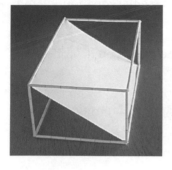

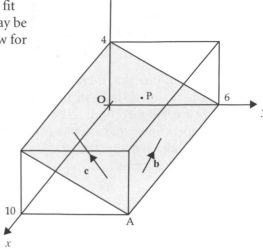

In question 1, you looked at describing any point in the plane using just two vectors in the plane. Consider a point P somewhere in the plane on your model.

The second diagram shows just the plane.

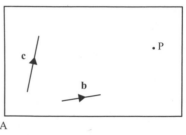

The vector $\overrightarrow{AP}$ can be expressed as a multiple of **b** plus a multiple of **c**, where **b** and **c** are any two non-parallel vectors in the plane.

This means that the position vector of P can be expressed as $\overrightarrow{OA} + \overrightarrow{AP} = \mathbf{a} + \lambda\mathbf{b} + \mu\mathbf{c}$. This is true for any point P in the plane. So you can say that $\mathbf{r} = \mathbf{a} + \lambda\mathbf{b} + \mu\mathbf{c}$ is the equation of the plane, where **a** is the position vector of one particular point in the plane, and **b** and **c** are any two non-parallel vectors in the plane.

For your model, using the 2.5 cm marks as units on the axes,

$$\overrightarrow{OA} = \begin{bmatrix} 10 \\ 6 \\ 0 \end{bmatrix}$$ and two vectors in the plane which are easy to find are the

ones along the bottom and far edges, $\begin{bmatrix} 10 \\ 0 \\ 0 \end{bmatrix}$ and $\begin{bmatrix} 0 \\ -6 \\ 4 \end{bmatrix}$.

Hence you can write the equation as

$$\mathbf{r} = \begin{bmatrix} 10 \\ 6 \\ 0 \end{bmatrix} + \lambda \begin{bmatrix} 10 \\ 0 \\ 0 \end{bmatrix} + \mu \begin{bmatrix} 0 \\ -6 \\ 4 \end{bmatrix}$$

There are many other possibilities for the equation of this plane.

2 Explain why this plane can be described by the equation

$$r = \begin{bmatrix} 0 \\ 0 \\ 4 \end{bmatrix} + \lambda \begin{bmatrix} 10 \\ 6 \\ -4 \end{bmatrix} + \mu \begin{bmatrix} 0 \\ 6 \\ -4 \end{bmatrix}$$

You will notice that there are two parameters in the equation – λ and μ. The reason is that you are describing a two-dimensional object; there are two directions in which the points on it can vary. When you describe a line, you have one parameter, and when you describe a point, there is no parameter.

A vector equation of a plane through a point with position vector

$\begin{bmatrix} a_1 \\ a_2 \\ a_3 \end{bmatrix}$ where the vectors $\begin{bmatrix} b_1 \\ b_2 \\ b_3 \end{bmatrix}$ and $\begin{bmatrix} c_1 \\ c_2 \\ c_3 \end{bmatrix}$ are parallel to the plane but

not to each other is $\begin{bmatrix} x \\ y \\ z \end{bmatrix} = \begin{bmatrix} a_1 \\ a_2 \\ a_3 \end{bmatrix} + \lambda \begin{bmatrix} b_1 \\ b_2 \\ b_3 \end{bmatrix} + \mu \begin{bmatrix} c_1 \\ c_2 \\ c_3 \end{bmatrix}$, where λ and μ are parameters.

> Position vector of *any* point on the plane

> Position vector of a *particular* point on the plane

> Vectors *parallel* to the plane but not parallel to each other

This can be written as $r = a + \lambda b + \mu c$.

The diagram shows a cube with sides of length 6 cm. The origin is at O.
The following questions all refer to this cube.

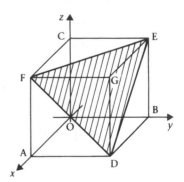

3 Consider the plane DEF. Find the vectors $\overrightarrow{DE}$ and $\overrightarrow{DF}$.

Explain why the position vector of any point in the plane DEF can be written as

$$\begin{bmatrix} x \\ y \\ z \end{bmatrix} = \begin{bmatrix} 6 \\ 6 \\ 0 \end{bmatrix} + \lambda \begin{bmatrix} -6 \\ 0 \\ 6 \end{bmatrix} + \mu \begin{bmatrix} 0 \\ -6 \\ 6 \end{bmatrix}$$

4 Find the coordinates of the points with the following values of λ and μ, and identify them on the diagram where possible.

(a) $\lambda = 0, \mu = 0$ (b) $\lambda = 1, \mu = 0$ (c) $\lambda = 0, \mu = 1$
(d) $\lambda = \frac{1}{2}, \mu = \frac{1}{2}$ (e) $\lambda = \frac{1}{3}, \mu = \frac{1}{3}$

5 Consider the equilateral triangle ABC.

What are the direction vectors $\overrightarrow{CB}$ and $\overrightarrow{CA}$?

Using $\overrightarrow{OC}$ as the position vector write down a vector equation of the plane ABC.

What do you notice about the planes ABC and DEF?

6 Repeat question 4 for the plane ABC.

7 (a) Suggest a possible vector equation for a plane parallel to ABC which passes through the origin.

(b) Likewise suggest an equation for a parallel plane through G.

8 If H is the mid-point of the line CF, find a vector equation for the plane DEH.

Example 7

Find a vector equation of the plane through the point $(2, 5, -6)$,

parallel to the vector $\begin{bmatrix} 4 \\ 1 \\ 3 \end{bmatrix}$ and to the z-axis.

Solution

Since the z-axis is parallel to the vector $\begin{bmatrix} 0 \\ 0 \\ 1 \end{bmatrix}$, a vector equation of the plane is

$$\begin{bmatrix} x \\ y \\ z \end{bmatrix} = \begin{bmatrix} 2 \\ 5 \\ -6 \end{bmatrix} + \lambda \begin{bmatrix} 4 \\ 1 \\ 3 \end{bmatrix} + \mu \begin{bmatrix} 0 \\ 0 \\ 1 \end{bmatrix}$$

9 Consider the plane through the three points A $(4, 0, 1)$, B $(3, 3, 4)$ and C $(1, 3, 0)$.

(a) Find $\overrightarrow{AB}$ and $\overrightarrow{AC}$.

(b) Find a vector equation for the plane.

10E (a) Find the mid-point of BC in question 9.

(b) Verify that this point lies in the plane.

11D What happens if you try to find the vector equation of the plane through the three points A $(2, 3, 1)$, B $(-1, 2, 4)$ and C $(-4, 1, 7)$? Why?

Exercise F (answers p. 147)

1 Find a vector equation for the plane through the three points
A (2, 3, 1), B (−1, 2, 4) and C (−4, 1, 5).

2 A plane cuts the x-, y- and z-axes at $x = 2$, $y = -1$ and $z = 3$.
Find a vector equation for the plane.

3 OABCD is a regular square-based pyramid with
base edges of length 4 and height 3.

(a) What is the position vector of the vertex D?

(b) Find vector equations for the faces OAD
and BCD.

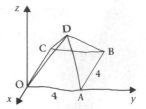

G Parametric and Cartesian equations of planes (answers p. 147)

Section F was concerned with writing the equation of a plane in vector
form. In this section we consider what the equation of a plane will look
like in parametric and Cartesian form, and the relationship between
the three forms, as well as an alternative vector form.

1D Consider the triangular plane through the points $(0, 0, 4)$, $(0, 4, 0)$
and $(4, 0, 0)$.

(a) List the coordinates of the points
marked with crosses.

(b) Suggest an equation linking x, y and z.

(c) One possible vector equation of the
plane is

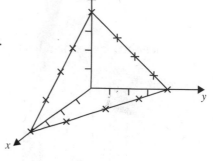

$$\begin{bmatrix} x \\ y \\ z \end{bmatrix} = \begin{bmatrix} 4 \\ 0 \\ 0 \end{bmatrix} + \lambda \begin{bmatrix} -4 \\ 4 \\ 0 \end{bmatrix} + \mu \begin{bmatrix} -4 \\ 0 \\ 4 \end{bmatrix}$$

Considering the components separately, you can write $x = 4 - 4\lambda - 4\mu$.

Write down the corresponding equations for the y and z components.

These are the parametric equations of the plane.

(d) Add the three parametric equations together and simplify. Is this what
you expected?

2D | Use the framework and plane made in section F to help with this question.

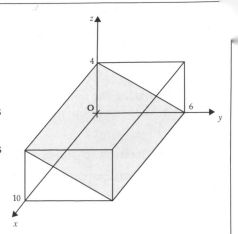

(a) Find the coordinates of several points along the top and bottom edges of the plane.

(b) Find the coordinates of a few points along the far edge of the plane.

(c) Find the coordinates of a few points along the near edge of the plane.

(d) Find the coordinates of the centre of the plane.

(e) Verify that all your points fit the equation $2y + 3z = 12$.

(f) Find a vector equation of the plane.

(g) Use your vector equation to find three parametric equations describing the plane.

(h) Verify that your parametric equations satisfy the equation $2y + 3z = 12$.

A plane with vector equation

$$\begin{bmatrix} x \\ y \\ z \end{bmatrix} = \begin{bmatrix} a_1 \\ a_2 \\ a_3 \end{bmatrix} + \lambda \begin{bmatrix} b_1 \\ b_2 \\ b_3 \end{bmatrix} + \mu \begin{bmatrix} c_1 \\ c_2 \\ c_3 \end{bmatrix}$$

has parametric equations:

$$x = a_1 + \lambda b_1 + \mu c_1$$
$$y = a_2 + \lambda b_2 + \mu c_2$$
$$z = a_3 + \lambda b_3 + \mu c_3$$

The Cartesian equation of the plane is of the form

$$px + qy + rz = s$$

It can be found by eliminating λ and μ from the parametric equations.

3   The vector equation of the plane DEF is

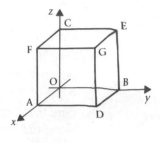

$$\begin{bmatrix} x \\ y \\ z \end{bmatrix} = \begin{bmatrix} 6 \\ 6 \\ 0 \end{bmatrix} + \lambda \begin{bmatrix} -6 \\ 0 \\ 6 \end{bmatrix} + \mu \begin{bmatrix} 0 \\ -6 \\ 6 \end{bmatrix}$$

Considering the components separately, you can write the x component as

$$x = 6 - 6\lambda$$

Write down the corresponding equations for the y and z components.

Add the three equations together and simplify. The result should involve x, y and z only and not λ and μ.

4   (a)   What is the Cartesian equation of the plane ABC? Check your suggestion by working from a vector equation as in question 3.

In section F you found that a possible equation is

$$\begin{bmatrix} x \\ y \\ z \end{bmatrix} = \begin{bmatrix} 0 \\ 0 \\ 6 \end{bmatrix} + \lambda \begin{bmatrix} 0 \\ 6 \\ -6 \end{bmatrix} + \mu \begin{bmatrix} 6 \\ 0 \\ -6 \end{bmatrix}$$

(b)   In section F vector equations of the planes through O and G parallel to ABC and DEF were found to be

$$\begin{bmatrix} x \\ y \\ z \end{bmatrix} = \lambda \begin{bmatrix} 0 \\ 6 \\ -6 \end{bmatrix} + \mu \begin{bmatrix} 6 \\ 0 \\ -6 \end{bmatrix} \quad \text{and} \quad \begin{bmatrix} x \\ y \\ z \end{bmatrix} = \begin{bmatrix} 6 \\ 6 \\ 6 \end{bmatrix} + \lambda \begin{bmatrix} 0 \\ 6 \\ -6 \end{bmatrix} + \mu \begin{bmatrix} 6 \\ 0 \\ -6 \end{bmatrix}$$

respectively. What are the Cartesian equations of these planes?

5   A vector equation of the plane DEH, where H is the mid-point of CF, is

$$\begin{bmatrix} x \\ y \\ z \end{bmatrix} = \begin{bmatrix} 6 \\ 6 \\ 0 \end{bmatrix} + \lambda \begin{bmatrix} -6 \\ 0 \\ 6 \end{bmatrix} + \mu \begin{bmatrix} -3 \\ -6 \\ 6 \end{bmatrix}$$

Write down equations for the x, y and z components.

By eliminating λ from the first and third equations and then eliminating μ, find the Cartesian equation of the plane DEH.

6   A plane has a vector equation $\begin{bmatrix} x \\ y \\ z \end{bmatrix} = \begin{bmatrix} 5 \\ 2 \\ 4 \end{bmatrix} + \lambda \begin{bmatrix} -3 \\ 0 \\ -6 \end{bmatrix} + \mu \begin{bmatrix} 2 \\ 3 \\ 1 \end{bmatrix}$.

Find the Cartesian equation of the plane.

7   Evaluate the scalar product $\begin{bmatrix} p \\ q \\ r \end{bmatrix} \cdot \begin{bmatrix} x \\ y \\ z \end{bmatrix}$.

The plane with Cartesian equation $px + qy + rz = s$ can also be written

as $\begin{bmatrix} p \\ q \\ r \end{bmatrix} \cdot \begin{bmatrix} x \\ y \\ z \end{bmatrix} = s$. This gives you a method for converting the Cartesian

equation of a plane to a vector equation, and a useful alternative form
for the vector equation.

8 The Cartesian equation of the plane DEF in question 3 is
$x + y + z = 12$.

Using scalar product notation, this could be written as $\begin{bmatrix} 1 \\ 1 \\ 1 \end{bmatrix} \cdot \begin{bmatrix} x \\ y \\ z \end{bmatrix} = 12$.

To investigate the significance of the vector $\begin{bmatrix} 1 \\ 1 \\ 1 \end{bmatrix}$, first note that it is in

the same direction as $\overrightarrow{OG}$, which is $\begin{bmatrix} 6 \\ 6 \\ 6 \end{bmatrix}$.

(a) How is this vector $\begin{bmatrix} 1 \\ 1 \\ 1 \end{bmatrix}$ related to the plane DEF?

(b) Calculate the scalar products of $\begin{bmatrix} 1 \\ 1 \\ 1 \end{bmatrix}$ with $\overrightarrow{DE}$ and $\overrightarrow{DF}$. What do the
results tell you?

9 In question 2, you looked at the plane with equation $2y + 3z = 12$. This

can be written as $\begin{bmatrix} 0 \\ 2 \\ 3 \end{bmatrix} \cdot \begin{bmatrix} x \\ y \\ z \end{bmatrix} = 12$.

With your model, hold a straw or pencil in the direction $\begin{bmatrix} 0 \\ 2 \\ 3 \end{bmatrix}$. What do
you notice?

10 (a) Write $\begin{bmatrix} 1 \\ 0 \\ 0 \end{bmatrix} \cdot \begin{bmatrix} x \\ y \\ z \end{bmatrix} = 10$ in Cartesian form.

(b) Which plane of your cuboid is this?

(c) Verify that $\begin{bmatrix} 1 \\ 0 \\ 0 \end{bmatrix}$ is perpendicular to this plane.

When a plane is described by the vector equation

$$\mathbf{n} \cdot \begin{bmatrix} x \\ y \\ z \end{bmatrix} = d \quad \text{or} \quad \mathbf{n} \cdot \mathbf{r} = d$$

$\mathbf{n}$ is known as the **normal vector** to the plane.

Using these ideas, the equation $x + y + z = 12$ can be written, using scalar product notation, as

$$\begin{bmatrix} 1 \\ 1 \\ 1 \end{bmatrix} \cdot \begin{bmatrix} x \\ y \\ z \end{bmatrix} = 12$$

You saw in question 8 that the vector $\begin{bmatrix} 1 \\ 1 \\ 1 \end{bmatrix}$ is at right angles to the plane.

Therefore this vector is the normal vector, $\mathbf{n}$, to the plane. For any point $\mathbf{r}$ in the plane, $\mathbf{n} \cdot \mathbf{r} = 12$.

Since a plane is two dimensional it is not possible to choose a single direction in which to measure the gradient. However, since the plane has a unique direction to which it is perpendicular, it is possible to specify its orientation using the normal vector.

You know that the vector equation of any plane can be written in the form

$$\mathbf{r} = \mathbf{a} + \lambda \mathbf{b} + \mu \mathbf{c}$$

where $\mathbf{r}$ is a general point on the plane, $\mathbf{a}$ is a particular point on the plane and $\mathbf{b}$ and $\mathbf{c}$ are two vectors parallel to the plane.

Choosing a vector $\mathbf{n}$, which is perpendicular to the plane, as the normal vector and considering the scalar product $\mathbf{n} \cdot \mathbf{r}$, you obtain

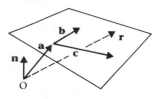

$$\mathbf{n} \cdot \mathbf{r} = \mathbf{n} \cdot (\mathbf{a} + \lambda \mathbf{b} + \mu \mathbf{c})$$
$$= \mathbf{n} \cdot \mathbf{a} + \lambda \mathbf{n} \cdot \mathbf{b} + \mu \mathbf{n} \cdot \mathbf{c}$$

Since the vector $\mathbf{n}$ is perpendicular to the plane, the dot products $\mathbf{n} \cdot \mathbf{b}$ and $\mathbf{n} \cdot \mathbf{c}$ will be zero. The product $\mathbf{n} \cdot \mathbf{a}$ will be a constant because $\mathbf{a}$ is a fixed point in the plane, so $\mathbf{n} \cdot \mathbf{a}$ is the product of two fixed vectors.

The equation therefore reduces to

$$\mathbf{n} \cdot \mathbf{r} = \mathbf{n} \cdot \mathbf{a} \quad \text{or} \quad \mathbf{n} \cdot \mathbf{r} = d \qquad \text{where } d \text{ is a constant}$$

In the case of $ax + by + cz = d$,

$$\mathbf{n} = \begin{bmatrix} a \\ b \\ c \end{bmatrix}, \qquad \mathbf{r} = \begin{bmatrix} x \\ y \\ z \end{bmatrix}$$

The equation of a plane can be written as $\mathbf{n} \cdot \mathbf{r} = d$, where $\mathbf{n}$ is a normal vector.

The normal vector to the plane $ax + by + cz = d$ is $\begin{bmatrix} a \\ b \\ c \end{bmatrix}$.

The value of d can be found by substituting in the position vector of a point in the plane.

Example 8

A plane through a point with position vector $\begin{bmatrix} 2 \\ 1 \\ 3 \end{bmatrix}$ has normal vector $\begin{bmatrix} 3 \\ -1 \\ 4 \end{bmatrix}$.

Find the Cartesian equation of the plane.

Solution

Using $\mathbf{n} \cdot \mathbf{r} = d$,

$$\begin{bmatrix} 3 \\ -1 \\ 4 \end{bmatrix} \cdot \begin{bmatrix} x \\ y \\ z \end{bmatrix} = d$$

Substituting,

$$\begin{bmatrix} 3 \\ -1 \\ 4 \end{bmatrix} \cdot \begin{bmatrix} 2 \\ 1 \\ 3 \end{bmatrix} = 6 - 1 + 12 = 17 = d$$

So

$$\begin{bmatrix} 3 \\ -1 \\ 4 \end{bmatrix} \cdot \begin{bmatrix} x \\ y \\ z \end{bmatrix} = 17 \quad \text{or} \quad 3x - y + 4z = 17$$

11 Find the Cartesian equation of the plane through $(4, 2, -1)$ with normal vector $\begin{bmatrix} 3 \\ -2 \\ 4 \end{bmatrix}$.

Exercise G (answers p. 148)

1 The diagram shows a parallelepiped, a
solid in which opposite faces are parallel.
The face OABC lies in the plane $z = 0$, and
D is the point $(0, 1, 4)$.

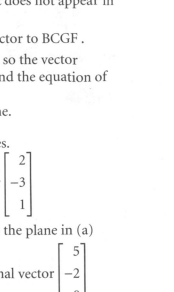

(a) Find $\overrightarrow{OB}$, $\overrightarrow{CB}$ and $\overrightarrow{CG}$.

(b) Find the equation of the plane BCGF
in the form $\mathbf{r} = \mathbf{a} + \lambda\mathbf{b} + \mu\mathbf{c}$.

(c) Find parametric equations for
BCGF.

(d) Find the Cartesian equation of BCGF. (Hint: x does not appear in
the equation.)

(e) From the Cartesian equation, find a normal vector to BCGF.

(f) You know that OAED is parallel to BCGF, and so the vector
found in (e) is also normal to OAED. Hence find the equation of
OAED in the form $\mathbf{r} \cdot \mathbf{n} = d$.

(g) Verify that $(0, 1, 4)$ and $(3, 1, 4)$ lie on this plane.

2 Find the Cartesian equations of the following planes.

(a) A plane through the origin with normal vector $\begin{bmatrix} 2 \\ -3 \\ 1 \end{bmatrix}$

(b) A plane through the point $(3, 1, -2)$ parallel to the plane in (a)

(c) A plane through the point $(3, 1, -2)$ with normal vector $\begin{bmatrix} 5 \\ -2 \\ 0 \end{bmatrix}$

3 OABCDEFG is a unit cube with x-, y- and z-axes as
shown.

For each of the following planes, use inspection to write
down a normal vector and give the Cartesian equation
of the plane.

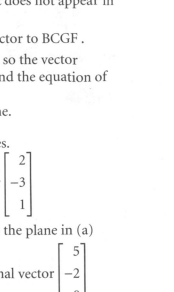

(a) ACGE   (b) OBFD   (c) ADC
(d) EGB   (e) OABC

4 A, B and C are 2, 3 and 4 units from the origin along
the x-, y- and z-axes.

(a) What is the position vector of C?

(b) Write down the vectors $\overrightarrow{CA}$ and $\overrightarrow{CB}$.

(c) What is a vector equation of the plane ABC?

(d) Write down equations for x, y and z in terms of the
parameters λ and μ.

(e) Eliminate λ and μ to find the Cartesian equation of the plane ABC.

(f) What is the normal vector to the plane ABC?

5 Three points have coordinates A $(2, 2, 2)$, B $(-1, 1, 6)$, C $(0, 2, 5)$.

(a) Find the vector equation of the plane ABC in the form
   (i) $\mathbf{r} = \overrightarrow{OC} + \lambda\overrightarrow{CA} + \mu\overrightarrow{CB}$ (ii) $\mathbf{r} = \overrightarrow{OA} + \lambda\overrightarrow{AB} + \mu\overrightarrow{AC}$

(b) Show that both vector equations give the same Cartesian equation
$$3x - y + 2z = 8$$

6E A regular octahedron ABCDEF is placed with its vertices on the x-, y- and z-axes, each at one unit from the origin.

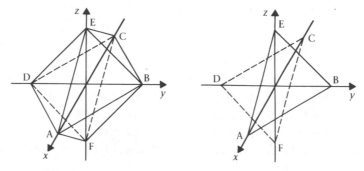

(a) Find the Cartesian equations of the planes AEB and DCF, shown in isolation on the second diagram.

(b) What do you notice about these two planes?

(c) Find the Cartesian equations of the planes ECB and FAD.

H Intersections and angles (answers p. 149)

In sections B and C, you learned to find the intersection of two lines, and the angles between them. In this section you will look at the intersections of lines and planes, and angles between planes or between lines and planes.

The intersection of a line and a plane is most easily dealt with by taking the parametric equations for the line and the Cartesian equation of the plane.

1 Consider the line $\begin{bmatrix} x \\ y \\ z \end{bmatrix} = \begin{bmatrix} 2 \\ 0 \\ -1 \end{bmatrix} + \lambda \begin{bmatrix} 0 \\ 3 \\ 2 \end{bmatrix}$ and the plane $\mathbf{r} \cdot \begin{bmatrix} 3 \\ 1 \\ -1 \end{bmatrix} = 10$.

(a) Find the Cartesian equation of the plane.

(b) Write down a set of parametric equations for the line.

(c) Find λ at the point of intersection, by substituting for x, y and z in the equation of the plane.

(d) Find the coordinates of the point of intersection.

2D

(a) Will a line and a plane always intersect in a single point?

(b) Attempt to find the intersection of

$$\mathbf{r} \cdot \begin{bmatrix} 3 \\ 1 \\ -1 \end{bmatrix} = 9 \quad \text{and} \quad \begin{bmatrix} x \\ y \\ z \end{bmatrix} = \begin{bmatrix} 3 \\ 1 \\ 1 \end{bmatrix} + \lambda \begin{bmatrix} 1 \\ -1 \\ 2 \end{bmatrix}$$

For what values of λ is the equation of the plane satisfied by the parametric equations of the line?

(c) Attempt to find the intersection of

$$\mathbf{r} \cdot \begin{bmatrix} 3 \\ 1 \\ -1 \end{bmatrix} = 10 \quad \text{and} \quad \begin{bmatrix} x \\ y \\ z \end{bmatrix} = \begin{bmatrix} 3 \\ 1 \\ 2 \end{bmatrix} + \lambda \begin{bmatrix} 1 \\ -1 \\ 2 \end{bmatrix}$$

For what values of λ is the equation of the plane satisfied by the parametric equations of the line?

A line and a plane may intersect at a single point, or the line may lie in the plane, as in 2(b), or parallel to the plane, as in 2(c).
In the latter two cases, the direction vector of the line will be perpendicular to the normal vector of the plane, and so their scalar product will be zero.

$$\begin{bmatrix} 3 \\ 1 \\ -1 \end{bmatrix} \cdot \begin{bmatrix} 1 \\ -1 \\ 2 \end{bmatrix} = 3 - 1 - 2 = 0$$

The intersection of a line and a plane may be found by substituting the parametric equations for the line into the Cartesian equation of the plane. The resulting equation may be true for a single value of the parameter, in which case the line and plane intersect.

If the equation is true for all values of the parameter, the line lies in the plane. If it is true for no values, the line is parallel to the plane.

In describing polyhedra or crystals, it is often useful to know the angle between adjacent faces, the **dihedral angle**.

3 This question is based on the model made earlier (p.101), using the units marked on the straws.

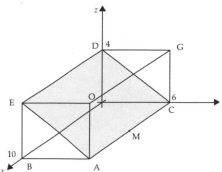

(a) Calculate angle DCO.

(b) If M is the mid-point of AC, use Pythagoras' theorem on triangle OCM to find the length OM.

(c) Calculate angle DMO.

(d) Calculate the length of OA.

(e) Calculate angle DAO.

(f) Comment on the angles DCO, DMO and DAO, all of which are angles between the planes ACDE and OBAC.

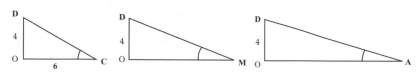

The dihedral angle is conventionally taken to be the angle between lines in the two planes which are perpendicular to the line of intersection. In the case above, this would be angle DCO.

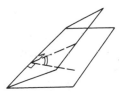

In this simple case, the angle can be calculated by looking at the diagram. However, you will usually need to use the scalar product as in section D. Moreover, you can make use of the normals to the planes, as shown below.

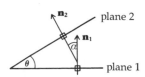

4D (a) Explain why the angle α between the two normals is equal to θ, the dihedral angle between the two planes.

(b) Explain how α can be calculated from the two normal vectors.

Example 9

Find the angle between the planes

$$3x + y - 2z = 4 \quad \text{and} \quad 2x - y + 5z = 1$$

Solution

$$n_1 = \begin{bmatrix} 3 \\ 1 \\ -2 \end{bmatrix}, \qquad n_2 = \begin{bmatrix} 2 \\ -1 \\ 5 \end{bmatrix}$$

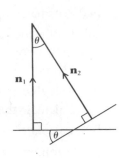

$$n_1 \cdot n_2 = 6 - 1 - 10 = -5$$

$$n_1 = \sqrt{9 + 1 + 4} = \sqrt{14}$$

$$n_2 = \sqrt{4 + 1 + 25} = \sqrt{30}$$

$$n_1 \cdot n_2 = n_1 n_2 \cos \theta \implies -5 = \sqrt{14}\sqrt{30} \cos \theta$$

$$\implies \quad \theta = 104°$$

The acute angle between the planes is 76°.

5 Find the angle between the planes $2x - y - z = 4$ and $3x + y - 2z = 5$.

Now consider the angle between a line and a plane.

The angle between a line and a plane is the angle between the line and a line AB in the plane as shown in the diagram.

The line AB is difficult to describe. However, you know the direction vectors for AC and BC (the normal vector to the plane). This enables you to calculate angle ACB using the scalar product, and hence find angle CAB.

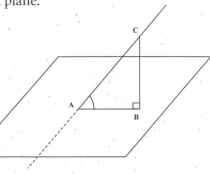

Example 10

Find the angle between the plane $3x + y - 2z = 4$ and the line $\begin{bmatrix} x \\ y \\ z \end{bmatrix} = \begin{bmatrix} 1 \\ 2 \\ 3 \end{bmatrix} + \lambda \begin{bmatrix} -1 \\ 3 \\ -5 \end{bmatrix}$.

Solution

The direction of the line is given by the vector $b = \begin{bmatrix} -1 \\ 3 \\ -5 \end{bmatrix}$.

Thus the angle between the line and the normal $n = \begin{bmatrix} 3 \\ 1 \\ -2 \end{bmatrix}$ is given by

$$b \cdot n = bn \cos \theta$$

$$\implies \quad 10 = \sqrt{35}\sqrt{14} \cos \theta$$

$$\implies \quad \theta = 63.1°$$

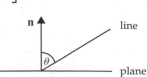

Thus the angle between the line and the plane is $90° - 63.1° = 26.9°$.

6 Find the angle between the plane $3x + 2y - z = 5$ and the line

$$\begin{bmatrix} x \\ y \\ z \end{bmatrix} = \begin{bmatrix} 0 \\ 0 \\ 2 \end{bmatrix} + \lambda \begin{bmatrix} 1 \\ 3 \\ -1 \end{bmatrix}.$$

> The angle between two planes is equal to the angle between their normal vectors, and can be found by using the scalar product of the normal vectors.
>
> The angle between a line and a plane is found by using the scalar product of the line's direction vector and the normal vector to the plane, and then subtracting from $90°$.

Exercise H (answers p. 150)

1 By substituting for x, y and z in the equation of the plane, find the value of the parameter t at the point of intersection of the line with vector equation

$$\begin{bmatrix} x \\ y \\ z \end{bmatrix} = \begin{bmatrix} 0 \\ 2 \\ 5 \end{bmatrix} + t \begin{bmatrix} 3 \\ -1 \\ -5 \end{bmatrix}$$

and the plane with Cartesian equation $2x + 3y + z = 7$.

Hence, write down the coordinates of the point of intersection.

2 Use the result $\cos \theta = \dfrac{\mathbf{a} \cdot \mathbf{b}}{ab}$ for the angle between two vectors to

calculate the angle between the normal vectors for each pair of planes.

What is the angle between the planes in each case?

(a) $x + y + z = 5$, $\quad 2x + 3y + z = 4$

(b) $x - 3y - 2z = 1$, $\quad 5x + 2z = -5$

(c) $x - 2z = 4$, $\quad y + 3z = 6$

3 Calculate the angle between the line $\begin{bmatrix} x \\ y \\ z \end{bmatrix} = \begin{bmatrix} 1 \\ -2 \\ 2 \end{bmatrix} + \lambda \begin{bmatrix} 2 \\ 1 \\ 1 \end{bmatrix}$ and the normal

vector to the plane $2x + 3y - z = 6$.

What is the angle between the line and the plane?

4   Find the angle between the line $\begin{bmatrix} x \\ y \\ z \end{bmatrix} = \begin{bmatrix} 1 \\ 4 \\ 2 \end{bmatrix} + \lambda \begin{bmatrix} 2 \\ 1 \\ -1 \end{bmatrix}$ and the plane

$3x - y + 2z = 4$.

5   The equations of the faces AEB and ECB of the regular octahedron in question 6E of exercise G are

$$x + y + z = 1 \quad \text{and} \quad -x + y + z = 1$$

Calculate the angle between the planes.

What is the dihedral angle of a regular octahedron?

6E   OABC is a tetrahedron where O is the origin and A, B, C are the points
$(1, 1, 0)$, $(0, 1, 1)$ and $(1, 0, 1)$.

(a) Draw a diagram to show the tetrahedron.

(b) Calculate the lengths of the six edges to show that the tetrahedron
is regular.

(c) Find the Cartesian equations of the faces OAB and OAC and
calculate the angle between them. What is the dihedral angle of a
regular tetrahedron?

(d) Write down vector equations of the edges BC and OA and find the
angle between them. What can be said about opposite pairs of
edges of a regular tetrahedron?

(e) Calculate the angle between the edge BC and the face OAC and
use the result to calculate the height of the tetrahedron, taking
OAC as base.

After working through this chapter you should

1   be able to use vectors in two and three dimensions

2   be familiar with vector equations of lines

3   be able to find the intersection of two lines and the distance from a
point to a line, using vector equations

4   understand the scalar product and know its main properties

5   be familiar with vector, parametric and Cartesian equations of
planes, and understand the significance of normal vectors

6   be able to find intersections of a line and a plane

7   be able to calculate angles in three-dimensional situations involving
lines and/or planes.

Answers

1 Cartesian and parametric equations

A Curves varying with time (p. 1)

1D (a)

x	0	1	2	3	4	5
y	10	9.6	8.4	6.4	3.6	0

(b)

t	0	0.2	0.4	0.6	0.8	1
x	0	1	2	3	4	5
y	0	9.6	8.4	6.4	3.6	0

(c) They give the same values for x and y.

(d) $y = 10 - 10\left(\dfrac{x}{5}\right)^2 = 10 - 0.4x^2$

$\qquad = 10 - \tfrac{2}{5}x^2$

2D (a)

t	0	1	2	3	4	5
x	−1	1	3	5	7	9
y	0	1	4	9	16	25

(b) It looks like a parabola; after section C you will be able to prove that this is the case.

3 $y = x^2 - 2x$

Exercise A (p. 2)

1 (a)

t	0	1	2	3	4	5
x	0	20	40	60	80	100
y	90	85	70	45	10	−35

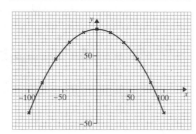

(b) Since $x = 20t$, negative values of t will simply give negative values of x and since $y = 90 - 5t^2$, the values of y will be unchanged. The result will be a graph that is symmetric about the y-axis.

(c) The curve is a parabola.

2

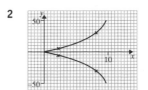

Note the symmetry in the x-axis. Note also that, since $x = 2t^2$, x will never be negative.

3E (a)

θ	0	$\dfrac{\pi}{4}$	$\dfrac{\pi}{3}$	$\dfrac{\pi}{2}$	$\dfrac{2\pi}{3}$	$\dfrac{3\pi}{4}$	π
x	0	0.08	0.18	0.57	1.23	1.65	3.14
y	0	0.29	0.5	1	1.5	1.71	2

θ	$\dfrac{5\pi}{4}$	$\dfrac{4\pi}{3}$	$\dfrac{3\pi}{2}$	$\dfrac{5\pi}{3}$	$\dfrac{7\pi}{4}$	2π
x	4.63	5.05	5.71	6.10	6.20	6.28
y	1.71	1.5	1	0.5	0.29	0

(c) The x values will continue to increase, although not steadily. The y values will oscillate between 0 and 2.

(d)

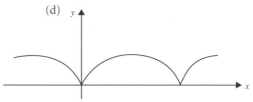

The resulting curve is a cycloid, the path taken by a point on a circle rolling along a line.

4E (a) $x = 0 \Rightarrow t = -1$, $y = \tfrac{1}{5}$

$y = 0 \Rightarrow t = -2$, $x = -\tfrac{1}{4}$

i.e. the curve cuts the axes at $(0, \tfrac{1}{5})$ and $(-\tfrac{1}{4}, 0)$.

(b) As $t \to 2^-$, $x \to +\infty$ and $y \to 2^-$;

i.e. $y = 2$ is an asymptote.

(c) As $t \to 4$ the graph approaches an asymptote since the denominator of y approaches zero.

As $t \to 4^+$, $x \to -\tfrac{5}{2}$ and $y \to -\infty$.

As $t \to 4^-$, $x \to -\tfrac{5}{2}$ and $y \to +\infty$.

(d) When $t = 0$, $x = \tfrac{1}{2}$ and $y = \tfrac{1}{2}$ (it may be necessary to find a few more points to increase your confidence).

(e)

B Conic sections (p. 3)

1D

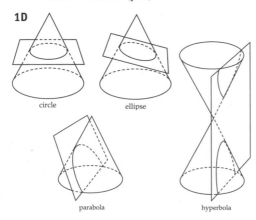

circle

ellipse

parabola

hyperbola

2 (a) $\cos\theta = \dfrac{x}{3}$, $\sin\theta = \dfrac{y}{3}$

(b) $x = 3\cos\theta$, $y = 3\sin\theta$

(c)

θ	0	$\dfrac{\pi}{2}$	π	$\dfrac{3\pi}{2}$	2π	$\dfrac{5\pi}{2}$	3π
x	3	0	-3	0	3	0	-3
y	0	3	0	-3	0	3	0

(d) These are the intersections with the axes, starting at the right and working anticlockwise. The whole circle is drawn by the time we reach $\theta = 2\pi$.

3 (a) $(3\cos\theta, 3\sin\theta)$

(b) $3\sin\theta$

(c) $6\cos\theta$

(d) $x = 6\cos\theta$, $y = 3\sin\theta$

(e) $R(0,3)$, $Q(3,0)$, $Q'(6,0)$

4 (a) $(5,0)$, $(0,4)$, $(-5,0)$, $(0,-4)$

(b)

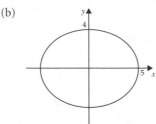

5 (a) (b) (c)

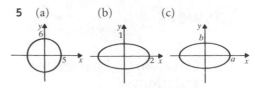

Axes 12, 10   Axes 4, 2   Axes 2a, 2b

6 (a) $x = a\cos\theta$, $y = b\sin\theta$

$\Rightarrow \cos\theta = \dfrac{x}{a}$, $\sin\theta = \dfrac{y}{b}$

So, since $\cos^2\theta + \sin^2\theta = 1$, it follows that

$$\left(\frac{x}{a}\right)^2 + \left(\frac{y}{b}\right)^2 = 1$$

or $\dfrac{x^2}{a^2} + \dfrac{y^2}{b^2} = 1$

which is the Cartesian equation of the ellipse.

(b) Comparing with $\dfrac{x^2}{a^2} + \dfrac{y^2}{b^2} = 1$,

$a = 2$, $b = 3$

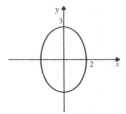

7E (a) The scale factors are a in the x direction, b in the y direction.

(b) $\pi \times 1^2 = \pi$

Since the circle is stretched by a factor a, followed by b, the area of the ellipse is $\pi \times a \times b = \pi ab$.

8 (a)

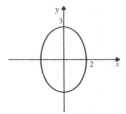

(b) Parabola, with horizontal line of symmetry

9 (a)

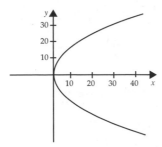

(b) $y^2 = 20x$

10 One possibility is $x = 4t^2$, $y = 8t$

11E (a) $y^2 = (2ap)^2 = 4a^2 p^2$
$4ax = 4a(ap^2) = 4a^2 p^2$

(b) Using $distance = $
$\sqrt{(x_1 - x_2)^2 + (y_1 - y_2)^2}$,
$a(p^2 + 1)$

(c) Nearest point on $x = -a$ is $(-a, 2ap)$,
so the distance is
$(ap^2 - (-a)) = a(p^2 + 1)$.

12D (a)

x	-3	-2	-1	1	2	3	t
y	$-\frac{1}{3}$	$-\frac{1}{2}$	-1	1	$\frac{1}{2}$	$\frac{1}{3}$	$\frac{1}{t}$

(b) One possibility is $x = t$, $y = \dfrac{1}{t}$

13 (a)

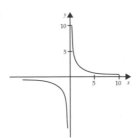

(b) $xy = 2t \times \left(\dfrac{2}{t}\right) = 4$

14 $xy = (ct)\left(\dfrac{c}{t}\right) = c^2$

15E (a), (b) You should find that a constant
added to the parametric equation for
x corresponds to a translation to the
right by that constant. Similarly, a
constant added to the equation for y
corresponds to a vertical translation.

$x = f(t) + a$, $y = g(t) + b$ corresponds
to $x = f(t)$, $y = g(t)$ translated by
vector $\begin{pmatrix} a \\ b \end{pmatrix}$.

(c) Add 2 to the parametric equation for
x, and 3 to the equation for y.

(d) $x = 4 \cos \theta + 1$, $y = 4 \sin \theta - 3$

Exercise B (p. 8)

1 Line 1: $x = 5 \cos \theta$, $y = 5 \sin \theta$

Line 2: Ellipse, $\dfrac{x^2}{9} + \dfrac{y^2}{25} = 1$

Line 3: Parabola, $y^2 = 8x$

Line 4: Rectangular hyperbola, $x = 4t$, $y = \dfrac{4}{t}$

Line 5: Rectangular hyperbola, $x = 3t$, $y = \dfrac{3}{t}$

Note that there are other possibilities for
the parametric equations.

2 $\dfrac{x^2}{2^2} + \dfrac{y^2}{3^2} = 1$
$x = 2 \cos \theta$, $y = 3 \sin \theta$

3 $4x^2 + 9y^2 = 1$

4 One possibility is $x = \dfrac{t^2}{2}$, $y = t$

5 $xy = \frac{1}{4}$ or $4xy = 1$

C Conversion (p. 8)

1 (a) $t = \dfrac{x}{20}$

2 (a) $16y = 40x - 5x^2$

(b) $xy = 5x - 18$

(c) $2x = 2y^2 - 3y$

3 (a) $2x = 6 + 4t$

(b) $2x + y = 12$

(c) This is the equation of a straight line.

4 (a) $x + y = 3$

(b) $3x - y = 13$

5E (a) $4y^2 = x^2 + 1$

(b) $9x^2 - 4y^2 = 36$

(c) $(x - 3)^2 + 4(y + 1)^2 = 4$ or
$x^2 - 6x + 4y^2 + 8y + 9 = 0$

Exercise C (p. 9)

1 (a) $5x + 3y = 22$

   (b) $4y = x^2 - 6x$

   (c) $y = x^2 - 2x$

   (d) $y = x^2 - 2x$

   (e) $y^2 = \dfrac{18}{6 - x}$

   (f) $x^2 y = 2$

2E (a) $4x^2 = 1 + \dfrac{y^2}{9}$ or $36x^2 = 9 + y^2$

   (b) $\dfrac{x^2}{16} + \dfrac{y^2}{9} = 1$ or $9x^2 + 16y^2 = 144$

   (c) $4y^2 + 1 = x^2$

   (d) $1 + (y-1)^2 = \left(\dfrac{x}{3}\right)^2$

      or $9y^2 - 18y + 18 = x^2$

3E Two possibilities are
   $x = t + 2, y = t^2 + 4$
   $x = 2 \pm \sqrt{t}, y = t + 4$

D Differentiating parametric equations (p. 10)

1D (b) Not defined, 0, not defined

2 (a) 10

   (b) $10t$

   (c) t

   (d) $(30, 45)$

   (e) 3

   (f) $y = 3x - 45$

   (g) $y = 55 - \dfrac{x}{3}$

3 (a) $y = \dfrac{x^2}{20}$

   (b) $\dfrac{dy}{dx} = \dfrac{x}{10}$

      When $t = 3$, $\dfrac{dy}{dx} = 3$

      $y = 3x - 45$, $y = 55 - \dfrac{x}{3}$

4 (a) $\dfrac{dy}{dx} = \dfrac{1}{t}$

      At $t = 2$, $\dfrac{dy}{dx} = \tfrac{1}{2}$

   (b) $t = -2$, so $\dfrac{dy}{dx} = -\tfrac{1}{2}$

Exercise D (p. 12)

1 $\dfrac{dy}{dx} = \dfrac{dy}{dt} \div \dfrac{dx}{dt}$

   $= -\dfrac{1}{t^2} \div 1$

   $= -\tfrac{1}{4}$ at $t = 2$

2 $\dfrac{dy}{dx} = \dfrac{4 \cos \theta}{-3 \sin \theta}$

   At $\theta = \dfrac{\pi}{2}$,

   $x = 0, y = 4, \dfrac{dy}{dx} = 0$

3 $\dfrac{dy}{dx} = \dfrac{u}{2}, y = x - 4, y = 12 - x$

4 $y = 3x - 1$

5 (a) $\dfrac{3(v^2 - 1)}{2}$ (b) $v = \pm 1$

   (c) $(2, -2)$ and $(-2, 2)$

6 Parametric: $\dfrac{dy}{dx} = \dfrac{2s}{3}$

   At $s = 1$ the gradient is $\tfrac{2}{3}$.

   Conversion: $s = \dfrac{x}{3}$, so $y = \left(\dfrac{x}{3}\right)^2 = \dfrac{x^2}{9}$

   $\dfrac{dy}{dx} = \dfrac{2x}{9}$

   When $s = 1$, $x = 3$, so the gradient at $x = 3$ is $\tfrac{6}{9}$ or $\tfrac{2}{3}$.

7 (a) Parametric differentiation is the only sensible method.

      $\dfrac{dy}{dx} = \dfrac{3t^2}{2(t+2)}$

   (b) It is easy to spot that $y = 3x - 4$, so

      $\dfrac{dy}{dx} = 3$

(c) Parametric differentiation is the only sensible method.

$$\frac{dy}{dx} = \frac{-3\cos\theta}{(2\sin\theta + \cos\theta)}$$

(d) Parametric differentiation is the only sensible method.

$$\frac{dy}{dx} = \frac{3\cos 3\theta}{2\cos 2\theta}$$

8 (a)
$$\frac{dy}{dx} = \frac{dy}{dt} \div \frac{dx}{dt}$$

$$= \frac{6t^2 + 4}{2t}$$

$$= 3t + \frac{2}{t}$$

$$\Rightarrow \left(\frac{dy}{dx}\right)^2 = 9t^2 + 12 + \frac{4}{t^2}$$

$$= \left(3t - \frac{2}{t}\right)^2 + 24$$

Since $\left(3t - \dfrac{2}{t}\right)^2 \geqslant 0$ for all t,

$$\left(\frac{dy}{dx}\right)^2 \geqslant 24.$$

(b)

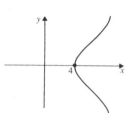

9E $\dfrac{dy}{dx} = \dfrac{\cos\theta}{1 + \sin\theta}$

At $\theta = \frac{1}{4}\pi$, $(x, y) \approx (0.0783, 0.707)$

and $\dfrac{dy}{dx} \approx 0.414$

$y - 0.707 \approx 0.414(x - 0.0783)$

$\qquad y \approx 0.414x + 0.675$

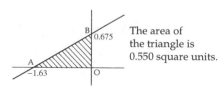

The area of the triangle is 0.550 square units.

10E (a) $p^2 y + x = 2cp$

(b) A: $(2cp, 0)$, B: $\left(0, \dfrac{2c}{p}\right)$

(c) $\left(cp, \dfrac{c}{p}\right)$. This is point P. Since any point on the curve can be written in the form $\left(cp, \dfrac{c}{p}\right)$, this result is true for any point on the curve.

E Implicit differentiation (p. 14)

1D (a) $\dfrac{dy}{dx} = \dfrac{-4x}{y}$

(b) $-4, 4$

(c) The part of the ellipse above the x-axis

(d) $\dfrac{dy}{dx} = \dfrac{-4x}{\sqrt{20 - 4x^2}}$

(e) -4. The equation differentiated in (d) did not apply to this part of the curve.

2 $-\frac{4}{5}$

3 (a) $\dfrac{dz}{dx} = 3y + 3x\dfrac{dy}{dx}$

(b) $3y + 3x\dfrac{dy}{dx} = 1 \implies \dfrac{dy}{dx} = \dfrac{1 - 3y}{3x}$

4 (a) $2xy + x^2\dfrac{dy}{dx}$

(b) $y^2 + 2xy\dfrac{dy}{dx}$

(c) $e^x y + e^x\dfrac{dy}{dx}$

5 (a) (i) $2y\dfrac{dy}{dx}$ (ii) $y + x\dfrac{dy}{dx}$

(iii) $2x$ (iv) 0

(b) $\dfrac{dy}{dx} = \dfrac{-y}{2y + x}$

6 (a) $\dfrac{\mathrm{d}y}{\mathrm{d}x} = \dfrac{4x - 3y}{3x}$

When $x = 2$ and $y = 2\frac{2}{3}$, $\dfrac{\mathrm{d}y}{\mathrm{d}x} = 0$,

so $(2,\ 2\frac{2}{3})$ is a stationary point.

When $x = -2$ and $y = -2\frac{2}{3}$, $\dfrac{\mathrm{d}y}{\mathrm{d}x} = 0$,

so $(-2,\ -2\frac{2}{3})$ is a stationary point.

(b) $3xy - 2x^2 = 8$

$\Rightarrow \quad 3xy = 8 + 2x^2$

$\Rightarrow \qquad y = \dfrac{8 + 2x^2}{3x}$

$\Rightarrow \quad \dfrac{\mathrm{d}y}{\mathrm{d}x} = \dfrac{12x^2 - 3(8 + 2x^2)}{9x^2} = \dfrac{6x^2 - 24}{9x^2}$

At the stationary points, $6x^2 = 24$,

so $x = \pm 2$.

$x = 2 \Rightarrow y = 2\frac{2}{3}$; $x = -2 \Rightarrow y = -2\frac{2}{3}$,

so $(2,\ 2\frac{2}{3})$ and $(-2,\ -2\frac{2}{3})$ are stationary points.

(c) It is clear that implicit differentiation is quicker for checking stationary points, but it is not well designed for *finding* stationary points.

Exercise E (p. 17)

1 (a) $4y\dfrac{\mathrm{d}y}{\mathrm{d}x} - 3\dfrac{\mathrm{d}y}{\mathrm{d}x} + 8x = 0$, so $\dfrac{\mathrm{d}y}{\mathrm{d}x} = \dfrac{-8x}{4y - 3}$

(b) $3x^2 + y\dfrac{\mathrm{d}y}{\mathrm{d}x} - 7 + 3\dfrac{\mathrm{d}y}{\mathrm{d}x} = 0$,

so $\dfrac{\mathrm{d}y}{\mathrm{d}x} = \dfrac{7 - 3x^2}{y + 3}$

2 (a) $18x + 8y\dfrac{\mathrm{d}y}{\mathrm{d}x} = 0$, so $\dfrac{\mathrm{d}y}{\mathrm{d}x} = \dfrac{-18x}{8y} = \dfrac{-9x}{4y}$

(b) When $x = 1$, $y^2 = 9$, so $y = \pm 3$.

At $(1, 3)$ the gradient is -0.75.

At $(1, -3)$ the gradient is 0.75.

3 (a) $4x + 3y + 3x\dfrac{\mathrm{d}y}{\mathrm{d}x} - 4\dfrac{\mathrm{d}y}{\mathrm{d}x} + 2y\dfrac{\mathrm{d}y}{\mathrm{d}x} = 0$

$\Rightarrow \quad (3x - 4 + 2y)\dfrac{\mathrm{d}y}{\mathrm{d}x} = -(4x + 3y)$

$\Rightarrow \qquad \dfrac{\mathrm{d}y}{\mathrm{d}x} = -\dfrac{4x + 3y}{3x + 2y - 4}$

(b) $\dfrac{2x + 2y - 3}{2y - 2x}$

(c) $\dfrac{2 - x}{4 + 4y}$

(d) $-\dfrac{3x^2 + y^2}{2xy + 3y^2}$

4 (a) $\dfrac{\mathrm{d}y}{\mathrm{d}x} = -\dfrac{y}{x}$

(b) $y = \dfrac{12}{x} \Rightarrow \dfrac{\mathrm{d}y}{\mathrm{d}x} = -\dfrac{12}{x^2}$

(c) Since $\dfrac{12}{x} = y$, $\dfrac{-12}{x^2} = -\dfrac{y}{x} = \dfrac{\mathrm{d}y}{\mathrm{d}x}$

5 (a) $2xy + x^2\dfrac{\mathrm{d}y}{\mathrm{d}x} + 3x^2 = 0$

$\Rightarrow \quad \dfrac{\mathrm{d}y}{\mathrm{d}x} = \dfrac{-(2xy + 3x^2)}{x^2}$

When $x = -2$ and $y = 3$, $\dfrac{\mathrm{d}y}{\mathrm{d}x} = 0$,

so $(-2, 3)$ is a stationary point on the curve.

(b) By the quotient rule,

$\dfrac{\mathrm{d}y}{\mathrm{d}x} = \dfrac{x^2(-3x^2) - 2x(4 - x^3)}{x^4}$

When $x = -2$, $\dfrac{\mathrm{d}y}{\mathrm{d}x} = \dfrac{(-48 + 4(4 + 8))}{4}$,

which is zero.

6 (a) $\dfrac{\mathrm{d}y}{\mathrm{d}x} = \dfrac{-(2x + 6)}{2y - 2}$

At $(1, 4)$ the gradient is $-\frac{4}{3}$.

The equation of the tangent is $3y + 4x = 16$.

(b) At $(1, -2)$ the gradient is $\frac{4}{3}$.

The radius joins $(1, -2)$ to $(-3, 1)$, so has gradient $-\frac{3}{4}$. Since this is the same as $-1 \div \frac{4}{3}$ the tangent and radius are perpendicular.

(c) Some other points on the circumference with integral coordinates are: $(0, 5)$, $(0, -3)$, $(-6, 5)$, $(-7, 4)$, $(-6, -3)$ and $(-7, -2)$. At all these points the gradient of the curve should be equal to

$$\dfrac{-1}{\text{gradient of radius}}$$

7 (a) $\dfrac{dy}{dx} = -\dfrac{9x}{4y} = -\dfrac{3}{2}$

(b) $\theta = \dfrac{\pi}{4}, \dfrac{dy}{dx} = \dfrac{-3}{2\tan\theta} = -\dfrac{3}{2}$

8 (a) $\dfrac{d}{dx}(\ln y) = \dfrac{d}{dy}(\ln y)\dfrac{dy}{dx}$,

by the chain rule

$= \dfrac{1}{y}\dfrac{dy}{dx}$

Now $\ln y = x \ln 2$

$\Rightarrow \dfrac{1}{y}\dfrac{dy}{dx} = \ln 2$

$\Rightarrow \dfrac{dy}{dx} = y \ln 2 = \ln 2 \times 2^x$

(b) $\dfrac{d}{dx}(3^x) = \ln 3 \times 3^x$

(c) $\dfrac{d}{dx}(a^x) = \ln a \times a^x$

(d) $\dfrac{d}{dx}(e^x) = \ln e \times e^x$

$= 1 \times e^x$

$= e^x$

9E (a), (b) You may have used either the product rule or the chain rule.

Chain rule:

$u = \dfrac{dy}{dx}$

$\dfrac{du}{dx} = \dfrac{d^2y}{dx^2}$

$\dfrac{d}{dx}(u^2) = \dfrac{d}{du}(u^2) \times \dfrac{du}{dx}$

$= 2u\dfrac{du}{dx}$

$= 2\dfrac{dy}{dx}\dfrac{d^2y}{dx^2}$

Similarly,

$\dfrac{d}{dx}(u^3) = 3u^2\dfrac{du}{dx}$

$= \left(\dfrac{dy}{dx}\right)^2 \dfrac{d^2y}{dx^2}$

Product rule:

$\dfrac{d}{dx}\left(\dfrac{dy}{dx} \times \dfrac{dy}{dx}\right) = \dfrac{d^2y}{dx^2}\dfrac{dy}{dx} + \dfrac{dy}{dx}\dfrac{d^2y}{dx^2}$

$= 2\dfrac{dy}{dx}\dfrac{d^2y}{dx^2}$

Using this result,

$\dfrac{d}{dx}\left(\dfrac{dy}{dx} \times \left(\dfrac{dy}{dx}\right)^2\right) = \dfrac{d^2y}{dx^2}\left(\dfrac{dy}{dx}\right)^2 + \dfrac{dy}{dx}\left(2\dfrac{dy}{dx}\dfrac{d^2y}{dx^2}\right)$

$= 3\left(\dfrac{dy}{dx}\right)^2 \dfrac{d^2y}{dx^2}$

S1.1 Further differentiation practice
(p. 19)

1 (a) Implicit differentiation:

$2xy + x^2\dfrac{dy}{dx} = 0$, so $\dfrac{dy}{dx} = \dfrac{-2xy}{x^2} = \dfrac{-2y}{x}$

Or $y = \dfrac{36}{x^2} = 36x^{-2}$,

so $\dfrac{dy}{dx} = -72x^{-3} = \dfrac{-72}{x^3}$

(b) Parametric differentiation:

$\dfrac{dy}{dx} = \dfrac{3\cos\theta}{-4\sin\theta} = -0.75\cot\theta$

(c) Parametric differentiation:

$\dfrac{dy}{dx} = \dfrac{-6\sin 3\theta}{2\cos 2\theta} = \dfrac{-3\sin 3\theta}{\cos 2\theta}$

(d) Implicit differentiation:

$2x + 2y\dfrac{dy}{dx} = 0$

$\dfrac{dy}{dx} = \dfrac{-x}{y}$

(e) Parametric differentiation:

$\dfrac{dy}{dx} = 3t^2 \div -\dfrac{1}{t^2} = -3t^4$

(f) Implicit differentiation:

$2x + 3y + 3x\dfrac{dy}{dx} + 4y\dfrac{dy}{dx} = 0$

$\dfrac{dy}{dx} = \dfrac{-(2x+3y)}{3x+4y}$

(g) Implicit differentiation:

$$3e^{3x}y + e^{3x}\frac{dy}{dx} = 2x$$

$$\frac{dy}{dx} = \frac{2x - 3ye^{3x}}{e^{3x}}$$

Or $y = \dfrac{x^2}{e^{3x}}$ and use the quotient rule to obtain

$$\frac{dy}{dx} = \frac{2x\,e^{3x} - 3x^2 e^{3x}}{(e^{3x})^2} = \frac{2x - 3x^2}{e^{3x}}$$

2 $y = \frac{1}{2}x + 2$

3 $\dfrac{dy}{dx} = \dfrac{2 - x}{y - 3}$

4 (a) $-\dfrac{6x}{5y}$ (b) $\dfrac{-2(1+y)}{x}$ (c) $\dfrac{-3}{\sin y}$

2 Binomial theorem

A Binomial expansions (p. 20)

1 $(a + b)^3 = (a + b)(a^2 + 2ab + b^2)$
$$= a^3 + 2a^2 b + ab^2 + a^2 b + 2ab^2 + b^3$$
$$= a^3 + 3a^2 b + 3ab^2 + b^3$$

2 $(a + b)^4 = (a + b)(a + b)^3$
$$= (a + b)(a^3 + 3a^2 b + 3ab^2 + b^3)$$
$$= a^4 + 4a^3 b + 6a^2 b^2 + 4ab^3 + b^4$$

3D (a) The coefficients form the rows of Pascal's triangle.

(b) The next row is 1   4   6   4   1,
as in the answer to question 2.

(c) $(a + b)^5 = a^5 + 5a^4 b + 10a^3 b^2$
$$+ 10a^2 b^3 + 5ab^4 + b^5$$

4E $a^4 + 4a^3(2b) + 6a^2(2b)^2 + 4a(2b)^3 + (2b)^4$
$$= a^4 + 8a^3 b + 24a^2 b^2 + 32ab^3 + 16b^4$$

5D $a \times 6a^2 b^2 + b \times 4a^3 b = 10a^3 b^2$. Coefficient is 10.

Exercise A (p. 21)

1 (a) $(a + b)^6 = a^6 + 6a^5 b + 15a^4 b^2 + 20a^3 b^3$
$$+ 15a^2 b^4 + 6ab^5 + b^6$$

(b) $(p - q)^5 = p^5 - 5p^4 q + 10p^3 q^2 - 10p^2 q^3$
$$+ 5pq^4 - q^5$$

(c) $(3x + y)^4 = (3x)^4 + 4(3x)^3 y + 6(3x)^2 y^2$
$$+ 4(3x)y^3 + y^4$$
$$= 81x^4 + 108x^3 y + 54x^2 y^2$$
$$+ 12xy^3 + y^4$$

(d) $(1 + z)^6 = 1 + 6z + 15z^2 + 20z^3 + 15z^4$
$$+ 6z^5 + z^6$$

2 (a) $(a + b)^3 = a^3 + 3a^2 b + 3ab^2 + b^3$
$$(a - b)^3 = a^3 - 3a^2 b + 3ab^2 - b^3$$

(b) Adding the results in (a),
$$(a + b)^3 + (a - b)^3 = 2a^3 + 6ab^2$$
$$= 2a(a^2 + 3b^2)$$

(c) Subtracting the results in (a),
$$(a + b)^3 - (a - b)^3 = 6a^2 b + 2b^3$$
$$= 2b(3a^2 + b^2)$$

3E (a) $p = a + b$ and $q = a - b$
$$\Rightarrow a = \tfrac{1}{2}(p + q) \text{ and } b = \tfrac{1}{2}(p - q)$$

Then
$$p^3 + q^3 = 2[\tfrac{1}{2}(p + q)]$$
$$\times [(\tfrac{1}{2}(p + q))^2 + 3(\tfrac{1}{2}(p - q))^2]$$
$$= (p + q)(p^2 - pq + q^2)$$

(b) $p^3 - q^3 = (p + (-q))$
$$\times (p^2 - p(-q) + (-q)^2)$$
$$= (p - q)(p^2 + pq + q^2)$$

4E Writing 11 as $10 + 1$,
$$11^2 = (10 + 1)^2 = 10^2 + 2 \times 10 + 1 = 121$$
$$11^3 = (10 + 1)^3$$
$$= 10^3 + 3 \times 10^2 \times 1 + 3 \times 10 \times 1^2 + 1^3$$
$$= 1331$$
$$11^4 = (10 + 1)^4$$
$$= 10^4 + 4 \times 10^3 \times 1 + 6 \times 10^2 \times 1^2$$
$$+ 4 \times 10 \times 1^3 + 1^4$$
$$= 14\,641$$
$$11^5 = 15 \;\boxed{10}\;\boxed{10}\; 51 = 161\,051$$

Pascal's triangle still applies, but you need to carry.

B Binomial coefficients (p. 21)

1 The reciprocals of $\frac{4}{1}$ and $\frac{3}{2}$ are $\frac{1}{4}$ and $\frac{2}{3}$.

2 (a) The multipliers for the 5th line are

$$\times\tfrac{5}{1} \quad \times\tfrac{4}{2} \quad \times\tfrac{3}{3} \quad \times\tfrac{2}{4} \quad \times\tfrac{1}{5}$$

$$1 \longrightarrow 5 \longrightarrow 10 \longrightarrow 10 \longrightarrow 5 \longrightarrow 1$$

(b) The sequence of multipliers is $\frac{5}{1}, \frac{4}{2}, \frac{3}{3}, \frac{2}{4}, \frac{1}{5}$, where numerators decrease by 1 and denominators increase by 1 .

3 (a) The multipliers for the 6th line are:

$\times \frac{6}{1} \quad \times \frac{5}{2} \quad \times \frac{4}{3} \quad \times \frac{3}{4} \quad \times \frac{2}{5} \quad \times \frac{1}{6}$

$1 \longrightarrow 6 \longrightarrow 15 \longrightarrow 20 \longrightarrow 15 \longrightarrow 6 \longrightarrow 1$

(b) This agrees with the result from Pascal's triangle.

4

$\times \frac{10}{1} \ \times \frac{9}{2} \ \times \frac{8}{3} \ \times \frac{7}{4} \ \times \frac{6}{5} \ \times \frac{5}{6} \ \times \frac{4}{7} \ \times \frac{3}{8} \ \times \frac{2}{9} \ \times \frac{1}{10}$

$1 \longrightarrow 10 \longrightarrow 45 \longrightarrow 120 \longrightarrow 210 \longrightarrow 252 \longrightarrow 210 \longrightarrow 120 \longrightarrow 45 \longrightarrow 10 \longrightarrow 1$

5E The sum is $1024 = 2^{10}$. The elements of the nth row of Pascal's triangle always sum to 2^n.

6    $\times \frac{80}{1} \quad \times \frac{79}{2} \quad \times \frac{78}{3}$

$1 \longrightarrow 80 \longrightarrow 3160 \longrightarrow 82\,160$

7 $\binom{12}{5} = \dfrac{12 \times 11 \times 10 \times 9 \times 8}{1 \times 2 \times 3 \times 4 \times 5}$

8 (a) $\dfrac{12!}{7!} = 12 \times 11 \times 10 \times 9 \times 8$

(b) $\binom{12}{5} = \dfrac{12 \times 11 \times 10 \times 9 \times 8}{1 \times 2 \times 3 \times 4 \times 5}$

$= \dfrac{12 \times 11 \times 10 \times 9 \times 8}{5!}$

$= \dfrac{12!}{5!7!}$ from (a)

(c) $\binom{12}{5} = 792$

9 $\binom{12}{4} = \dfrac{12!}{4!8!}$ and $\binom{12}{8} = \dfrac{12!}{8!4!}$

$\Rightarrow \binom{12}{8} = \binom{12}{4}$

10 (a) 220   (b) 792   (c) 12

11 $\binom{n}{r} = \dfrac{n!}{r!(n-r)!}$

12 (a) $\binom{12}{0} = \binom{12}{12} = 1$ (b) $\dfrac{12!}{0!12!} = 1$ (c) $0! = 1$

Exercise B (p. 25)

1 (a) 56   (b) 10   (c) 84   (d) 4950

2 $(a+b)^7 = a^7 + 7a^6 b + 21a^5 b^2 + 35a^4 b^3$
$+ 35a^3 b^4 + 21a^2 b^5 + 7ab^6 + b^7$

3 (a) $(a-b)^8 = a^8 - 8a^7 b + 28a^6 b^2$
$-56a^5 b^3 + \ldots$

(b) $(2a - 3b)^{10} = (2a)^{10} - 10(2a)^9(3b)$
$+ 45(2a)^8(3b)^2$
$- 120(2a)^7(3b)^3 + \ldots$
$= 1024a^{10} - 15\,360a^9 b$
$+ 103\,680a^8 b^2$
$- 414\,720a^7 b^3 + \ldots$

(c) $\left(x^2 - \dfrac{1}{x^2}\right)^6 = (x^2)^6 - 6(x^2)^5\left(\dfrac{1}{x^2}\right)$
$+ 15(x^2)^4\left(\dfrac{1}{x^2}\right)^2$
$- 20(x^2)^3\left(\dfrac{1}{x^2}\right)^3 + \ldots$
$= x^{12} - 6x^8 + 15x^4 - 20 + \ldots$

4 $a = 11$ from the symmetry of the binomial coefficients.

5 (a) 0.0158   (b) 3.05

6E (a) $\binom{9}{3} = 84$, $\binom{9}{4} = 126$,

$\binom{10}{4} = 210 = \binom{9}{3} + \binom{9}{4}$

(b) $\binom{n+1}{r} = \binom{n}{r} + \binom{n}{r-1}$

$\binom{n}{r} = \dfrac{n!}{(n-r)!r!} = \dfrac{n!(n-r+1)}{(n-r+1)!r!}$

and

$\binom{n}{r-1} = \dfrac{n!}{(n-r+1)!(r-1)!}$
$= \dfrac{n!r}{(n-r+1)!r!}$

So $\binom{n}{r} + \binom{n}{r-1} = \dfrac{n!(n-r+1) + n!r}{(n-r+1)!r!}$
$= \dfrac{(n+1)!}{(n+1-r)!r!}$
$= \binom{n+1}{r}$

C   Binomial series (p. 25)

1D (b) $y = 1 + 3x$ is the tangent of $y = (1 + x)^3$ at $x = 0$, $y = 1$ and is a good approximation to the function for values of x near zero.

(c)

x	0.05	0.1	0.15	0.2	0.25
$1 + 3x$	1.15	1.3	1.45	1.6	1.75
$(1 + x)^3$	1.157 625	1.331	1.520 875	1.728	1.953 125

The results are close for small values of x but diverge as x increases.

2D (b)

x	0.05	0.1	0.15	0.2	0.25
$1 + 3x + 3x^2$	1.1575	1.33	1.5175	1.72	1.9375

$1 + 3x + 3x^2$ gives a better approximation than $1 + 3x$.

3 (a) $(1 + x)^8 = 1 + 8x + 28x^2 + \ldots$ so $1 + 8x + 28x^2$ is a quadratic approximation to $(1 + x)^8$.

(b) The approximation looks good for small positive and negative values of x. It is within about 10% of the correct value for $-0.1 < x < 0.17$.

4 (a) With $n = -1$, $1 + nx + \dfrac{n(n-1)}{2!} x^2$ becomes

$$1 + (-1)x + \frac{(-1)(-2)}{2!} x^2 = 1 - x + x^2$$

(b) For $-0.464 < x < 0.464$, the value of the quadratic is within 10% of the true value.

5 (a) $\sqrt{1 + x} = (1 + x)^{\frac{1}{2}}$

If $n = \frac{1}{2}$, the first three terms of the series are

$$1 + \frac{1}{2}x + \frac{(\frac{1}{2})(-\frac{1}{2})}{2!} x^2 = 1 + \frac{1}{2}x + \frac{(-\frac{1}{4})}{2} x^2$$

$$= 1 + \frac{1}{2}x - \frac{1}{8}x^2$$

(b) The value of $1 + \dfrac{1}{2}x - \dfrac{1}{8}x^2$ is within 10% of the value of $\sqrt{1 + x}$ for $-0.7 < x < 1.7$.

6 The next term in the series is

$$\frac{n(n-1)(n-2)}{3!} x^3.$$

So, putting $n = \dfrac{1}{2}$ gives

$$\frac{\frac{1}{2}(-\frac{1}{2})(-\frac{3}{2})}{3!} x^3 = \frac{\frac{3}{8}}{6} x^3 = \frac{3}{48} x^3 = \frac{1}{16} x^3$$

and a sensible cubic approximation would be $1 + \dfrac{1}{2}x - \dfrac{1}{8}x^2 + \dfrac{1}{16}x^3$.

This is a better approximation than the quadratic, but again is good only for small values of x.

7E (a) The series is a geometric series, common ratio $-x$.

The sum is $\dfrac{1}{1 - (-x)} = \dfrac{1}{1 + x}$, provided $-1 < x < 1$.

(b) Substituting $n = -1$ gives

$$(1 + x)^{-1} = 1 - x + x^2 - x^3 + \ldots,$$

whose sum is known to be $\dfrac{1}{1 + x}$ from (a).

If the binomial series is summed to infinity, then the series is *equal* to $(1 + x)^n$ for $-1 < x < 1$ and is not merely an approximation.

8E $1 + x - \dfrac{x^3}{8} + \dfrac{x^4}{64}$

Note that $1 + \frac{1}{2}x - \frac{1}{8}x^2 \approx \sqrt{1 + x}$; $(\sqrt{1 + x})^2$ is of course $1 + x$.

9D (a) $(a + x)^n = a^n + na^{n-1}x$

$$+ \frac{n(n-1)}{2!} a^{n-2} x^2$$

$$+ \frac{n(n-1)(n-2)}{3!} a^{n-3} x^3 + \ldots$$

(b) The expansion of $\left(1 + \dfrac{x}{a}\right)^n$ is valid for

$$\left| \frac{x}{a} \right| < 1 \Longrightarrow |x| < |a|$$

Exercise C (p. 28)

1 (a) $(1+x)^{\frac{1}{3}} = 1 + \frac{1}{3}x - \frac{1}{9}x^2 + \frac{5}{81}x^3 + \dots$

(b) $(1+x)^{-3} = 1 - 3x + 6x^2 - 10x^3 + \dots$

2 (a) $(1+x)^{\frac{1}{2}}$ (b) $(1+x)^{-3}$

(c) $(1+x)^{\frac{1}{5}}$ (d) $(1+x)^{-\frac{1}{3}}$

3 (a) $1 - 4x + 10x^2 - 20x^3$

(b) $1 - x - \frac{1}{2}x^2 - \frac{1}{2}x^3$

(c) $1 - \frac{1}{2}x^2$

4 (a) $\sqrt{9 - 18x} = \sqrt{9(1-2x)}$

$\qquad = \sqrt{9}\sqrt{1-2x} = 3\sqrt{1-2x}$

(b) $\sqrt{9 - 18x} = 3(1-2x)^{\frac{1}{2}}$

$= 3\left(1 + \frac{1}{2}(-2x) + \frac{(\frac{1}{2})(-\frac{1}{2})}{2!}(-2x)^2\right.$

$+ \frac{(\frac{1}{2})(-\frac{1}{2})(-\frac{3}{2})}{3!}(-2x)^3$

$\left. + \frac{(\frac{1}{2})(-\frac{1}{2})(-\frac{3}{2})(-\frac{5}{2})}{4!}(-2x)^4 + \dots\right)$

$= 3 - 3x - \frac{3}{2}x^2 - \frac{3}{2}x^3 - \frac{15}{8}x^4 - \dots$

$-1 < 2x < 1 \Rightarrow -\frac{1}{2} < x < \frac{1}{2}$

5 (a) $\frac{1}{2}(1+x)^{-\frac{1}{2}} \approx \frac{1}{2} - \frac{1}{4}x + \frac{3}{16}x^2$

(b) $\frac{1}{9}(1+x)^{-2} \approx \frac{1}{9} - \frac{2}{9}x + \frac{1}{3}x^2$

6 (a) The binomial series is only valid for $-1 < x < 1$.

(b) $7\sqrt{1 + \frac{1}{49}} = \sqrt{49\left(1 + \frac{1}{49}\right)} = \sqrt{50}$

$\sqrt{50} = 7\left(1 + \frac{1}{2}\left(\frac{1}{49}\right) - \frac{1}{8}\left(\frac{1}{49}\right)^2\right.$

$\left. + \frac{1}{16}\left(\frac{1}{49}\right)^3 - \dots\right) \approx 7.071\,068$

7E (a) $(1+x)^{\frac{1}{2}} \approx 1 + \frac{1}{2}x$

$\Rightarrow \left(1 - \frac{v^2}{c^2}\right)^{\frac{1}{2}} \approx 1 + \frac{1}{2}\left(-\frac{v^2}{c^2}\right)$

$= 1 - \frac{v^2}{2c^2}$

(b) $1 - \frac{1}{2}\left(\frac{1}{3}\right)^2 = \frac{17}{18} = 0.94$ (to 2 s.f.)

3 Maclaurin's series (p. 30)

A **Introduction** (p. 30)

1D Both graphs go through $(0, 1)$ with the same gradient.

2D (a) Yes

(b) Neither is very good for large x.

3 (a) $f'(x) = \frac{1}{3}(1+x)^{-\frac{2}{3}}$, $f''(x) = -\frac{2}{9}(1+x)^{-\frac{5}{3}}$

$f(0) = 1$, $f'(0) = \frac{1}{3}$, $f''(0) = -\frac{2}{9}$

(b) $g'(x) = \frac{1}{3} - \frac{2}{9}x$, $g''(x) = -\frac{2}{9}$

$g(0) = 1$, $g'(0) = \frac{1}{3}$, $g''(0) = -\frac{2}{9}$

(c) $f(0) = g(0)$, $f'(0) = g'(0)$, $f''(0) = g''(0)$

4E (a) $f^{(3)}(x) = \frac{10}{27}(1+x)^{-\frac{8}{3}}$

$f^{(3)}(0) = \frac{10}{27}$

(b) $\frac{10}{27} = 6 \times \frac{5}{81}$

5 (a) $y = 4x + 10$

(b) $f(x) = a + bx + cx^2$, $f(0) = a = 10$

$f'(x) = b + 2cx$, $f'(0) - b = 4$

6D They all go through $(0, 10)$ with gradient 4.

7 $f(x) \approx 10 + 4x + x^2$

8 $\begin{aligned} p(0) &= 12 & \Rightarrow a &= 12 \\ p'(0) &= 11 & \Rightarrow b &= 11 \\ p''(0) &= 10 & \Rightarrow 2c &= 10 \\ p^{(3)}(0) &= 6 & \Rightarrow 6d &= 6 \end{aligned}$

Hence $a = 12$, $b = 11$, $c = 5$, $d = 1$

9 (a) If $p(x) = a + bx + cx^2 + dx^3$

$\begin{aligned} p(0) &= a & \Rightarrow a &= p(0) \\ p'(0) &= b & \Rightarrow b &= p'(0) \\ p''(0) &= 2c & \Rightarrow c &= p''(0) \div 2 \\ p^{(3)}(0) &= 6d & \Rightarrow d &= p^{(3)}(0) \div 6 \end{aligned}$

Hence

$p(x) = p(0) + p'(0)x + p''(0)\frac{x^2}{2} + p^{(3)}(0)\frac{x^3}{6}$

(b) Under differentiation,

$ax^n \to n \times ax^{n-1}$

So

$cx^2 \to 2 \times cx \to 1 \times 2 \times c$

and

$dx^3 \to 3 \times dx^2 \to 2 \times 3 \times dx \to 1 \times 2 \times 3d$

10   If $p(x)$ is a polynomial of degree 4, then

$p(x) = a + bx + cx^2 + dx^3 + ex^4$

$\implies$ $p'(x)$ $= b + 2cx + 3dx^2 + 4ex^3$

$\qquad$ $p''(x)$ $= \qquad 2c + 6dx + 12ex^2$

$\qquad$ $p^{(3)}(x) = \qquad\qquad 6d + 24ex$

$\qquad$ $p^{(4)}(x) \qquad\qquad\qquad 24e$

$\implies$ $p(0)$ $= a$

$\qquad$ $p'(0)$ $= b$

$\qquad$ $p''(0)$ $= 2c$

$\qquad$ $p^{(3)}(0) = 6d$

$\qquad$ $p^{(4)}(0) = 24e$

But $24 = 4 \times 3 \times 2 \times 1$ is usually written as $4!$

So $e = p^{(4)}(0) \div 4!$

In a similar way, $d = p^{(3)}(0) \div 3!$ and $c = p''(0) \div 2!$

Hence

$$p(x) = p(0) + p'(0)x + p''(0)\frac{x^2}{2!} + p^{(3)}(0)\frac{x^3}{3!}$$
$$+ p^{(4)}(0)\frac{x^4}{4!}$$

11   (a) $p(x) = p(0) + p'(0)x + p''(0)\frac{x^2}{2!}$
$$+ p^{(3)}(0)\frac{x^3}{3!} + p^{(4)}\frac{x^4}{4!} + p^{(5)}(0)\frac{x^5}{5!}$$

(b) $p(x) = p(0) + p'(0)x + p''(0)\frac{x^2}{2!}$
$$+ p^{(3)}(0)\frac{x^{3!}}{3!} + p^{(4)}\frac{x^4}{4!} + \dots$$
$$+ p^{(n)}(0)\frac{x^n}{n!}$$

12 $f(x)$ $= e^{2x}$

$\implies$ $f'(x)$ $= 2e^{2x}$

$\qquad$ $f''(x)$ $= 2^2 e^{2x}$

$\qquad$ $f^{(3)}(x) = 2^3 e^{2x}$

$\qquad$ $f^{(4)}(x) = 2^4 e^{2x}$

$\implies$ $f(0)$ $= 1$

$\qquad$ $f'(0)$ $= 2$

$\qquad$ $f''(0)$ $= 2^2$

$\qquad$ $f^{(3)}(0) = 2^3$

$\qquad$ $f^{(4)}(0) = 2^4$

The polynomial

$$1 + 2x + 2x^2 + \frac{4x^3}{3} + \frac{2x^4}{3}$$

will pass through the same point with the same gradient, and with the same second derivative, third derivative and fourth derivative, as the function e^{2x} does when $x = 0$.

Hence it is a good approximation to e^{2x} for values of x near $x = 0$, and this is confirmed by plotting the functions. The approximation gives an error of within $\pm 1\%$ for $-0.45 < x < 0.64$.

Exercise A (p. 33)

1   (a) $f(x)$ $= \cos x$ $\implies f(0) = 1$

$\qquad$ $f'(x)$ $= -\sin x \implies f'(0) = 0$

$\qquad$ $f''(x)$ $= -\cos x \implies f''(0) = -1$

$\qquad$ $f^{(3)}(x) = \sin x$ $\implies f^{(3)}(0) = 0$

$\qquad$ $f^{(4)}(x) = \cos x$ $\implies f^{(4)}(0) = 1$

and the cycle repeats itself.

$$\implies \cos x = 1 + 0x + \frac{(-1)x^2}{2!} + \frac{0x^3}{3!} + \frac{1x^4}{4!}$$
$$+ \frac{0x^5}{5!} + \frac{(-1)x^6}{6!} + \dots$$
$$= 1 - \frac{x^2}{2!} + \frac{x^4}{4!} - \frac{x^6}{6!} + \dots$$

(b) $f(x) = e^x \implies f(0) = 1$

$\qquad$ $f'(x) = e^x \implies f'(0) = 1$

and it is clear that all derivatives will take the value 1 when $x = 0$.

$$\implies e^x = 1 + x + \frac{x^2}{2!} + \frac{x^3}{3!} + \frac{x^4}{4!} + \dots$$

(c) (i) $f(x) = \sin 2x$ $\implies f(0) = 0$

$\qquad$ $f'(x) = 2\cos 2x$ $\implies f'(0) = 2$

$\qquad$ $f''(x) = -2^2 \sin 2x$ $\implies f''(0) = 0$

$\qquad$ $f^{(3)}(x) = -2^3 \cos 2x \implies f^{(3)}(0) = -2^3$

$\qquad$ $f^{(4)}(x) = 2^4 \sin 2x$ $\implies f^{(4)}(0) = 0$

and the pattern will continue with higher odd powers of 2 that alternate in sign.

$\implies \sin 2x$
$$= 2x - \frac{2^3 x^3}{3!} + \frac{2^5 x^5}{5!} - \frac{2^7 x^7}{7!} + \dots$$

(ii) $f(x) = e^{3x}$ $\implies f(0) = 1$

$\qquad$ $f'(x) = 3e^{3x}$ $\implies f'(0) = 3$

$\qquad$ $f''(x) = 3^2 e^{3x}$ $\implies f''(0) = 3^2$

$\qquad$ $f^{(3)}(x) = 3^3 e^{3x}$ $\implies f^{(3)}(0) = 3^3$

and the pattern will continue with higher powers of 3.

$\implies e^{3x} = 1 + 3x$
$$+ \frac{3^2 x^2}{2!} + \frac{3^3 x^3}{3!} + \frac{3^4 x^4}{4!} + \dots$$

2   (a)   ln 0 is undefined.

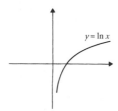

$y = \ln x$

(b)   Since f(0) cannot be found, it is not possible to find a Maclaurin's series. Geometrically, it is not possible to approximate a function at a point that is not defined!

3   (a) $f'(x) = \dfrac{1}{1+x}$

(b) $f''(x) = -1(1+x)^{-2} = -(1+x)^{-2}$

(c) $f^{(3)}(x) = -(-2)(1+x)^{-3} = 2(1+x)^{-3}$

$f^{(4)}(x) = 2 \times -3(1+x)^{-4}$

$\quad\quad = -3!(1+x)^{-4}$

$f^{(5)}(x) = 4!(1+x)^{-5}$

(d) $f(0) = 0, \quad f'(0) = 1, \quad f''(0) = -1,$

$f^{(3)}(0) = 2, \; f^{(4)}(0) = -3!, \; f^{(5)}(0) = 4!$

(e) $\ln(1+x) = 0 + 1x + \dfrac{-1x^2}{2!} + \dfrac{2x^3}{3!}$

$\quad\quad + \dfrac{-3!x^4}{4!} + \dfrac{4!x^5}{5!}$

Note that $\dfrac{2}{3!} = \dfrac{2}{3 \times 2} = \dfrac{1}{3}$,

$\dfrac{3!}{4!} = \dfrac{3 \times 2 \times 1}{4 \times 3 \times 2 \times 1} = \dfrac{1}{4}$ and $\dfrac{4!}{5!} = \dfrac{1}{5}$ gives

$\ln(1+x) = x - \dfrac{x^2}{2} + \dfrac{x^3}{3} - \dfrac{x^4}{4} + \dfrac{x^5}{5} - \cdots$

4   (a) $\sin x = x - \dfrac{x^3}{3!} + \dfrac{x^5}{5!} - \dfrac{x^7}{7!} + \dfrac{x^9}{9!} - \cdots$

$\dfrac{d}{dx}(\sin x)$

$\quad = 1 - \dfrac{3x^2}{3!} + \dfrac{5x^4}{5!} - \dfrac{7x^6}{7!} + \dfrac{9x^8}{9!} - \cdots$

$\quad = 1 - \dfrac{x^2}{2!} + \dfrac{x^4}{4!} - \dfrac{x^6}{6!} + \dfrac{x^8}{8!} - \cdots$

$\quad = \cos x$

(b) $\dfrac{d}{dx}(\cos x)$

$\quad = 0 - \dfrac{2x}{2!} + \dfrac{4x^3}{4!} - \dfrac{6x^5}{6!} + \dfrac{8x^7}{8!} - \cdots$

$\quad = -x + \dfrac{x^3}{3!} - \dfrac{x^5}{5!} + \dfrac{x^7}{7!} - \cdots$

$\quad = -\sin x$

5E   (a) $n(1+x)^{n-1}$

(b) $f''(x) = n(n-1)(1+x)^{n-2}$

$f^{(3)}(x) = n(n-1)(n-2)(1+x)^{n-3}$

(c) $f(0) = 1, f'(0) = n, \; f''(0) = n(n-1),$

$f^{(3)}(0) = n(n-1)(n-2)$

$(1+x)^n = 1 + nx + \dfrac{n(n-1)}{2!}x^2$

$\quad\quad + \dfrac{n(n-1)(n-2)}{3!}x^3 + \cdots$

6 $e^x = 1 + x + \dfrac{x^2}{2!} + \dfrac{x^3}{3!} + \dfrac{x^4}{4!} + \cdots$

$\dfrac{d}{dx}(e^x) = 0 + 1 + \dfrac{2x}{2!} + \dfrac{3x^2}{3!} + \dfrac{4x^3}{4!} + \cdots$

$\quad = 1 + x + \dfrac{x^2}{2!} + \dfrac{x^3}{3!} + \cdots$

$\quad = e^x$

B   Using Maclaurin's series (p. 34)

1   (a) $1 + 2x + 2x^2 + \frac{4}{3}x^3$ (all x)

(b) $-x - \dfrac{x^2}{2} - \dfrac{x^3}{3} - \dfrac{x^4}{4}$ $(-1 \leqslant x < 1)$

(c) $1 + x - \frac{1}{2}x^2 + \frac{1}{3}x^3$ $(-\frac{1}{2} < x < \frac{1}{2})$

2   (a) $-x^2 - \frac{1}{2}x^4 - \frac{1}{3}x^6 - \cdots$

(b) $-x^2 - \frac{1}{2}x^4 - \frac{1}{3}x^6 - \cdots$

(c) $\ln(1+x) + \ln(1-x) = \ln[(1+x)(1-x)]$

$\quad\quad = \ln(1-x^2)$

3 $1 + x - \dfrac{x^2}{2!} - \dfrac{x^3}{3!} + \dfrac{x^4}{4!} + \dfrac{x^5}{5!} - \dfrac{x^6}{6!} + \cdots$

4 $x - \frac{2}{3}x^3 + \frac{2}{15}x^5$

5D   When x is small (in particular, between -1 and 1), so that high powers of x become very small.
This will be explored in section C.

Exercise B (p. 37)

1 (a) $2x - \frac{4}{3}x^3 + \frac{4}{15}x^5$

   (b) $\sin 2x = 2(\sin x \cos x)$

2 (a) $1 + 3x + \frac{9}{2}x^2 + \frac{9}{2}x^3$

   (b) $1 + x^2 + \frac{x^4}{2} + \frac{x^6}{6}$

   (c) $1 - x + \frac{x^2}{2} - \frac{x^3}{6}$

3 (a) $\dfrac{x^{n-1}}{(n-1)!}$ (b) $\dfrac{x^{2n-2}}{(2n-2)!}$ (c) $\dfrac{x^{2(n-1)}}{(n-1)!}$

4 (a) $1 + x - x^2 + \frac{5}{3}x^3$, $-\frac{1}{3} < x < \frac{1}{3}$

   (b) $-x - \dfrac{x^2}{2} - \dfrac{x^3}{3} - \dfrac{x^4}{4}$, $-1 \leqslant x < 1$

   (c) $\frac{1}{2}x - \frac{1}{8}x^2 + \frac{1}{24}x^3 - \frac{1}{64}x^4$, $-2 < x \leqslant 2$

   (d) $1 - x - \frac{1}{2}x^2 - \frac{1}{2}x^3$, $-\frac{1}{2} < x < \frac{1}{2}$

5 (a) $2 + x^2 + \dfrac{x^4}{12} + \dfrac{x^6}{360}$

   (b) $-\frac{3}{2}x^2 - \frac{5}{8}x^4 - \frac{7}{80}x^6$

6 $\left(1 + x + \dfrac{x^2}{2} + \dfrac{x^3}{6} + \dfrac{x^4}{24}\right)\left(1 - \dfrac{x^2}{2} + \dfrac{x^4}{24}\right)$

   $= 1 + x - \dfrac{x^3}{3} - \dfrac{x^4}{6}$

7 $\left(1 + x + \dfrac{x^2}{2} + \dfrac{x^3}{6} + \dfrac{x^4}{24}\right)(1 + 2x + x^2)$

   $= 1 + 3x + \frac{7}{2}x^2 + \frac{13}{6}x^3 + \frac{7}{8}x^4$

8 $(1 + 2x + 2x^2 + \frac{4}{3}x^3 + \frac{2}{3}x^4 + \frac{4}{15}x^5 + \frac{4}{45}x^6)$

   $\times \left(1 - \dfrac{1}{2!}x^2 + \dfrac{1}{4!}x^4 - \dfrac{1}{6!}x^6\right)$

   $= 1 + 2x + \frac{3}{2}x^2 + \frac{1}{3}x^3 - \frac{7}{24}x^4 - \frac{19}{60}x^5 - \frac{117}{720}x^6$

9 (a) $1 - 2x^2 + \frac{2}{3}x^4 - \frac{4}{45}x^6$

   (b) $1 - x^2 + \frac{1}{3}x^4 - \frac{2}{45}x^6$

10E (a) The terms would each contain a power of $x + 1$ to be expanded.

   (b) $e^{x+1} = e^x e^1 = e\left(1 + x + \dfrac{x^2}{2!} + \dfrac{x^3}{3!} \cdots\right)$

11E $e^{ix} = 1 + ix - \dfrac{x^2}{2!} - \dfrac{ix^3}{3!} + \dfrac{x^4}{4!} + \dfrac{ix^5}{5!} + \cdots$

   $= \left(1 - \dfrac{x^2}{2!} + \dfrac{x^4}{4!} - \dfrac{x^6}{6!} + \cdots\right)$

   $\qquad + i\left(x - \dfrac{x^3}{3!} + \dfrac{x^5}{5!} - \dfrac{x^7}{7!} + \cdots\right)$

   $= \cos x + i \sin x$

C   Accuracy of approximations (p. 38)

1D (a) 0.980 066 6   (b) 3   (c) 3
    (d) 4   (e) 9

2 (a) 4   (b) 5   (c) 7   (d) 11

3 (a) 3   (b) 13

   (c) It gets further and further from the value of $\ln 6$.

4 (a) $e^{-x} = 1 - x + \dfrac{x^2}{2!} - \dfrac{x^3}{3!} + \cdots$

   $\approx 1 - x$

   (b) $x \approx 1 - e^{-x}$

   $\sqrt{x} \approx \sqrt{1 - e^{-x}}$

   (c) $\sqrt{1 - e^{-0.1}} = 0.308\ 484\ 330\ 2$

   $\sqrt{0.1} = 0.316\ 227\ 766$

   Percentage error = 2.5%

5 | (a) | (b) | (c) |
   |---|---|---|
   | 1 | 0.1 | 0.01 |
   | $0.1\dot{6}$ | $1.\dot{6} \times 10^{-4}$ | $0.1\dot{6} \times 10^{-7}$ |
   | $8.\dot{3} \times 10^{-3}$ | $8.\dot{3} \times 10^{-8}$ | $8.\dot{3} \times 10^{-13}$ |
   | 1.984×10^{-4} | 1.984×10^{-11} | 1.984×10^{-18} |

   (d) (i) 4   (ii) 2   (iii) 1

Exercise C (p. 39)

1 (a) 0.7174   (b) 0.9950
   (c) 7.3891   (d) 1.0914

2 $x - \dfrac{x^2}{2} + \dfrac{x^3}{3} = 0.41\dot{6}$

   $\ln(1 + x) = 0.405\ 465\ 108\ 1$

   Percentage error = 2.76%

3 (a) 4.29   (b) 0.17   (c) 0.0017

4 Algebraic fractions

A Partial fractions (p. 40)

1 $\dfrac{5x+4}{(x+3)(3x-2)} = \dfrac{1}{x+3} + \dfrac{2}{3x-2}$

2 (a) x^2, x and number terms give conflicting values.

(b) $A = \frac{7}{9}$, $B = -\frac{7}{9}$, $C = -\frac{19}{9}$

(c) $A = \frac{7}{9}$, $D = -\frac{7}{9}$, $E = -\frac{4}{3}$

(d) $\dfrac{-\frac{7}{9}}{x+1} + \dfrac{-\frac{4}{3}}{(x+1)^2} = \dfrac{-\frac{7}{9}(x+1) - \frac{12}{9}}{(x+1)^2}$

$\qquad = \dfrac{-\frac{7}{9}x - \frac{19}{9}}{(x+1)^2}$

3 $\dfrac{4x-3}{2x+1} = 2 - \dfrac{5}{2x+1}$

Exercise A (p. 43)

1 (a) $\dfrac{3}{x+3} - \dfrac{2}{x+2}$ (b) $\dfrac{6}{2x+1} - \dfrac{3}{x+1}$

(c) $\dfrac{3}{2x-1} - \dfrac{1}{x+2}$ (d) $\dfrac{5}{x-1} + \dfrac{2}{x-2}$

(e) $\dfrac{3}{2x+1} - \dfrac{2}{3x+2}$ (f) $\dfrac{2}{x+1} - \dfrac{1}{x}$

2 $A = -5$, $B = 5$, $C = -12$

3 (a) $1 + \dfrac{3}{2(x-3)} - \dfrac{3}{2(x+3)}$

(b) $3 + \dfrac{1}{1-x} + \dfrac{16}{x-4}$

4 (a) $2x + \dfrac{1}{x+2} + \dfrac{2}{x-2}$

(b) $x - 2 + \dfrac{31}{2(x+5)} + \dfrac{7}{2(x-3)}$

B Using the binomial series to expand algebraic fractions (p. 43)

1D (a) $\dfrac{1}{(1+x)^n} = 1 + (-n)x + \dfrac{(-n)(-n-1)}{2!}x^2$

$\qquad + \dfrac{(-n)(-n-1)(-n-2)}{3!}x^3 + \ldots,$

$\qquad |x| < 1$

(b) $\dfrac{3}{(1+x)^2} = 3 - 6x + 9x^2 - 12x^3 + \ldots,$

$\qquad |x| < 1$

(c) $\dfrac{1}{(a+x)^n} = a^{-n}$

$\qquad + (-n)a^{-n-1}x + \dfrac{(-n)(-n-1)}{2!}a^{-n-2}x^2$

$\qquad + \dfrac{(-n)(-n-1)(-n-2)}{3!}a^{-n-3}x^3 + \ldots,$

$\qquad |x| < a$

(d) $\dfrac{1+2x}{1+x} = 1 + x - x^2 + x^3 - \ldots, \quad |x| < 1$

(e) $\dfrac{1}{(1+2x)(x-1)}$

$\qquad = -\dfrac{2}{3(1+2x)} - \dfrac{1}{3(1-x)}$

$\qquad = -1 + x - 3x^2 + 5x^3 - \ldots, |x| < \frac{1}{2}$

Exercise B (p. 44)

1 (a) $\dfrac{x+1}{x-1} = 1 - 2(1-x)^{-1}$

$\qquad = -1 - 2x - 2x^2 - 2x^3 - \ldots,$

$\qquad |x| < 1$

(b) $\dfrac{x+1}{x-4} = 1 - 5(4-x)^{-1}$

$\qquad = -\dfrac{1}{4} - \dfrac{5}{16}x - \dfrac{5}{64}x^2 - \dfrac{5}{256}x^3 - \ldots,$

$\qquad |x| < 4$

(c) $\dfrac{x+9}{(x-1)(x-4)}$

$\qquad = \dfrac{10}{3}(1-x)^{-1} - \dfrac{13}{3}(4-x)^{-1}$

$\qquad = \dfrac{9}{4} + \dfrac{49}{16}x + \dfrac{209}{64}x^2 + \dfrac{849}{256}x^3 + \ldots,$

$\qquad |x| < 1$

2 (a) $\dfrac{x^2+3}{2x+1} - \dfrac{1}{2}x - \dfrac{1}{4} + \dfrac{13}{4}(1+2x)^{-1}$

$\qquad = 3 - 6x + 13x^2 - 26x^3 + \ldots,$

$\qquad |x| < \frac{1}{2}$

(b) $\dfrac{4x^3 + 2x + 1}{(2x-1)^2} = x + 1 + 5x(1-2x)^{-2}$

$\qquad = 1 + 6x + 20x^2 + 60x^3 + \ldots, |x| < \frac{1}{2}$

3 (a) $\dfrac{3x^2 - x - 2}{(x+1)(x-1)^2}$

$= \dfrac{1}{2}(1+x)^{-1} - \dfrac{5}{2}(1-x)^{-1}$

$= -2 - 3x - 2x^2 - 3x^3 - \ldots, |x| < 1$

3 (a) $\dfrac{9 + 2x^2}{(2x+1)(x-3)^2}$

$= \dfrac{38}{49}(1+2x)^{-1} + \left(\dfrac{30}{49}x + \dfrac{99}{49}\right)(3-x)^{-2}$

$= 1 - \dfrac{196}{147}x + \dfrac{1421}{441}x^2 - \dfrac{8134}{1323}x^3 + \ldots,$

$|x| < \dfrac{1}{2}$

C Revision of integration techniques already met (p. 44)

1D Possibilities include the logarithmic function, inverse trigonometric functions, and functions which are already algebraic fractions.

2D Strategies are discussed in the rest of the section.

3 (a) $\dfrac{-4}{(x+1)^5}$ (b) $\dfrac{-6}{(2x+1)^4}$

(c) $\dfrac{-6a}{(ax+b)^7}$

4 (a) $\dfrac{-1}{6(x+3)^6} + c$ (b) $\dfrac{-1}{12(3x-1)^4} + c$

5 (a) Let $u = \dfrac{x}{a}$.

$\dfrac{d}{dx}(\sin^{-1} u) = \dfrac{1}{\sqrt{1-u^2}} \times \dfrac{1}{a}$

$= \dfrac{1}{a\sqrt{1 - \dfrac{x^2}{a^2}}}$

$= \dfrac{1}{\sqrt{a^2 - x^2}}$

(b) Similarly,

$\dfrac{d}{dx}\left(\dfrac{1}{a}\tan^{-1} u\right) = \dfrac{1}{a} \times \dfrac{1}{1 + u^2} \times \dfrac{1}{a}$

$= \dfrac{1}{a^2\left(1 + \dfrac{x^2}{a^2}\right)}$

$= \dfrac{1}{a^2 + x^2}$

6 (a) $\dfrac{1}{3}\tan^{-1}\dfrac{x}{3} + c$

(b) $\sin^{-1}\dfrac{x}{2} + c$

(c) $\dfrac{1}{2}\tan^{-1} 2x + c$

7 (a) $\ln|3x^2 - 2| + c$

(b) $-\ln|\cos x| + c$

(c) $\dfrac{1}{2}\ln|x^2 - 2x + 3| + c$

(d) $\dfrac{1}{3}\ln|x^6 - 3x| + c$

(e) $3\ln|x^2 - x| + c$

(f) $\ln|x^2 + x + 1| + c$

8E (b) (i) $\dfrac{-1}{3(2x+1)^3} + c$

(ii) $\dfrac{-1}{2(x^3+1)^2} + c$

9 $\dfrac{1}{2}\ln|x^2 + 1| + 3\tan^{-1} x + c$

10D (a) -0.980 (to 3 d.p.)

(b) -0.981 (to 3 d.p.)

(c) $\dfrac{5}{(x-3)(x+2)} = \dfrac{1}{x-3} - \dfrac{1}{x+2}$

11 (a) $\dfrac{2}{x+3} + \dfrac{3}{x-4}$

(b) $2\ln|x+3| + 3\ln|x-4| + c$

Exercise C (p. 49)

1 (a) $\dfrac{2}{3}\ln|3x+1|$

(b) $\dfrac{1}{3}\ln|2x^3 - 3x|$

(c) $\ln|e^x + x|$

(d) $\dfrac{2}{3}\tan^{-1}\dfrac{x}{3}$

(e) $-2\ln|3 - x|$

(f) $2\tan^{-1} x - \dfrac{1}{2}\ln|x^2 + 1|$

2 (a) $[\frac{1}{2}\ln|2x-1|]_1^5 = 1.098\,612\,3$

(b) $[\frac{1}{2}\ln|x^2+3|]_0^1 = 0.143\,841\,0$

(c) $[\tan^{-1} 2x]_0^{0.25} = 0.463\,647\,6$

(d) $[\ln|x+1|]_0^1 = 0.693\,147\,2$

(e) $[\ln|1 - \cos x|]_{\frac{\pi}{3}}^{\frac{\pi}{2}} = 0.693\,147\,2$

(f) Can't be done, as the function is not continuous in this range.

3 (a) $\ln\left|\dfrac{(x-2)^3}{(x-1)^2}\right| + c$

(b) $\dfrac{1}{4}\ln\left|\dfrac{x-2}{x+2}\right| + c$

(c) $\ln\left|\dfrac{(x+3)^2}{x+2}\right| + c$

4 (a) $\dfrac{1}{2(1-x)} + \dfrac{1}{4}\ln\left|\dfrac{x+1}{x-1}\right| + c$

(b) $\frac{1}{4}\ln(\frac{3}{2}) + \frac{1}{4} = 0.3514$

5 $\dfrac{x^2 + 3x + 2 + 5x + 7}{x^2 + 3x + 2} = 1 + \dfrac{5x + 7}{x^2 + 3x + 2}$

$= 1 + \dfrac{2}{x+1} + \dfrac{3}{x+2}$

$\displaystyle\int_0^1 \left(1 + \dfrac{2}{x+1} + \dfrac{3}{x+2}\right) dx$

$= [x + 2\ln|x+1| + 3\ln|x+2|]_0^1$

$= 3.6027$ (to 4 d.p.)

6 $\displaystyle\int \dfrac{2x^2 + 3x + 1}{x^2 + x}\, dx = \int \left(2 + \dfrac{x+1}{x^2 + 2x}\right) dx$

$= 2x + \frac{1}{2}\ln|x^2 + 2x| + c$

7E $\displaystyle\int \dfrac{3x^3 - 2x^2 - 3x + 1}{x^2 - x}\, dx$

$= \displaystyle\int \left(3x + 1 + \dfrac{1 - 2x}{x^2 - x}\right) dx$

$= \frac{3}{2}x^2 + x - \ln|x^2 - x| + c$

5 Differential equations

A Introduction (p. 50)

1D You will probably have assumed that the temperature fell at a constant rate of 1 °C every 10 minutes, suggesting that death was at 4:00 a.m.

A more sophisticated model is examined later in the chapter.

2D (c) A linear relation (straight-line graph)

(d) Rate of cooling

(e) $\dfrac{dy}{dt}$

(f) $\dfrac{dy}{dt} = -ky$

where k is the gradient of your graph in (b), and around 0.03 .

3D (a) One reason might be that different amounts of milk were added.

(b), (c) The three gradients are the same.

(d) The starting temperature does not affect the relationship between the rate of cooling and the temperature difference.

(e) Middle curve.

(f) $\dfrac{dy}{dt} = -ky$, where $k \approx 0.03$

4 $\dfrac{dy}{dt}$: rate of cooling

y : temperature difference

k : a constant

5 (a) $y = x^3 - 5x + c$

(b) $c = 5$

6 $y = \frac{3}{2}x^2 + 2x + \frac{1}{2}$

7 $y = e^2 - \sin 2 - 1 = 5.48$

Exercise A (p. 54)

1 (a) $y = e^x + c$

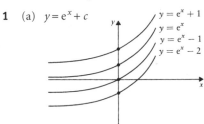

(b) $y = \frac{1}{2}\sin 2x + c$

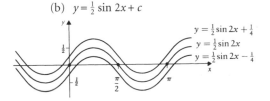

(c) $\dfrac{dy}{dx} = \dfrac{-1}{x^2} \Rightarrow y = \dfrac{1}{x} + c$

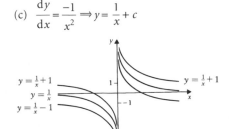

2 (a) $y = x^4 - 1$; when $x = 3$, $y = 80$

(b) $y = x^3 - x^2 + 2x - 2$; when $x = 3$, $y = 22$

(c) $y = \frac{1}{2} - \frac{1}{2}x^{-2}$; when $x = 3$, $y = \frac{4}{9}$

(d) $y = e^{2x} - e^2$; when $x = 3$, $y \approx 396$

3 (a) $y = 8t - \dfrac{2t^2}{3} + 32$; so when $t = 4$, $y = 53\frac{1}{3}$

(b) $\dfrac{dy}{dt} = 0$ when $t = 6$. After this time, $\dfrac{dy}{dt} < 0$ and so the water is no longer being heated. The model is probably no longer valid.

4E (a) $y = -\frac{1}{3}\cos(3x + 2) - 0.139$ (to 3 d.p.); when $x = 2$, $y \approx -0.090$

(b) $y = \frac{1}{3}e^{x^3} - \frac{1}{3}$; when $x = 2$, $y \approx 993$

(c) $y = \frac{1}{2}\sin(x^2 + 1) - 0.421$ (to 3 d.p.); when $x = 2$, $y \approx -0.900$

B   Numerical methods (p. 55)

1D (a) $y = \frac{3}{2}x^2 + 2x + 1$

(b) $y = x^3 - x^2 - x + 1$

(c) $y = x\sin x + \cos x$ using integration by parts.

(d) $y = \frac{1}{2}\sin x^2 + 1$ using the substitution $u = x^2$.

(e) The integral here is not one you know how to do other than by a numerical method.

(f) You cannot integrate a function of both y and x with respect to x.

2 (a) 2.4   (b) 0.24   (c) 1.3, 4.66

(d) $x + \delta x = 1.4$, $y + \delta y = 4.92$

3D (a) $= 2 * \text{A1}$ (and equivalents copied to rest of column)

(b) $= \text{C1} * \text{D1}$ (and equivalents)

(c) The calculation would become more accurate with a smaller increment, but more iterations would be required to reach $x = 2$. Note that if you use the formula $= \text{D1}$ in cell D2, and equivalents for the rest of the column, you will be able to change the whole column just by changing cell D1.

(d) The formula in the whole of the dy/dx column would need to be changed, as would the starting point given in cells A1 and B1.

4 (a) $y = x^2 + 3$ (b) 7

(c) The error is only about 1.4%.

5 $y \approx 7.9$

6 $y \approx 7.7$. The second solution should be more accurate.

7 (a) $y = -\frac{1}{2}\cos 2x$

(b) An exact solution is $-\frac{1}{2}\cos 2 \approx 0.208$. The numerical solution is 0.160.

Percentage error $= \dfrac{0.048}{0.208} \times 100 \approx 23\%$

Exercise B (p. 58)

1 (a) $y = \sin x$

(b)

x	0	0.5	1.0	1.5	2.0	2.5	3.0	3.5	4.0	4.5	5.0
Numerical y	0	0.5	0.9	1.0	1.0	0.7	0.2	−0.3	−0.7	−0.9	−0.9
Exact y	0	0.5	0.8	1.0	0.9	0.6	0.1	−0.4	−0.8	−1.0	−1.0

From the table you can see that the numerical and exact values appear to differ by at most 0.1.

2 (a) $y = x^4 + c \Longrightarrow y = x^4 - 1$; when $x = 2$, $y = 15$

(b) To 1 decimal place, successive points are $(1, 0)$, $(1.2, 0.8)$, $(1.4, 2.2)$, $(1.6, 4.4)$, $(1.8, 7.7)$, $(2, 12.3)$ When $x = 2$, $y \approx 12.3$

3 $y \approx 5.0$

4 (a) $y \approx -2.46$

(b) $y \approx -2.55$

(c) $x \approx 4.4$

5 (a) $y = x^2 + 1$

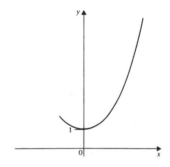

(b) With a step of $\delta x = 0.2$,

x	1	1.2	1.4	1.6	1.8	2.0	2.2	2.4	2.6	2.8	3.0
y	2	2.4	2.9	3.4	4.1	4.8	5.6	6.5	7.4	8.5	9.6

With a step of $\delta x = -0.2$,

x	1	0.8	0.6	0.4	0.2	0.0	−0.2	−0.4	−0.6	−0.8	−1.0
y	2	1.6	1.3	1.0	0.9	0.8	0.8	0.9	1.0	1.3	1.6

(c) Halving the step size approximately halves the error.

6E The solution to the equation is $y = e^x + k$. The particular solution through $(0, 1)$ is $y = e^x$.
The values for a step size of 0.1 will be (to 3 s.f.):

x	0	0.1	0.2	0.3	0.4	...	
y	1.00	1.10	1.21	1.33	1.47	...	and so on

C Growth and decay (p. 59)

1 (a) 5

(b) 1.84

(c) $5e^{-0.2t} = 2.5$
$e^{-0.2t} = 0.5$
$-0.2t = \ln 0.5$
$-0.2t = -0.693$
$t = 3.47$

(d) 6.93

(e) The answer in (d) is twice that in (c). It always takes the same length of time for the amount of the drug remaining to halve.

(f) $\dfrac{dy}{dt} = -0.2 \times 5e^{-0.2t} = -0.2 \times y$

2 (a) $\dfrac{dy}{dx} = 2 \times 3e^{2x} = 2 \times y$

(b) $\dfrac{dy}{dx} = -3 \times 5e^{-3x} = -3 \times y$

(c) $\dfrac{dy}{dx} = -3 \times 2e^{-3x} = -3 \times y$

(d) $\dfrac{dy}{dx} = \lambda \times Ae^{\lambda x} = \lambda \times y$

3 (a) $y = 100e^{2t}$

(b) 2 202 646

4 Modelling with $y = Ae^{\lambda t}$, and taking 3 p.m. as $t = 0$, you find that
$$y = 3e^{(\ln \frac{2}{3})t}$$
where y is the amount of the drug.
Substituting $y = 6$, we get $t = -1.71$ hours, and so the drug was probably injected at about 1:17 p.m.

5 About 1920 years (to nearest 10 years)

Exercise C (p. 63)

1 $y = Ae^{-x}$
$y = 2$ when $x = 0$, therefore $A = 2$
$y = 2e^{-x}$

2 (a) $m = Ae^{-0.1t} \Longrightarrow m = 2e^{-0.1t}$

(b) $\qquad 1 = 2e^{-0.1t}$
$\Longrightarrow \qquad e^{-0.1t} = 0.5$
$\Longrightarrow \qquad -0.1t = \ln 0.5$
$\Longrightarrow \qquad -0.1t \approx -0.693$
$\Longrightarrow \qquad t \approx 6.93$ hours

It takes approximately 6 hours 56 minutes.

3 Assume Newton's law of cooling. y is the temperature in °C above room temperature; t is the time in minutes after boiling.
$$\frac{dy}{dt} = \lambda y \Longrightarrow y = Ae^{\lambda t}$$
When $t = 0$, $y = 80 \Longrightarrow A = 80$
When $t = 5$, $y = 70 \Longrightarrow 70 = 80e^{5\lambda}$
$$\Longrightarrow \lambda = \frac{1}{5} \ln\left(\frac{70}{80}\right) = -0.0267$$
The water cools to 60 °C when $y = 40$.
$40 = 80e^{-0.0267t} \Longrightarrow t = 26$ minutes

4 The differential equation is $\dfrac{dN}{dt} = \lambda N$.
N is the number of insects; t is the time in days.
When $N = 100$, $\dfrac{dN}{dt} = 50 \Longrightarrow \lambda = 0.5$
$$\frac{dN}{dt} = 0.5N \Longrightarrow N = Ae^{0.5t}$$
When $t = 0$, $N = 100 \Longrightarrow A = 100$
Therefore $N = 100e^{0.5t}$ and so when $t = 10$, $N = 14\,841$.
There will be nearly 15 000 insects after 10 days.

5 (a) $\dfrac{dm}{dt} = \lambda m$

When $m = 0.020$,

$\dfrac{dm}{dt} = -0.001 \implies \lambda = -0.05$

The differential equation is

$\dfrac{dm}{dt} = -0.05m$

(b) $\dfrac{dm}{dt} = -0.05m \implies m = Ae^{-0.05t}$

A is the mass when $t = 0$, so
$A = 0.020 \implies m = 0.020e^{-0.05t}$

When $m = 0.010$, $0.010 = 0.020e^{-0.05t}$
$\implies t = -20 \ln 0.5$
$= 13.86$

The substance will decay to half its mass after 13.86 days. This is called the **half-life** of the substance.

6 2700 BC is about 4700 years ago.

2550 BC is about 4550 years ago.

Assuming a radioactivity level of 6.68 when alive, $t = 8300 \ln\left(\dfrac{6.68}{3.8}\right) = 4680$ years

This agrees with historical records.

7 4500 BC is about 6500 years ago.

Assuming an original radioactivity level of 6.68, $t = 8300 \ln\left(\dfrac{6.68}{2.8}\right) = 7200$ years

There was strong evidence that the origins of agriculture were even earlier than first thought.

8E 5750 years

D Separating the variables (p. 64)

1D y is a function of x which is not known; in fact, it is this function that you are trying to find.

2 (a) $\ln |y| + c_1$

(b) $\frac{1}{2}x^2 + c_2$

3D a, b, d, e (take out x as a factor), f, g, h (by writing e^{x+y} as $e^x e^y$)

4 $\frac{1}{2}y^3 = \sin x + c$

5 $y = -\ln\left|10 - \frac{1}{3}x^3\right|$

6 $v = \dfrac{10}{t+1}$

$v = 2 \text{ m s}^{-1}$

Exercise D (p. 68)

1 (a) $\dfrac{dy}{dx} = xy$

$\displaystyle\int \frac{1}{y}\, dy = \int x \, dx$

$\ln |y| = \frac{1}{2}x^2 + k$

$y = \pm e^{(\frac{1}{2}x^2 + k)}$

$y = Ae^{\frac{1}{2}x^2}$

(b) $p^2 = t^2 + k$ (c) $m = Ae^{2t}$

(d) $y^2 = 2e^x + k$ (e) $y + 1 = k(x+1)$

2 $y = \frac{3}{2}(1 - e^{-2x})$

3 (a) $y = 10e^x$ (b) $y = 3.297e^{-\frac{1}{2}x^2}$

(c) $y = \dfrac{2}{2x+1}$

4 (a) $y = \ln\left|\frac{1}{2}\sin 2x + 1\right|$

(b) $y = -\ln\left|2 - x^4\right|$

E Formulating differential equations (p. 69)

1D (a) $\dfrac{dN}{dt} = 3\sqrt{N}$

(b) $2\sqrt{N} = 3t - 4$

(c)

(d) The number of animals infected will continue to grow forever. Obviously the number cannot grow once all animals are infected.

(e) The extra term is subtracting half the infected animals.

(f) About 37

(g) 36

2D The water rushes in through the gap. It may be related to the difference in height between the river above and the water in the lock. This would give a differential equation

$$\frac{dh}{dt} = k(H - h)$$

where h is the depth of the water in the lock and H is the height of the water in the river.

3 (a) $\dfrac{dN}{dt} = kN$

(b) $100 - 2t$

(c) $\dfrac{N}{100 - 2t}$

(d) $\dfrac{2N}{100 - 2t} = \dfrac{N}{50 - t}$

(e) $\dfrac{dN}{dt} = kN - \dfrac{N}{50 - t}$

 or $\dfrac{dN}{dt} = kN - \dfrac{2N}{100 - 2t}$

(f) Depending on whether you took out the factor of 2 in (d)

$$\ln N = 0.7t + \ln|100 - 2t|$$

 or

$$\ln N = 0.7t + \ln|50 - t| + \ln 2$$

giving $N = 2980$.

Exercise E (p. 74)

1 $I = 25e^{-0.04t}$
After 5 seconds, $I = 20.5$ mA
After 10 seconds, $I = 16.8$ mA

2 (a) $\dfrac{dh}{dt} = 0.4\sqrt{h}$

$$5\sqrt{h} = t + 25$$

(b) (i) 25 weeks   (ii) 75 weeks

(c) The tree will continue growing forever. After 1000 weeks (20 years), it would be 400 m tall, which doesn't sound reasonable.

3 (a) $\dfrac{dh}{dt} = -0.0025(12 + 14h)$

$$t = -\frac{200}{7}\ln\left|\frac{6 + 7h}{20}\right|$$

(b) 34.4 hours

4 (a) $\dfrac{dA}{dt} = kr$,   where k is constant

(b) $\dfrac{dA}{dr} = 2\pi r$

(c) $\dfrac{dr}{dt} = \dfrac{k}{2\pi}$

The rate at which the radius is increasing is constant.

5 (a) $\dfrac{dV}{dt} = -0.1\sqrt{h}$

(b) $\dfrac{dV}{dh} = 2$

(c) $\dfrac{dh}{dt} = -0.05\sqrt{h}$

(d) $2\sqrt{h} = -0.05t + 4$; 80 minutes

6 (a) 950

(b) 5

(c) $\dfrac{W}{1000}$

(d) $\dfrac{W}{200}$

(e) $\dfrac{dW}{dt} = 5 - \dfrac{W}{200}$

(f) $\dfrac{t}{200} = \ln 100 - \ln|1000 - W|$; 139 minutes

7 (a) For a snowball of radius r cm and time t days

$$\frac{dV}{dt} = -4k\pi r^2 \implies \frac{dr}{dt} = -k$$

(b) $r = c - kt$
$r = 30$ when $t = 0$ and $r = 0$ when $t = 10$, so $r = 30 - 3t$

(c) (i) $15 = 30 - 3t \implies t = 5$
The radius will be halved after 5 days.

(ii) $\dfrac{30}{\sqrt[3]{2}} = 30 - 3t \implies t = 2.1$
The volume will be halved after 2.1 days.

8   (a) $0.1 = 10\%$; -0.1 is used because there
is a reduction of 10%.
$a = 2000$.

(b) y is the number of fish and $\dfrac{dy}{dt}$ is the
change in the number of fish per year.

(c)   About 16 years

(d) $\dfrac{dy}{dt} = 2500 - 0.12y$

9 $\dfrac{dP}{dt} = 0.04P - 0.2\sqrt{P}$

$\sqrt{P} = 5 + 45e^{\frac{1}{50}t}$

113 911 rabbits

10E   The population remains stable if $\dfrac{dP}{dt} = 0$.

$0.04P = 0.2\sqrt{P} \Rightarrow P = 25$

11E $\dfrac{dP}{dt} = kP(2000 - P)$

$\ln\left|\dfrac{P}{2000 - P}\right| = \dfrac{2000}{1999}t + \ln\left(\dfrac{1}{1999}\right)$

8 days

6   Vector geometry

A   Vectors and position vectors (p. 77)

1   (a) $\begin{bmatrix} 5 \\ 4 \end{bmatrix}$ (b) $\begin{bmatrix} -2 \\ -2 \end{bmatrix}$ (c) $\begin{bmatrix} 1 \\ 1 \end{bmatrix}$

(d) $\begin{bmatrix} a_1 \\ a_2 \end{bmatrix} + \begin{bmatrix} b_1 \\ b_2 \end{bmatrix} = \begin{bmatrix} a_1 + b_1 \\ a_2 + b_2 \end{bmatrix}$

(e) $\begin{bmatrix} 5 \\ 4 \end{bmatrix}$; $a + b = b + a$

2   (a) $\begin{bmatrix} -2 \\ -2 \end{bmatrix}$ (b) $\begin{bmatrix} 3 \\ -4 \end{bmatrix}$ (c) $\begin{bmatrix} -1 \\ 4 \end{bmatrix}$

(d) $\overrightarrow{AB} = b - a$

3 $\overrightarrow{PQ} = q - p$
$\overrightarrow{QP} = p - q$

4   (a) $\begin{bmatrix} 5 \\ 1 \end{bmatrix}$ (b) $\begin{bmatrix} -1 \\ 1 \end{bmatrix}$ (c) $\begin{bmatrix} 5 \\ 1 \end{bmatrix}$ (d) $\begin{bmatrix} 7 \\ 2 \end{bmatrix}$

(e) $\begin{bmatrix} 0 \\ 3 \end{bmatrix}$ (f) $\begin{bmatrix} -3 \\ 3 \end{bmatrix}$ (g) $\begin{bmatrix} -3 \\ 3 \end{bmatrix}$ (h) $\begin{bmatrix} 1 \\ 0 \end{bmatrix}$

5   (a) $c = \frac{3}{2}a$
$d = 2b$
$e = b - a$
$f = -b$

(b) $\overrightarrow{AB} = b - a$
$\overrightarrow{CD} = d - c = 2b - \frac{3}{2}a$
$\overrightarrow{DE} = e - d = (b - a) - 2b = -a - b$
$\overrightarrow{EF} = f - e = -b - (b - a) = a - 2b$
$\overrightarrow{FC} = c - f = \frac{3}{2}a + b$

(c) $\overrightarrow{CD} + \overrightarrow{DE} + \overrightarrow{EF} + \overrightarrow{FC}$
$= 2b - \frac{3}{2}a - a - b + a - 2b + \frac{3}{2}a + b$
$= 0$

The sum of the vectors is zero because
the net displacement around the
quadrilateral CDEFC is zero, i.e. the
vectors have returned to their starting
point.

(d) $\overrightarrow{AD} = 2b - a = -\overrightarrow{EF}$
$\overrightarrow{EF}$ is of the same magnitude as $\overrightarrow{AD}$
but in the opposite direction.

6   For each set: the vectors are parallel, the
components are in the same ratios, and
the vectors are multiples of one another.

7   (a) $\begin{bmatrix} 5 \\ 1 \\ 0 \end{bmatrix}$ (b) $\begin{bmatrix} 1 \\ 1 \\ 4 \end{bmatrix}$ (c) $\begin{bmatrix} -1 \\ -1 \\ -4 \end{bmatrix}$

(d) $\begin{bmatrix} 3 \\ -1 \\ -8 \end{bmatrix}$ (e) $\begin{bmatrix} 1 \\ 0 \\ -1 \end{bmatrix}$ (f) $\begin{bmatrix} 13 \\ 4 \\ 7 \end{bmatrix}$

8   (a) $A\begin{bmatrix} 6 \\ 0 \\ 0 \end{bmatrix}$, $B\begin{bmatrix} 6 \\ 6 \\ 0 \end{bmatrix}$, $C\begin{bmatrix} 0 \\ 6 \\ 0 \end{bmatrix}$, $D\begin{bmatrix} 0 \\ 0 \\ 6 \end{bmatrix}$,

$E\begin{bmatrix} 6 \\ 0 \\ 6 \end{bmatrix}$, $F\begin{bmatrix} 6 \\ 6 \\ 6 \end{bmatrix}$, $G\begin{bmatrix} 0 \\ 6 \\ 6 \end{bmatrix}$

(b) $P\begin{bmatrix} 6 \\ 3 \\ 6 \end{bmatrix}$, $Q\begin{bmatrix} 3 \\ 6 \\ 6 \end{bmatrix}$, $R\begin{bmatrix} 6 \\ 6 \\ 3 \end{bmatrix}$

9   (a) $\sqrt{5}$ (b) 5   (c) $\sqrt{10}$

10   (a) $\sqrt{5}$ (b) $\sqrt{5 + 5^2} = \sqrt{30}$

11   (a) $\sqrt{a^2 + b^2}$ (b) $\sqrt{(a^2 + b^2) + c^2}$

Exercise A (p. 82)

1 (a) $\begin{bmatrix} 11 \\ 7 \\ 2 \end{bmatrix}$ (b) $\begin{bmatrix} -10 \\ -10 \\ 4 \end{bmatrix}$ (c) $\begin{bmatrix} 6 \\ 2 \\ 4 \end{bmatrix}$

(d) $\sqrt{14}$ (e) $\sqrt{69}$ (f) $\begin{bmatrix} 1 \\ 2 \\ -2 \end{bmatrix}$

(g) $\begin{bmatrix} -2 \\ -4 \\ 4 \end{bmatrix}$ (h) $\begin{bmatrix} 2 \\ -1 \\ 4 \end{bmatrix} = \overrightarrow{OC}$

2 (a) By definition of vector addition,
$\overrightarrow{OA} + \overrightarrow{AB} + \overrightarrow{BC} = \overrightarrow{OC}$.

(b) $\mathbf{b} + \mathbf{c} = 2\mathbf{a}$

3 (a) $\overrightarrow{PQ} = \mathbf{q} - \mathbf{p} = \begin{bmatrix} 5 \\ -2 \end{bmatrix} - \begin{bmatrix} 3 \\ 1 \end{bmatrix} = \begin{bmatrix} 2 \\ -3 \end{bmatrix}$

$\overrightarrow{SR} = \mathbf{r} - \mathbf{s} = \begin{bmatrix} 2 \\ -4 \end{bmatrix} - \begin{bmatrix} 0 \\ -1 \end{bmatrix} = \begin{bmatrix} 2 \\ -3 \end{bmatrix}$

Since $\overrightarrow{PQ} = \overrightarrow{SR}$
the vectors are of
the same length
and direction
(i.e. PQ is
parallel to SR
and equal in length), PQRS
is a parallelogram.

(b) It follows also that $\overrightarrow{PS}$ must equal $\overrightarrow{QR}$.

4 (a) (i) $\overrightarrow{OD} = \begin{bmatrix} 6 \\ 0 \\ 10 \end{bmatrix}$, $\overrightarrow{OE} = \begin{bmatrix} 0 \\ 8 \\ 10 \end{bmatrix}$

(ii) $\overrightarrow{AB} = \mathbf{b} - \mathbf{a} = \begin{bmatrix} -6 \\ 8 \\ 0 \end{bmatrix}$

$\overrightarrow{AD} = \begin{bmatrix} 0 \\ 0 \\ 10 \end{bmatrix}$, $\overrightarrow{AC} = \begin{bmatrix} -6 \\ 0 \\ 10 \end{bmatrix}$

$\overrightarrow{AE} = \begin{bmatrix} 0 \\ 8 \\ 10 \end{bmatrix}$, $\overrightarrow{DE} = \begin{bmatrix} -6 \\ 8 \\ 0 \end{bmatrix}$

(b) (i) $\overrightarrow{OM} = \overrightarrow{OA} + \tfrac{1}{2}\overrightarrow{AB} = \begin{bmatrix} 3 \\ 4 \\ 0 \end{bmatrix}$

$\overrightarrow{ON} = \overrightarrow{OD} + \tfrac{1}{2}\overrightarrow{DE} = \begin{bmatrix} 3 \\ 4 \\ 10 \end{bmatrix}$

(ii) $\overrightarrow{AN} = \begin{bmatrix} -3 \\ 4 \\ 10 \end{bmatrix}$, $\overrightarrow{ME} = \begin{bmatrix} -3 \\ 4 \\ 10 \end{bmatrix}$

(iii) $\overrightarrow{AN} = \overrightarrow{ME}$, which is to be
expected since AN is parallel to
ME and of equal length.

5 (a) $\mathbf{a} = \begin{bmatrix} 8 \\ 0 \\ 0 \end{bmatrix}$, $\mathbf{b} = \begin{bmatrix} 8 \\ 10 \\ 0 \end{bmatrix}$, $\mathbf{c} = \begin{bmatrix} 0 \\ 10 \\ 0 \end{bmatrix}$

$\mathbf{d} = \begin{bmatrix} 4 \\ 2 \\ 3 \end{bmatrix}$, $\mathbf{e} = \begin{bmatrix} 4 \\ 8 \\ 3 \end{bmatrix}$

You can find $\mathbf{d}$ and $\mathbf{e}$ by viewing the
roof from above.

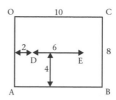

(b) $\overrightarrow{AD} = \mathbf{d} - \mathbf{a} = \begin{bmatrix} -4 \\ 2 \\ 3 \end{bmatrix}$, $\overrightarrow{OD} = \begin{bmatrix} 4 \\ 2 \\ 3 \end{bmatrix}$

$\overrightarrow{BE} = \begin{bmatrix} -4 \\ -2 \\ 3 \end{bmatrix}$, $\overrightarrow{CE} = \begin{bmatrix} 4 \\ -2 \\ 3 \end{bmatrix}$

(c) By Pythagoras, the length of $\overrightarrow{AD}$ is
$\sqrt{4^2 + 2^2 + 3^2} = \sqrt{29} = 5.4$ m.

B Vector equations of lines (p. 83)

1D (a) Values of t generate the position vectors.

t	-3	-2	-1	0	1	2	3
$\begin{bmatrix} x \\ y \end{bmatrix}$	$\begin{bmatrix} -6 \\ -9 \end{bmatrix}$	$\begin{bmatrix} -4 \\ -6 \end{bmatrix}$	$\begin{bmatrix} -2 \\ -3 \end{bmatrix}$	$\begin{bmatrix} 0 \\ 0 \end{bmatrix}$	$\begin{bmatrix} 2 \\ 3 \end{bmatrix}$	$\begin{bmatrix} 4 \\ 6 \end{bmatrix}$	$\begin{bmatrix} 6 \\ 9 \end{bmatrix}$

These give the graph of the straight line.

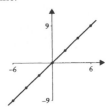

You can apply a similar method to (b) and (c).

(b)

(c)

(d) In each case the graph is a straight line.

(e) The vector $\begin{bmatrix} 2 \\ 3 \end{bmatrix}$ gives the *direction* of the line.

2 All three equations describe the same line.

3 One possibility is $\begin{bmatrix} x \\ y \end{bmatrix} = \begin{bmatrix} -2 \\ 1 \end{bmatrix} + \lambda \begin{bmatrix} 5 \\ -5 \end{bmatrix}$.

4 (a) $t = \frac{1}{2}(x - 3)$

(b) $y = -1 + 3 \times \frac{1}{2}(x - 3) \Rightarrow y = \frac{3}{2}x - \frac{11}{2}$

(c) The gradient is $\frac{3}{2}$. The vector $\begin{bmatrix} 2 \\ 3 \end{bmatrix}$ has gradient $\frac{3}{2}$.

5 (a) $\begin{aligned} x &= 3 - 2s \\ y &= -2 + s \\ \Rightarrow y &= -\tfrac{1}{2}x - \tfrac{1}{2} \end{aligned}$
   (b) $\begin{aligned} x &= 1 + 2t \\ y &= -1 - t \\ \Rightarrow y &= -\tfrac{1}{2}x - \tfrac{1}{2} \end{aligned}$

The two vector equations give the same straight line.

They have the same direction, $\begin{bmatrix} -2 \\ 1 \end{bmatrix}$ or $\begin{bmatrix} 2 \\ -1 \end{bmatrix}$, but appear to be different since different points on the line have been chosen.

6 $\mathbf{d} = \begin{bmatrix} 4 \\ 6 \\ 0 \end{bmatrix}$, $\mathbf{e} = \begin{bmatrix} 0 \\ 6 \\ 3 \end{bmatrix}$

$\mathbf{f} = \begin{bmatrix} 4 \\ 0 \\ 3 \end{bmatrix}$, $\mathbf{g} = \begin{bmatrix} 4 \\ 6 \\ 3 \end{bmatrix}$

7 (a) $\lambda = 0 \Rightarrow \begin{bmatrix} x \\ y \\ z \end{bmatrix} = \begin{bmatrix} 0 \\ 0 \\ 0 \end{bmatrix}$

$\lambda = 1 \Rightarrow \begin{bmatrix} x \\ y \\ z \end{bmatrix} = \begin{bmatrix} 4 \\ 6 \\ 0 \end{bmatrix}$

So $\lambda = 0$ gives O, $\lambda = 1$ gives D.

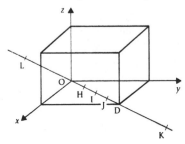

H, I, J, K and L correspond to $\lambda = \frac{1}{4}, \frac{1}{2}, \frac{3}{4}$, 2 and -1 respectively.

(b) H, I and J are on the line between O and D.

(c) K and L are on the same line but outside OD.

8 (a) Since $\overrightarrow{OC} = \begin{bmatrix} 0 \\ 0 \\ 3 \end{bmatrix}$ the vector equation

corresponds to the line OC.

(b) OE (c) $\begin{bmatrix} x \\ y \\ z \end{bmatrix} = \lambda \begin{bmatrix} 0 \\ 6 \\ 0 \end{bmatrix}$

(d) $\begin{bmatrix} x \\ y \\ z \end{bmatrix} = \lambda \begin{bmatrix} 4 \\ 0 \\ 3 \end{bmatrix}$ (e) $\begin{bmatrix} x \\ y \\ z \end{bmatrix} = \lambda \begin{bmatrix} 4 \\ 6 \\ 3 \end{bmatrix}$

9 (a) When $\lambda = 0$, $\begin{bmatrix} x \\ y \\ z \end{bmatrix} = \begin{bmatrix} 0 \\ 6 \\ 0 \end{bmatrix}$, i.e. point B.

When $\lambda = 1$, $\begin{bmatrix} x \\ y \\ z \end{bmatrix} = \begin{bmatrix} 0 \\ 6 \\ 3 \end{bmatrix}$, i.e. point E.

Hence the line is BE.

(b) $\lambda = 0$ gives F, $\lambda = 1$ gives E, so the line is FE.

In each case the vector specifies the *direction* of the line.

10 (a) The line AD passes through A and

has direction $\overrightarrow{AD} = \begin{bmatrix} 0 \\ 6 \\ 0 \end{bmatrix}$ so it has

equation $\begin{bmatrix} x \\ y \\ z \end{bmatrix} = \begin{bmatrix} 4 \\ 0 \\ 0 \end{bmatrix} + \lambda \begin{bmatrix} 0 \\ 6 \\ 0 \end{bmatrix}$.

(b) $\begin{bmatrix} x \\ y \\ z \end{bmatrix} = \begin{bmatrix} 4 \\ 0 \\ 0 \end{bmatrix} + \lambda \begin{bmatrix} 0 \\ 6 \\ 3 \end{bmatrix}$

(c) $\begin{bmatrix} x \\ y \\ z \end{bmatrix} = \begin{bmatrix} 4 \\ 0 \\ 0 \end{bmatrix} + \lambda \begin{bmatrix} -4 \\ 6 \\ 3 \end{bmatrix}$

These are *not* unique equations. For example, AE also passes through E and has

equation $\begin{bmatrix} x \\ y \\ z \end{bmatrix} = \begin{bmatrix} 0 \\ 6 \\ 3 \end{bmatrix} + \mu \begin{bmatrix} 4 \\ -6 \\ -3 \end{bmatrix}$. Thus the

point $(-4, 12, 6)$ is found either by starting from A and putting $\lambda = 2$, or by starting from E and putting $\mu = -1$.

11 One possibility is $\begin{bmatrix} x \\ y \\ z \end{bmatrix} = \begin{bmatrix} 0 \\ 2 \\ -3 \end{bmatrix} + \lambda \begin{bmatrix} 1 \\ 2 \\ 3 \end{bmatrix}$.

Exercise B (p. 87)

1 (a) The direction vector is $\begin{bmatrix} 7 \\ 7 \end{bmatrix} - \begin{bmatrix} 4 \\ 1 \end{bmatrix} = \begin{bmatrix} 3 \\ 6 \end{bmatrix}$,

so the line is $\begin{bmatrix} x \\ y \end{bmatrix} = \begin{bmatrix} 4 \\ 1 \end{bmatrix} + t \begin{bmatrix} 3 \\ 6 \end{bmatrix}$

(b) $\begin{bmatrix} x \\ y \end{bmatrix} = \begin{bmatrix} 2 \\ 1 \end{bmatrix} + t \begin{bmatrix} -3 \\ 4 \end{bmatrix}$ (c) $\begin{bmatrix} x \\ y \end{bmatrix} = \begin{bmatrix} 5 \\ 1 \end{bmatrix} + t \begin{bmatrix} -2 \\ 4 \end{bmatrix}$

(d) $\begin{bmatrix} x \\ y \end{bmatrix} = t \begin{bmatrix} 1 \\ 1 \end{bmatrix}$ (e) $\begin{bmatrix} x \\ y \end{bmatrix} = t \begin{bmatrix} 0 \\ 1 \end{bmatrix}$

2 (a) $\begin{bmatrix} x \\ y \\ z \end{bmatrix} = \begin{bmatrix} 2 \\ 1 \\ 0 \end{bmatrix} + \lambda \begin{bmatrix} 1 \\ 3 \\ 4 \end{bmatrix}$

(b) $\begin{bmatrix} x \\ y \\ z \end{bmatrix} = \begin{bmatrix} -1 \\ 0 \\ 3 \end{bmatrix} + \lambda \begin{bmatrix} 3 \\ 2 \\ 0 \end{bmatrix}$

(c) $\begin{bmatrix} x \\ y \\ z \end{bmatrix} = \begin{bmatrix} 1 \\ 2 \\ 2 \end{bmatrix} + \lambda \begin{bmatrix} 3 \\ -1 \\ 2 \end{bmatrix}$

(d) $\begin{bmatrix} x \\ y \\ z \end{bmatrix} = \lambda \begin{bmatrix} 1 \\ 0 \\ 0 \end{bmatrix}$

Remember that these are not unique.

3 (a) OG

(b) $\lambda = 0$ gives $\begin{bmatrix} 4 \\ 0 \\ 3 \end{bmatrix}$

$\lambda = 1$ gives $\begin{bmatrix} 0 \\ 5 \\ 3 \end{bmatrix}$, i.e. EG

(c) CE (d) BD

4   Writing **r** for $\begin{bmatrix} x \\ y \\ z \end{bmatrix}$ gives the following.

(a) $\mathbf{r} = \overrightarrow{OA} + \lambda\overrightarrow{AB} = \begin{bmatrix} 4 \\ 0 \\ 0 \end{bmatrix} + \lambda \begin{bmatrix} 0 \\ 5 \\ 0 \end{bmatrix}$

(b) $\mathbf{r} = \overrightarrow{OA} + \lambda\overrightarrow{AC} = \begin{bmatrix} 4 \\ 0 \\ 0 \end{bmatrix} + \lambda \begin{bmatrix} -4 \\ 5 \\ 0 \end{bmatrix}$

(c) $\mathbf{r} = \overrightarrow{OA} + \lambda\overrightarrow{AF} = \begin{bmatrix} 4 \\ 0 \\ 0 \end{bmatrix} + \lambda \begin{bmatrix} 0 \\ 5 \\ 3 \end{bmatrix}$

(d) $\mathbf{r} = \overrightarrow{OA} + \lambda\overrightarrow{AG} = \begin{bmatrix} 4 \\ 0 \\ 0 \end{bmatrix} + \lambda \begin{bmatrix} -4 \\ 5 \\ 3 \end{bmatrix}$

C   Intersections of lines (p. 88)

1D   (a)

λ	-2	-1	0	1	2
$\begin{bmatrix} x \\ y \end{bmatrix}$	$\begin{bmatrix} -1 \\ -2 \end{bmatrix}$	$\begin{bmatrix} 0 \\ -1 \end{bmatrix}$	$\begin{bmatrix} 1 \\ 0 \end{bmatrix}$	$\begin{bmatrix} 2 \\ 1 \end{bmatrix}$	$\begin{bmatrix} 3 \\ 2 \end{bmatrix}$

μ	-2	-1	0	1	2
$\begin{bmatrix} x \\ y \end{bmatrix}$	$\begin{bmatrix} -3 \\ 5 \end{bmatrix}$	$\begin{bmatrix} -1 \\ 4 \end{bmatrix}$	$\begin{bmatrix} 1 \\ 3 \end{bmatrix}$	$\begin{bmatrix} 3 \\ 2 \end{bmatrix}$	$\begin{bmatrix} 5 \\ 1 \end{bmatrix}$

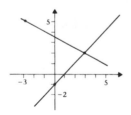

(b)   The lines intersect at $(3, 2)$.

(c) $\lambda = 2, \mu = 1$ at the point of intersection.

(d)   Since at the point of intersection both x- and y-coordinates are equal,

$$1 + \lambda = 1 + 2\mu \quad \text{and} \quad \lambda = 3 - \mu$$

(e)   Solving these gives $\lambda = 2, \mu = 1$.

2   The intersection is at $(2\frac{1}{5}, 2\frac{2}{5})$.

3D   (a)   The direction vectors would be multiples of one another.

(b)   The direction vectors would be multiples of one another. In addition, they would have points in common.

4D   (a)   Perpendicular, intersect at right angles

(b)   Parallel

(c)   Don't intersect, not perpendicular or parallel

5 $\begin{bmatrix} 7 \\ 4 \\ -3 \end{bmatrix}$

6   The x and y components give $t = 1, s = 2$, but with these values the z components are not equal.

Exercise C (p. 92)

1   (a)   Intersect at $\begin{bmatrix} 7 \\ 15 \end{bmatrix}$

(b)   Parallel

(c)   Coincident

(d)   Intersect at $\begin{bmatrix} 18 \\ 8 \end{bmatrix}$

2   When the y components are equal, $3 - \lambda = -3 + \mu$, and when the z components are equal, $\lambda = \mu$, i.e.

$$\lambda = \mu = 3$$
$$\lambda = 3 \Rightarrow x = 4 - 3 = 1$$
$$\mu = 3 \Rightarrow x = 4 - 3 = 1$$

Hence the vertex is at $(1, 0, 3)$.

3   (a)   They meet at $(5, 3, 11)$.

(b)   Parallel, no intersection

(c)   They meet at $(6, 3, -2)$.

(d)   Skew, no intersection

4   They meet at $(-9, 3.5, -1.5)$.

5E $s = 3, t = -2, p = 2$

D Scalar product (p. 93)

1 (a) $a = \sqrt{a_1^2 + a_2^2} \Rightarrow a^2 = a_1^2 + a_2^2$
Similarly $b^2 = b_1^2 + b_2^2$

(b) $c^2 = (b_1 - a_1)^2 + (b_2 - a_2)^2$
$= b_1^2 - 2a_1 b_1 + a_1^2 + b_2^2 - 2a_2 b_2 + a_2^2$
$= (a_1^2 + a_2^2) + (b_1^2 + b_2^2) - 2a_1 b_1 - 2a_2 b_2$
$= a^2 + b^2 - 2(a_1 b_1 + a_2 b_2)$

(c) By the cosine rule,
$c^2 = a^2 + b^2 - 2ab \cos \theta$
So $a_1 b_1 + a_2 b_2 = ab \cos \theta$, since the two expressions are otherwise identical.

2 $\theta = 37.9°$

3 (a) $26.6°$
(b) $19.7°$
(c) $90°$

4 (a)

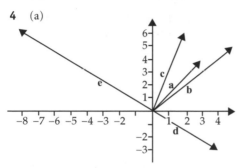

(b) **d** is parallel to **e**
a is perpendicular to **d** and **e**

5 (a) $a = 5$, $b = \sqrt{50}$, $c = \sqrt{40}$
$d = 5$, $e = 10$

(b) $\mathbf{a} \cdot \mathbf{a} = 25$, $\mathbf{b} \cdot \mathbf{b} = 50$, $\mathbf{c} \cdot \mathbf{c} = 40$
$\mathbf{d} \cdot \mathbf{d} = 25$, $\mathbf{e} \cdot \mathbf{e} = 100$

(c) $\mathbf{a} \cdot \mathbf{a} = a^2$
The scalar product of a vector with itself is equal to the square of its magnitude.

(d) $\theta = 0 \Rightarrow \cos \theta = 1 \Rightarrow \mathbf{a} \cdot \mathbf{a} = 1 \times a \times a$

6 (a) $\mathbf{a} \cdot \mathbf{b} = 35$, $\mathbf{b} \cdot \mathbf{a} = 35$

(b) $\mathbf{a} \cdot \mathbf{c} = 30$, $\mathbf{c} \cdot \mathbf{a} = 30$

(c) $\mathbf{a} \cdot \mathbf{b} = \mathbf{b} \cdot \mathbf{a}$, $\mathbf{a} \cdot \mathbf{c} = \mathbf{c} \cdot \mathbf{a}$
You can conclude that scalar multiplication is **commutative** as a consequence of the commutativity of ordinary multiplication.

7 (a) $\mathbf{a} \cdot \mathbf{b} + \mathbf{a} \cdot \mathbf{c} = 35 + 30 = 65$

(b) $\mathbf{a} \cdot (\mathbf{b} + \mathbf{c}) = \begin{bmatrix} 3 \\ 4 \end{bmatrix} \cdot \begin{bmatrix} 7 \\ 11 \end{bmatrix} = 21 + 44 = 65$

(c) So the **distributive law** appears to hold, i.e. $\mathbf{a} \cdot \mathbf{b} + \mathbf{a} \cdot \mathbf{c} = \mathbf{a} \cdot (\mathbf{b} + \mathbf{c})$.
In fact, it can be shown that the distributive law holds for all vectors **a, b, c**.

8 (a) $\mathbf{a} \cdot \mathbf{b} = 35$, $\mathbf{a} \cdot \mathbf{d} = 0$, $\mathbf{a} \cdot \mathbf{e} = 0$

(b) If the vectors are perpendicular, then their scalar product is zero.

(c) $\cos 90° = 0 \Rightarrow ab \cos 90° = 0$

(d) If the magnitude of either vector is zero.

9

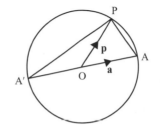

(a) $\overrightarrow{OA'} = -\overrightarrow{OA} = -\mathbf{a}$
$\overrightarrow{AP} = \mathbf{p} - \mathbf{a}$
$\overrightarrow{A'P} = \mathbf{p} - \mathbf{a'} = \mathbf{p} + \mathbf{a}$

(b) $\overrightarrow{AP} \cdot \overrightarrow{A'P} = (\mathbf{p} - \mathbf{a}) \cdot (\mathbf{p} + \mathbf{a})$
$= p^2 - a^2$
But, since $p = a$, $p^2 - a^2 = 0$

(c) $\overrightarrow{AP}$ is perpendicular to $\overrightarrow{A'P}$, i.e. the angle in a semicircle is a right angle.

10 (a) $\overrightarrow{OA} = \begin{bmatrix} 3 \\ 0 \\ 0 \end{bmatrix}$, $\overrightarrow{OB} = \begin{bmatrix} 3 \\ 3 \\ 0 \end{bmatrix}$, $\overrightarrow{OD} = \begin{bmatrix} 0 \\ 0 \\ 2 \end{bmatrix}$,

$\overrightarrow{DE} = \begin{bmatrix} 3 \\ 0 \\ 0 \end{bmatrix}$, $\overrightarrow{DF} = \begin{bmatrix} 3 \\ 3 \\ 0 \end{bmatrix}$, $\overrightarrow{DG} = \begin{bmatrix} 0 \\ 3 \\ 0 \end{bmatrix}$

(b) (i) $45°$ (ii) $90°$ (iii) $0°$
(iv) $90°$ (v) $45°$ (vi) $90°$

Exercise D (p. 97)

1 (a) $\mathbf{a} \cdot \mathbf{b} = 0$, $\mathbf{b} \cdot \mathbf{c} = 0$, $\mathbf{c} \cdot \mathbf{a} = 0$

(b) All three pairs of vectors are mutually perpendicular.

2 (a) Using $\cos\theta = \dfrac{\mathbf{a}\cdot\mathbf{b}}{ab}$ gives

$$\cos\theta = \frac{\begin{bmatrix}5\\2\end{bmatrix}\cdot\begin{bmatrix}3\\2\end{bmatrix}}{\sqrt{25+4}\,\sqrt{9+4}}$$

$$= \frac{5\times 3 + 2\times 2}{\sqrt{29}\,\sqrt{13}} = \frac{19}{\sqrt{377}}$$

$\Rightarrow\ \theta = 11.9°$

(b) $\theta = 124.5°$

3

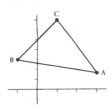

(a) $\overrightarrow{AB} = \mathbf{b} - \mathbf{a} = \begin{bmatrix}-1\\3\end{bmatrix} - \begin{bmatrix}3\\2\end{bmatrix} = \begin{bmatrix}-4\\1\end{bmatrix}$

$\overrightarrow{AC} = \begin{bmatrix}-2\\5\end{bmatrix}$

(b) Both vectors must be pointing away from A.

$$\cos A = \frac{\overrightarrow{AB}\cdot\overrightarrow{AC}}{|AB||AC|}$$

$$= \frac{8+5}{\sqrt{17}\,\sqrt{29}} = \frac{13}{\sqrt{493}}$$

$\Rightarrow\ A = 54.2°$

4 (a) $\theta = 54.9°$ (b) $\theta = 46.3°$

5 $\overrightarrow{PQ} = \begin{bmatrix}-7\\4\\4\end{bmatrix},\quad \overrightarrow{PR} = \begin{bmatrix}4\\8\\-1\end{bmatrix}$

$\Rightarrow \cos P = \dfrac{-28+32-4}{\sqrt{49+16+16}\,\sqrt{16+64+1}} = 0$

$\Rightarrow P = 90°$

$\overrightarrow{QP} = -\overrightarrow{PQ} = \begin{bmatrix}7\\-4\\-4\end{bmatrix},\quad \overrightarrow{QR} = \begin{bmatrix}11\\4\\-5\end{bmatrix}$

$\Rightarrow \cos Q = \dfrac{77-16+20}{\sqrt{49+16+16}\,\sqrt{121+16+25}}$

$$= \frac{81}{9\sqrt{162}} = \frac{9}{\sqrt{2}\,\sqrt{81}} = \frac{1}{\sqrt{2}}$$

$\Rightarrow Q = 45°$ and $R = 180° - 90° - 45° = 45°$

6 (a) $\mathbf{c} = \begin{bmatrix}2\\4\end{bmatrix}$

(b) $\mathbf{d} = \mathbf{a} - \mathbf{b} = \begin{bmatrix}16\\-8\end{bmatrix}$

(c) $\mathbf{c}\cdot\mathbf{d} = 32 - 32 = 0$

(d) Since $\mathbf{c}\cdot\mathbf{d} = 0$, $\mathbf{c}$ is perpendicular to $\mathbf{d}$, i.e. OC is perpendicular to AB.

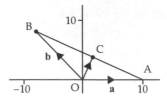

7 One way is to find vectors for all four sides, show that the magnitudes are equal, and show that the scalar product of two of them is zero.

8E (a) $\mathbf{b} - \mathbf{h}$ is the vector $\overrightarrow{HB}$ and since $\overrightarrow{HB}$ is perpendicular to $\overrightarrow{OA}$, $\mathbf{a}\cdot(\mathbf{b}-\mathbf{h}) = 0$

(b) $\overrightarrow{HA}$ is perpendicular to $\overrightarrow{OB}$ so $\mathbf{b}\cdot(\mathbf{a}-\mathbf{h}) = 0$

(c) $\mathbf{b}\cdot(\mathbf{a}-\mathbf{h}) - \mathbf{a}\cdot(\mathbf{b}-\mathbf{h}) = 0$

$\Rightarrow \mathbf{b}\cdot\mathbf{a} - \mathbf{b}\cdot\mathbf{h} - \mathbf{a}\cdot\mathbf{b} + \mathbf{a}\cdot\mathbf{h} = 0$

$\Rightarrow \mathbf{a}\cdot\mathbf{h} - \mathbf{b}\cdot\mathbf{h} = 0$ (since $\mathbf{b}\cdot\mathbf{a} = \mathbf{a}\cdot\mathbf{b}$)

$\Rightarrow (\mathbf{a}-\mathbf{b})\cdot\mathbf{h} = 0$

(d) $\mathbf{a} - \mathbf{b}$ is the vector $\overrightarrow{BA}$ and this is perpendicular to $\overrightarrow{OH}$.

Thus $\overrightarrow{OH}$ is also an altitude of the triangle; i.e. in any triangle, the three altitudes are concurrent. (They intersect in a single point.)

9E (a) $\overrightarrow{OR} = \overrightarrow{OP} + \overrightarrow{PR} = \overrightarrow{OP} + \overrightarrow{OQ} = \mathbf{p} + \mathbf{q}$

$\overrightarrow{QP} = \mathbf{p} - \mathbf{q}$

(b) Using the result that

$\mathbf{a}\cdot(\mathbf{b}+\mathbf{c}) = \mathbf{a}\cdot\mathbf{b} + \mathbf{a}\cdot\mathbf{c}$,

$(\mathbf{p}+\mathbf{q})\cdot(\mathbf{p}-\mathbf{q})$

$= \mathbf{p}\cdot\mathbf{p} - \mathbf{p}\cdot\mathbf{q} + \mathbf{q}\cdot\mathbf{p} - \mathbf{q}\cdot\mathbf{q}$

$= p^2 - q^2$

(since $\mathbf{p}\cdot\mathbf{p} = p^2$ and $\mathbf{p}\cdot\mathbf{q} = \mathbf{q}\cdot\mathbf{p}$)

(c) (i) $\overrightarrow{OR} \cdot \overrightarrow{QP} = 0 \Rightarrow \overrightarrow{OR}$ is perpendicular to $\overrightarrow{QP}$.

(ii) If $\overrightarrow{OR} \cdot \overrightarrow{QP} = 0$
then $(\mathbf{p} + \mathbf{q}) \cdot (\mathbf{p} - \mathbf{q}) = 0$
i.e. $p^2 - q^2 = 0$
$\Rightarrow p = q$ and the parallelogram is a rhombus.

This proves the well-known result that if the diagonals of a parallelogram intersect at right angles, the parallelogram is a rhombus.

10E Consider a unit cube as shown.

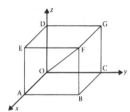

A longest diagonal is $\overrightarrow{OF} = \begin{bmatrix} 1 \\ 1 \\ 1 \end{bmatrix}$.

(a) You require DOF.

$$\cos DOF = \frac{\overrightarrow{OD} \cdot \overrightarrow{OF}}{|OD||OF|}$$

$$= \frac{\begin{bmatrix} 0 \\ 0 \\ 1 \end{bmatrix} \cdot \begin{bmatrix} 1 \\ 1 \\ 1 \end{bmatrix}}{1 \times \sqrt{3}} = \frac{1}{\sqrt{3}}$$

$\Rightarrow$ angle DOF = $54.7°$

(b) One face diagonal is OE.

$$\cos EOF = \frac{\overrightarrow{OE} \cdot \overrightarrow{OF}}{|OE||OF|}$$

$$= \frac{\begin{bmatrix} 1 \\ 0 \\ 1 \end{bmatrix} \cdot \begin{bmatrix} 1 \\ 1 \\ 1 \end{bmatrix}}{\sqrt{2}\sqrt{3}} = \frac{2}{\sqrt{6}}$$

$\Rightarrow$ angle EOF = $35.3°$

(c) One other longest diagonal is CE, represented by

$$\begin{bmatrix} 1 \\ 0 \\ 1 \end{bmatrix} - \begin{bmatrix} 0 \\ 1 \\ 0 \end{bmatrix} = \begin{bmatrix} 1 \\ -1 \\ 1 \end{bmatrix}$$

If the angle between the diagonals is θ,

$$\cos\theta = \frac{\overrightarrow{CE} \cdot \overrightarrow{OF}}{|CE||OF|}$$

$$= \frac{\begin{bmatrix} 1 \\ -1 \\ 1 \end{bmatrix} \cdot \begin{bmatrix} 1 \\ 1 \\ 1 \end{bmatrix}}{\sqrt{3}\sqrt{3}} = \frac{1}{3}$$

$\Rightarrow \theta = 70.5°$

E Perpendicular lines (p. 98)

1D (c) They are both perpendicular to the line.

(d) It is the hypotenuse of the right-angled triangle.

2 $3\sqrt{5}$

3D (a) $\begin{bmatrix} 1 + 2\lambda_1 \\ 2\lambda_1 \\ 2 - \lambda_1 \end{bmatrix}$ (b) $\begin{bmatrix} 2\lambda_1 - 9 \\ 2\lambda_1 - 9 \\ -\lambda_1 - 9 \end{bmatrix}$

(c) $9\lambda_1 - 27$ (d) $\lambda_1 = 3$

(e) $(7, 6, -1)$ (f) $9\sqrt{2}$

4 $\lambda_1 = -2$

Foot of perpendicular is $(3, -7, 0)$
Distance = $6\sqrt{2}$

Exercise E (p. 100)

1 $s = 3$
Distance = $2\sqrt{10}$

2 $t = 2$
Distance = $3\sqrt{14}$

3 (a) One possibility is

$$\begin{bmatrix} x \\ y \\ z \end{bmatrix} = \begin{bmatrix} 2 \\ 0 \\ -3 \end{bmatrix} + \mu \begin{bmatrix} 3 \\ 3 \\ 6 \end{bmatrix}$$

(b) $3\sqrt{6}$

(c) Distance = $\sqrt{3}$

Area = $\dfrac{9}{\sqrt{2}}$

4 (a) $\overrightarrow{AB} = \overrightarrow{DC} = \begin{bmatrix} 6 \\ 3 \\ 6 \end{bmatrix}$

$\overrightarrow{BC} = \overrightarrow{AD} = \begin{bmatrix} 4 \\ 5 \\ -2 \end{bmatrix}$

Opposite sides are equal and parallel.

(b) 9

(c) Distance = 6
Area = 54 square units

F   Vector equations of planes (p. 100)

1D (a) $c = 3a$, $d = 2b$, $e = -2b$
$f = -2b + a$, $g = 2a + 2b$
$h = 2b - 2a$, $i = \frac{1}{2}a + \frac{1}{2}b$

(b) Yes, if the multiples of **a** and **b** do not have to be whole numbers.

2 $\begin{bmatrix} 0 \\ 0 \\ 4 \end{bmatrix}$ is the vertical in the back corner of the

cuboid and is the position vector of a point in the plane.

$\begin{bmatrix} 10 \\ 6 \\ -4 \end{bmatrix}$ is one of the diagonals of the shaded

plane.

$\begin{bmatrix} 0 \\ 6 \\ -4 \end{bmatrix}$ is one of the end edges of the shaded

plane.

3 $\overrightarrow{DE} = \begin{bmatrix} 0 \\ 6 \\ 6 \end{bmatrix} - \begin{bmatrix} 6 \\ 6 \\ 0 \end{bmatrix} = \begin{bmatrix} -6 \\ 0 \\ 6 \end{bmatrix}$

$\overrightarrow{DF} = \begin{bmatrix} 6 \\ 0 \\ 6 \end{bmatrix} - \begin{bmatrix} 6 \\ 6 \\ 0 \end{bmatrix} = \begin{bmatrix} 0 \\ -6 \\ 6 \end{bmatrix}$

In order to reach any point in the plane DEF, it is necessary to go from O to D, followed by some combination of $\overrightarrow{DE}$ and $\overrightarrow{DF}$. Thus, if P is some point on the plane,

$$\overrightarrow{OP} = \overrightarrow{OD} + \overrightarrow{DP} = \overrightarrow{OD} + \lambda\overrightarrow{DE} + \mu\overrightarrow{DE}$$

for some λ and μ, i.e.

$$\begin{bmatrix} x \\ y \\ z \end{bmatrix} = \begin{bmatrix} 6 \\ 6 \\ 0 \end{bmatrix} + \lambda\begin{bmatrix} -6 \\ 0 \\ 6 \end{bmatrix} + \mu\begin{bmatrix} 0 \\ -6 \\ 6 \end{bmatrix}$$

4 The coordinates of each point are as follows:
(a) $(6, 6, 0)$ i.e. D   (b) $(0, 6, 6)$ i.e. E
(c) $(6, 0, 6)$ i.e. F   (d) $(3, 3, 6)$
(e) $(4, 4, 4)$

5 $\overrightarrow{CB} = \begin{bmatrix} 0 \\ 6 \\ -6 \end{bmatrix}$, $\overrightarrow{CA} = \begin{bmatrix} 6 \\ 0 \\ -6 \end{bmatrix}$

ABC has equation

$$\begin{bmatrix} x \\ y \\ z \end{bmatrix} = \begin{bmatrix} 0 \\ 0 \\ 6 \end{bmatrix} + \lambda\begin{bmatrix} 0 \\ 6 \\ -6 \end{bmatrix} + \mu\begin{bmatrix} 6 \\ 0 \\ -6 \end{bmatrix}$$

The planes are parallel.

6 (a) $(0, 0, 6)$ i.e. C   (b) $(0, 6, 0)$ i.e. B
(c) $(6, 0, 0)$ i.e. A   (d) $(3, 3, 0)$
(e) $(2, 2, 2)$

7 (a) If the plane is parallel to ABC, then its direction will still be specified by vectors $\overrightarrow{CB}$ and $\overrightarrow{CA}$, but will pass through O instead of C.

The equation will therefore be

$$\begin{bmatrix} x \\ y \\ z \end{bmatrix} = \begin{bmatrix} 0 \\ 0 \\ 0 \end{bmatrix} + \lambda\begin{bmatrix} 0 \\ 6 \\ -6 \end{bmatrix} + \mu\begin{bmatrix} 6 \\ 0 \\ -6 \end{bmatrix}$$

(b) Similarly the parallel plane through G will be

$$\begin{bmatrix} x \\ y \\ z \end{bmatrix} = \begin{bmatrix} 6 \\ 6 \\ 6 \end{bmatrix} + \lambda\begin{bmatrix} 0 \\ 6 \\ -6 \end{bmatrix} + \mu\begin{bmatrix} 6 \\ 0 \\ -6 \end{bmatrix}$$

8 $\overrightarrow{OH}$ is $\begin{bmatrix} 3 \\ 0 \\ 6 \end{bmatrix}$, $\overrightarrow{HD}$ is $\begin{bmatrix} 3 \\ 6 \\ -6 \end{bmatrix}$, $\overrightarrow{HE}$ is $\begin{bmatrix} -3 \\ 6 \\ 0 \end{bmatrix}$

Plane DEH is

$$\begin{bmatrix} x \\ y \\ z \end{bmatrix} = \begin{bmatrix} 3 \\ 0 \\ 6 \end{bmatrix} + \lambda \begin{bmatrix} 3 \\ 6 \\ -6 \end{bmatrix} + \mu \begin{bmatrix} -3 \\ 6 \\ 0 \end{bmatrix}$$

9   (a) $\begin{bmatrix} -1 \\ 3 \\ 3 \end{bmatrix}$, $\begin{bmatrix} -3 \\ 3 \\ -1 \end{bmatrix}$

(b)   One possibility is

$$\mathbf{r} = \begin{bmatrix} 4 \\ 0 \\ 1 \end{bmatrix} + \lambda \begin{bmatrix} -1 \\ 3 \\ 3 \end{bmatrix} + \mu \begin{bmatrix} -3 \\ 3 \\ -1 \end{bmatrix}$$

10E   (a) $(2, 3, 2)$

(b)   Set the x and y components of the equation of the plane equal to 2 and 3.

Solve for λ and μ. Then check that these values give equal z components.

11D   You cannot find two non-parallel vectors in the plane, as the three points are in fact co-linear (they lie in a straight line).

Exercise F (p. 104)

1   Taking A as the particular point on the plane,

$$\overrightarrow{AB} = \begin{bmatrix} -3 \\ -1 \\ 3 \end{bmatrix}, \quad \overrightarrow{AC} = \begin{bmatrix} -6 \\ -2 \\ 4 \end{bmatrix}$$

$$\text{so} \begin{bmatrix} x \\ y \\ z \end{bmatrix} = \begin{bmatrix} 2 \\ 3 \\ 1 \end{bmatrix} + \lambda \begin{bmatrix} -3 \\ -1 \\ 3 \end{bmatrix} + \mu \begin{bmatrix} -6 \\ -2 \\ 4 \end{bmatrix}$$

2   The three points at which the plane cuts the axes are

A $(2, 0, 0)$,   B $(0, -1, 0)$,   C $(0, 0, 3)$

$$\overrightarrow{AB} = \begin{bmatrix} -2 \\ -1 \\ 0 \end{bmatrix}, \quad \overrightarrow{AC} = \begin{bmatrix} -2 \\ 0 \\ 3 \end{bmatrix}$$

$$\text{so} \begin{bmatrix} x \\ y \\ z \end{bmatrix} = \begin{bmatrix} 2 \\ 0 \\ 0 \end{bmatrix} + \lambda \begin{bmatrix} -2 \\ -1 \\ 0 \end{bmatrix} + \mu \begin{bmatrix} -2 \\ 0 \\ 3 \end{bmatrix}$$

3   (a) $\overrightarrow{OD} = \begin{bmatrix} -2 \\ 2 \\ 3 \end{bmatrix}$

(b)   Taking O as the particular point on OAD,

$$\begin{bmatrix} x \\ y \\ z \end{bmatrix} = \lambda \begin{bmatrix} -2 \\ 2 \\ 3 \end{bmatrix} + \mu \begin{bmatrix} 0 \\ 4 \\ 0 \end{bmatrix}$$

$$\overrightarrow{DC} = \begin{bmatrix} -2 \\ -2 \\ -3 \end{bmatrix}, \quad \overrightarrow{DB} = \begin{bmatrix} -2 \\ 2 \\ -3 \end{bmatrix}$$

$$\text{so} \begin{bmatrix} x \\ y \\ z \end{bmatrix} = \begin{bmatrix} -2 \\ 2 \\ 3 \end{bmatrix} + \lambda \begin{bmatrix} -2 \\ -2 \\ -3 \end{bmatrix} + \mu \begin{bmatrix} -2 \\ 2 \\ -3 \end{bmatrix}$$

for BCD.

G   **Parametric and Cartesian equations of planes** (p. 104)

1D   (a)   Starting at the left and going clockwise:

$(4, 0, 0), (3, 0, 1), (2, 0, 2), (1, 0, 3),$
$(0, 0, 4), (0, 1, 3), (0, 2, 2), (0, 3, 1),$
$(0, 4, 0), (1, 3, 0), (2, 2, 0), (3, 1, 0)$

(b) $x + y + z = 4$

(c) $y = 4\lambda$, $z = 4\mu$

(d) $x + y + z = 4$, as in (b)

2D   Many answers are possible. (e) and (h) should help you to check!

3
$$\begin{array}{llr} x = 6 - 6\lambda & & ① \\ y = 6 & - 6\mu & ② \\ z = & 6\lambda + 6\mu & ③ \\ & ① + ② + ③ \Rightarrow x + y + z = 12 \end{array}$$

4 (a) A is $(6, 0, 0)$, B is $(0, 6, 0)$, C is $(0, 0, 6)$, which suggests that $x + y + z = 6$.

$x = \qquad\qquad 6\mu \qquad$ ①

$y = \qquad 6\lambda \qquad\qquad$ ②

$z = 6 - 6\lambda \quad - 6\mu \qquad$ ③

$\qquad$ ① + ② + ③ $\Rightarrow x + y + z = 6$

(b) For the plane through O,

$x = \qquad\qquad 6\mu$

$y = \qquad 6\lambda$

$z = \qquad - 6\lambda \quad - 6\mu$

$\Rightarrow x + y + z = 0$

For the plane through G,

$x = 6 \qquad\quad + 6\mu$

$y = 6 + 6\lambda$

$z = 6 - 6\lambda - 6\mu$

$\Rightarrow x + y + z = 18$

5 $x = 6 - 6\lambda - 3\mu \qquad$ ①

$y = 6 \qquad - 6\mu \qquad$ ②

$z = \qquad 6\lambda + 6\mu \qquad$ ③

① + ③ $\Rightarrow x + z = 6 + 3\mu \qquad$ ④

Eliminating μ between equations ② and ④, ② + 2 × ④

$\Rightarrow y + 2(x + z) = 6 - 6\mu + 2(6 + 3\mu)$

$\Rightarrow 2x + y + 2z = 18$

6 Using the method of question 5,

$x = 5 - 3\lambda + 2\mu \qquad$ ①

$y = 2 \qquad + 3\mu \qquad$ ②

$z = 4 - 6\lambda + \mu \qquad$ ③

$2 \times$ ① $-$ ③ $\Rightarrow 2x - z = 6 + 3\mu \qquad$ ④

④ $-$ ② $\Rightarrow 2x - y - z = 4$

7 $px + qy + rz$

8 (a) It is perpendicular to the plane.

(b) They are both zero, so it is perpendicular to these vectors, which lie in the plane.

9 This vector is perpendicular to the plane.

10 (a) $x = 10$

(b) The near end of the cuboid, where all the x-coordinates are 10.

11 $\mathbf{r} \cdot \begin{bmatrix} 3 \\ -2 \\ 4 \end{bmatrix} = \begin{bmatrix} 4 \\ 2 \\ -1 \end{bmatrix} \cdot \begin{bmatrix} 3 \\ -2 \\ 4 \end{bmatrix} = 4$

$3x - 2y + 4z = 4$

Exercise G (p. 110)

1 (a) $\begin{bmatrix} 3 \\ 5 \\ 0 \end{bmatrix}, \begin{bmatrix} 3 \\ 0 \\ 0 \end{bmatrix}, \begin{bmatrix} 0 \\ 1 \\ 4 \end{bmatrix}$

(b) One possibility is

$\mathbf{r} = \begin{bmatrix} 3 \\ 5 \\ 0 \end{bmatrix} + \lambda \begin{bmatrix} 3 \\ 0 \\ 0 \end{bmatrix} + \mu \begin{bmatrix} 0 \\ 1 \\ 4 \end{bmatrix}$

(c) $x = 3 + 3\lambda$

$y = 5 + \mu$

$z = 4\mu$

(d) $4y - z = 20$

(e) $\begin{bmatrix} 0 \\ 4 \\ -1 \end{bmatrix}$

(f) $\mathbf{r} \cdot \begin{bmatrix} 0 \\ 4 \\ -1 \end{bmatrix} = 0$

2 (a) $\mathbf{n} \cdot \mathbf{r} = \mathbf{n} \cdot \mathbf{a}$

$\Rightarrow \begin{bmatrix} 2 \\ -3 \\ 1 \end{bmatrix} \cdot \begin{bmatrix} x \\ y \\ z \end{bmatrix} = \begin{bmatrix} 2 \\ -3 \\ 1 \end{bmatrix} \cdot \begin{bmatrix} 0 \\ 0 \\ 0 \end{bmatrix}$

i.e. $2x - 3y + z = 0$

(b) $2x - 3y + z = 1$ (c) $5x - 2y = 13$

3 (a) $\mathbf{n} = \begin{bmatrix} 1 \\ 1 \\ 0 \end{bmatrix}$

$\begin{bmatrix} 1 \\ 1 \\ 0 \end{bmatrix} \cdot \begin{bmatrix} x \\ y \\ z \end{bmatrix} = \begin{bmatrix} 1 \\ 1 \\ 0 \end{bmatrix} \cdot \begin{bmatrix} 1 \\ 0 \\ 0 \end{bmatrix}$

i.e. $x + y = 1$

Although this looks like the equation of a line, it represents a plane, formed by the lines $x + y = 1$ corresponding to various values of z.

(b) $\mathbf{n} = \begin{bmatrix} -1 \\ 1 \\ 0 \end{bmatrix}$

$\begin{bmatrix} -1 \\ 1 \\ 0 \end{bmatrix} \cdot \begin{bmatrix} x \\ y \\ z \end{bmatrix} = \begin{bmatrix} -1 \\ 1 \\ 0 \end{bmatrix} \cdot \begin{bmatrix} 0 \\ 0 \\ 0 \end{bmatrix}$

i.e. $-x + y = 0$ or $y = x$

(c) $\mathbf{n} = \begin{bmatrix} 1 \\ 1 \\ 1 \end{bmatrix}$, $x + y + z = 1$

(d) $\mathbf{n} = \begin{bmatrix} 1 \\ 1 \\ 1 \end{bmatrix}$, $x + y + z = 2$

(e) $\mathbf{n} = \begin{bmatrix} 0 \\ 0 \\ 1 \end{bmatrix}$, $z = 0$

4   (a) $\mathbf{c} = \begin{bmatrix} 0 \\ 0 \\ 4 \end{bmatrix}$

(b) $\overrightarrow{CA} = \begin{bmatrix} 2 \\ 0 \\ -4 \end{bmatrix}$, $\overrightarrow{CB} = \begin{bmatrix} 0 \\ 3 \\ -4 \end{bmatrix}$

(c) $\mathbf{r} = \begin{bmatrix} 0 \\ 0 \\ 4 \end{bmatrix} + \lambda \begin{bmatrix} 2 \\ 0 \\ -4 \end{bmatrix} + \mu \begin{bmatrix} 0 \\ 3 \\ -4 \end{bmatrix}$

(d) $x = 2\lambda$ ①

$y = 3\mu$ ②

$z = 4 - 4\lambda - 4\mu$ ③

(e) $6x + 4y + 3z = 12$

(f) $\mathbf{n} = \begin{bmatrix} 6 \\ 4 \\ 3 \end{bmatrix}$

5   (a) (i) $\mathbf{r} = \begin{bmatrix} 0 \\ 2 \\ 5 \end{bmatrix} + \lambda \begin{bmatrix} 2 \\ 0 \\ -3 \end{bmatrix} + \mu \begin{bmatrix} -1 \\ -1 \\ 1 \end{bmatrix}$

(ii) $\mathbf{r} = \begin{bmatrix} 2 \\ 2 \\ 2 \end{bmatrix} + \lambda \begin{bmatrix} -3 \\ -1 \\ 4 \end{bmatrix} + \mu \begin{bmatrix} -2 \\ 0 \\ 3 \end{bmatrix}$

(b) (i) $x = 2\lambda - \mu$ ①

$y = 2 \quad - \mu$ ②

$z = 5 - 3\lambda + \mu$ ③

$\Rightarrow 3x - y + 2z = 8$

(ii) $x = 2 - 3\lambda - 2\mu$ ①

$y = 2 - \lambda$ ②

$z = 2 + 4\lambda + 3\mu$ ③

$\Rightarrow 3x - y + 2z = 8$ as before

6E   The coordinates of the vertices are
A $(1, 0, 0)$, B $(0, 1, 0)$, C $(-1, 0, 0)$,
D $(0, -1, 0)$, E $(0, 0, 1)$, F $(0, 0, -1)$.

(a)   The vector equation of AEB is

$\begin{bmatrix} x \\ y \\ z \end{bmatrix} = \begin{bmatrix} 1 \\ 0 \\ 0 \end{bmatrix} + \lambda \begin{bmatrix} -1 \\ 0 \\ 1 \end{bmatrix} + \mu \begin{bmatrix} -1 \\ 1 \\ 0 \end{bmatrix}$

giving the Cartesian equation
$x + y + z = 1$.

The vector equation of DCF is

$\begin{bmatrix} x \\ y \\ z \end{bmatrix} = \begin{bmatrix} 0 \\ -1 \\ 0 \end{bmatrix} + \lambda \begin{bmatrix} -1 \\ 1 \\ 0 \end{bmatrix} + \mu \begin{bmatrix} 0 \\ 1 \\ -1 \end{bmatrix}$

giving $x + y + z = -1$.

(Or both planes may be found by inspection.)

(b)   Since both have normal vector $\begin{bmatrix} 1 \\ 1 \\ 1 \end{bmatrix}$ the planes are parallel.

(c)   ECB is $x - y - z = -1$ and FAD is $x - y - z = 1$

H   **Intersections and angles** (p. 111)

1   (a) $3x + y - z = 10$

(b) $x = 2$, $y = 3\lambda$, $z = 2\lambda - 1$

(c) $\lambda = 3$

(d) $(2, 9, 5)$

2D   (a)   No; the line could be parallel to the plane, or lie in the plane.

(b)   All values of λ; all points on the line are in the plane.

(c)   No values of λ; the line lies parallel to the plane, so never intersects it.

3   (a) $33.7°$ (b) $\sqrt{61}$ (c) $27.1°$

(d) $\sqrt{136}$ (e) $18.9°$

(f)   They are not equal.

4D (a) The unmarked angle in the quadrilateral is $180 - \theta$; by angles on a straight line, $\alpha = 180 - (180 - \theta) = \theta$.

(b) $\cos \alpha = \dfrac{\mathbf{n}_1 \cdot \mathbf{n}_2}{n_1 n_2}$

5 $\cos \alpha = \dfrac{7}{\sqrt{6}\sqrt{14}}$

$\alpha = 40.2°$

6 53.7°

Exercise H (p. 115)

1 $t = 2$

$(6, 0, -5)$

2 (a) $\mathbf{n}_1 = \begin{bmatrix} 1 \\ 1 \\ 1 \end{bmatrix}$, $\mathbf{n}_2 = \begin{bmatrix} 2 \\ 3 \\ 1 \end{bmatrix}$

$\cos \theta = \dfrac{2 + 3 + 1}{\sqrt{3}\sqrt{14}} = \dfrac{6}{\sqrt{42}}$

$\Rightarrow \theta = 22.2°$

(b) $\mathbf{n}_1 = \begin{bmatrix} 1 \\ -3 \\ -2 \end{bmatrix}$, $\mathbf{n}_2 = \begin{bmatrix} 5 \\ 0 \\ 2 \end{bmatrix}$

$\Rightarrow \theta = 87.2°$

(c) $\mathbf{n}_1 = \begin{bmatrix} 1 \\ 0 \\ -2 \end{bmatrix}$, $\mathbf{n}_2 = \begin{bmatrix} 0 \\ 1 \\ 3 \end{bmatrix}$

$\Rightarrow \theta = 148.1°$ or, taking the acute angle, 31.9°

3 $\cos^{-1}\left(\dfrac{6}{\sqrt{6}\sqrt{14}}\right) = 49.1°$

40.9°

4 19.1°

5 $\mathbf{n}_1 = \begin{bmatrix} 1 \\ 1 \\ 1 \end{bmatrix}$, $\mathbf{n}_2 = \begin{bmatrix} -1 \\ 1 \\ 1 \end{bmatrix}$

$\cos \theta = \dfrac{-1 + 1 + 1}{\sqrt{3}\sqrt{3}} = \dfrac{1}{3} \Rightarrow \theta = 70.5°$

However, the dihedral angle is obtuse in this case, so

dihedral angle $= 180° - 70.5° = 109.5°$

6E (a)

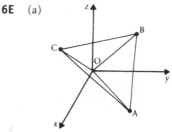

(b) $OA = \sqrt{2}$, $OB = \sqrt{2}$, $OC = \sqrt{2}$

$\overrightarrow{AB} = \begin{bmatrix} -1 \\ 0 \\ 1 \end{bmatrix}$

$\Rightarrow |AB| = \sqrt{1^2 + 0^2 + 1^2} = \sqrt{2}$

$\overrightarrow{AC} = \begin{bmatrix} 0 \\ -1 \\ 1 \end{bmatrix} \Rightarrow |AC| = \sqrt{2}$

$\overrightarrow{BC} = \begin{bmatrix} 1 \\ -1 \\ 0 \end{bmatrix} \Rightarrow |BC| = \sqrt{2}$

(c) $x - y + z = 0$, $x - y - z = 0$

60°

(d) They are perpendicular.

(e) 0.816

Index